D0915616

Political Science and Area Studies

Rivals or Partners?

Edited by Lucian W. Pye

Political Science and Area Studies

Rivals or Partners?

CONTRIBUTORS

Harry Eckstein

Samuel P. Huntington

Chalmers Johnson

Martin Kilson

Leon N. Lindberg

Alfred G. Meyer

Lucian W. Pye ✓

Dankwart A. Rustow

Kalman H. Silvert

Robert E. Ward

Myron Weiner

INDIANA UNIVERSITY PRESS BLOOMINGTON & LONDON

Published in Canada by Fitzhenry & Whiteside Limited,
Don Mills, Ontario
Manufactured in the United States of America

Library of Congress Cataloging in Publication Data
Pye, Lucian W   1921-
    Political science and area studies, rivals or
partners?

    Includes bibliographical references.
    1. Political science--Addresses, essays, lectures.
2. Area studies--Addresses, essays, lectures.
I. Eckstein, Harry. II. Title.
JA71.P89   320'.09   74-15711
ISBN 0-253-34540-5   75 76 77 78 79 1 2 3 4 5

Contents

Preface

In recent years there has been considerable latent tension in the academic community between advocates of foreign area specialization and defenders of the supremacy of the traditional disciplines. Substantial sums for foreign area research have led to the establishment of area institutions and centers, but academic promotion has remained with the disciplines. Intellectually there has been a running conflict between those who are sensitive to the unique and distinctive features of particular regions and countries, and those whose interests lie with general theoretical developments.

This book seeks to explore all dimensions of this conflict through the contributions of leading political scientists who are specialists of different regions and cultures. Although this book originated out of plenary sessions and the presidential address at the 1973 meeting of the American Political Science Association and thus the focus is on the problem in political science, the issue has emerged in all of the social sciences. Therefore this study is addressed to more than just political scientists, but to all social scientists who are sensitive to the pull between general theory building and competence in specific cultures.

Although the explicit theme throughout this book is the confrontation between discipline and area specialization, it is also possible to read the volume from the perspective of comparing the experiences of the different area specializations. There is surprising variety and similarity in the intellectual and organizational histories of Soviet, Latin American, African, East Asian, South Asian, and the other area specialists. Some, such as the East Asian specialists, have had to break from earlier humanistic traditions in order to incorporate a social science orientation, while others, such as the Africanists, have begun with a more contemporary social science basis and have moved back toward a greater appreciation of history.

Finally, this volume reveals uncertainties and anxieties about the potential of the social sciences. Comparative study in foreign areas does raise in acute form the issues of the proper relationship between scholars and governments. Similarly the relationship of area studies to the discipline highlights questions about the objectivity and professional biases of the social "sciences."

It is hoped that the study will be of not only general interest to all social scientists and area specialists but of special interest to graduate students and younger scholars who are concerned over defining their professional identities. It is important for all scholars to appreciate where we have come from and where we seem to be moving toward, and above all to understand that tensions can produce intellectual growth if they are approached in a constructive manner.

L.W.P.

SEPTEMBER, 1974
CAMBRIDGE, MASSACHUSETTS

Political Science and Area Studies
Rivals or Partners?

The Confrontation between Discipline and Area Studies

Lucian W. Pye

MASSACHUSETTS INSTITUTE OF TECHNOLOGY

For an age already deadened by endless analysis of "turmoil on the campus" it may seem like mere academic specter-hunting for a group of scholars to unearth yet another divisive issue which they claim has unsuspectedly and profoundly reshaped higher education in the social sciences. Yet it is the thesis of this book that for the last twenty-odd years there has been a quiet but fundamental struggle between the conventional disciplines and area studies which has affected the self-identities of aspiring scholars, the designing, funding, and execution of research, and even the organizing and hiring of faculties. By the early 1970s this tension had receded, but its aftermath has exacerbated the newly emerging issue which is now dividing the social sciences, and this is the question, how objective and nonideological are the social sciences.

Although the structure of knowledge and training organized around separate academic disciplines has not been altered by the establishment of innumerable area studies and training programs, the emergence of area specialization has changed perspectives and raised questions which go to the foundations of the social sciences.

What is the proper balance between the understanding which can only come from deep immersion into the ways of a particular culture and theoretical knowledge which depends upon abstract generalizations? To what extent is it possible in the contemporary world to rely primarily upon Western experiences for the advancement of social science theories? How is it possible to break the bonds of parochialism in a world of cultural diversities and achieve the universal foundations expected of science?

These are some of the issues which dominated the first rounds of the conflict when it was presumed that there was a neat division of functions between theory builders and data collectors, between discipline specialists and area experts. As we shall see, the resolution of these initial tensions occurred as area specialists became more methodologically sophisticated and as discipline specialists became less confident about the nature of science. It now seems that at a time when the culture of science is under attack the orientations of the new breed of area specialists may be of great help to a discipline confronted with new ideological confrontations which seek to blur distinctions between objective measurement and subjective preferences, between analysis and advocacy.

Before we speculate about the possible fruits of a marriage between discipline and area studies, we need to review the history of the confrontation. Initially, the conflict between the traditional disciplines and area specialization was exacerbated because it was an early case of the academic world being buffeted about by the currents of international politics and domestic change. The need for area specialization came about because of changes in the world, and raised in very vivid form such questions as: How responsive should universities be to public problems? How readily should the academy follow the path that has been paved with foundation funds? In a rapidly changing world what can guide those who seek only integrity in the cause of knowledge? The explosive growth of American higher education in the 1950s and 1960s coincided with the discovery that the classical European traditions and perspectives could no longer describe the diverse richness of the real world. Change sparked by demographic and economic forces—which in themselves would have revolutionized the size and vitality of American universities—was given broader dimensions by a national need to understand better the non-Western world. Africa and Asia in bidding for attention suggested the need for new intellectual approaches and the end of older academic traditions. And, of course, the emergence of the Cold War stimulated greater interest in, and resources for, the study of Russia and China.

World War II and the problem of understanding distant national enemies had already proved the limits of the conventional ways of organizing knowledge and the need for new approaches for learning about foreign societies. The unprecedented demand for trained interpreters, analysts, and ultimately, administrators to deal with the military conquests and then the occupations of Germany, and especially Japan, had forced a banding together of all disciplines, and the emergence of interdisciplinary area studies. World War II stimulated tremendous changes in the scale and form of social organizations in nearly every aspect of American life, and it is therefore not surprising that in the universities questions should have been raised about the desirability of new arrangements for the administration of teaching and research. If the urgencies of wartime called for trampling down the boundaries of disciplines, should they be resurrected again with the return to civilian patterns of education? The issue of the legitimacy of area studies was thus an immediate consequence of war.

Given the powerful pull of inertia in the academic world and an instinctive urge for a return to normalcy immediately after the war, it is not surprising that in the first postwar years the traditional disciplines had little difficulty in maintaining their status and supremacy. Indeed, the spectacular growth of graduate education in the postwar period, with its focus on the training of professionals in the disciplines, contributed directly to the reestablishment of the intellectual authority of the old divisions of knowledge. Yet the challenge of the area approach lingered, and indeed grew as research monies were channeled into the universities to stimulate a rapid expansion in knowledge about parts of the world which had been traditionally ignored.

Under these conditions there emerged within the social sciences a division between the ardent champions of the disciplines as the citadels of universal knowledge and the advocates of area studies as centers of highly specialized knowledge of the particular. At the most abstract or theoretical level this confrontation between the disciplines and area studies revolved around the question of how generalized or particularized scientific knowledge about human behavior can or should be. In part, thus, the division has been one between those who crave knowledge in the form of universal propositions and discount the merit of "mere description," and those who revere the unending uniqueness of human experiences and see mainly empty words in abstract formulations. The limits of knowledge have always been defined by the narrows between the great expanses of truism and of trivia, and the seeker of knowledge has constantly been in danger of losing himself in the empty wastes of generalities or the dense details of the specific. Long before knowledge became identified with science, philosophers and laymen equally recognized that wisdom and truth lay somewhere between the two poles of unqualified generalizations and the specification of unique particulars. Modern science has struggled constantly with the dilemma of seeking universality while making fully comprehensible the specific. Consequently, social scientists have readily divided themselves between those who would be the boldest in striving for the outermost limits of generality and those who would be the most precise and penetrating in understanding the individual case.

The dilemma of the general and the particular in science became the source of increasing strain as the essentially Eurocentric social sciences sought to become truly global. Evidence of the inherent Western parochialism of much of contemporary social science can be found in the standard practice of giving universal, mankind-wide titles to studies based on European or American data while expecting a limiting designation for comparable studies focusing on some other part of the world. A study of, say, voting behavior or legislative practices conducted in America is normally given a title which would suggest a general investigation of the topic, while such a study carried out in an Asian or African country would almost invariably be given a title that would reveal its specific aspects.

Interestingly, the founders of modern social science strove to incorporate all available knowledge about the rest of the world into their theorizing. From Montesquieu to Max Weber the mark of erudition was to generalize about distant as well as near-at-hand cultures. Yet, strangely, the more self-conscious social scientists became about being scientific, the more they tended to work with a parochial Western data base. In part the explanation for this paradox seems to be that as social scientists became more methodologically sophisticated they also became more ambitious to make scientific, and universalistic, statements which would not have to be bound by either time or space. Proceeding from the assumption of modern social science that human behavior reflects certain universal consistencies, and therefore the same theories should apply to all men, all societies, all economies, some social scientists jumped to the convenient conclusion that since all must adhere to the same rules, then any generalization about the immediate can be taken to apply to all, and therefore it should be possible to focus on what is most conveniently researched.

This legerdemain in logic thus dismissed, faster than the academic eye could see, the difference between inflated generalizations about Western behavior and universal scientific truth. To the extent that this view was accepted without critical examination it strengthened the notion that science lay with the disciplines and that the work of area specialists somehow fell outside the scientific tradition. All this was encouraged because rigor in scientific research, which was one dimension of the scientific or behavioral revolution in political science, could be practiced far more easily when the "laboratory" was near at hand and where, of course, the data were more bountifully available. On the other side, those who were interested in exotic places and cultures did often tend to scorn the notion of science in the study of man and dwelt on the importance of other, and particularly linguistic, skills. This was at least true of those who before World War II gave authority to such fields as Sinology, Egyptology, and Semitic studies. The stereotype of these scholars of esoteric and distant cultures as being aggressively antimodern in methodology was frequently and unfairly applied to the post-World War II area specialists who sought to join the mainstream of the social sciences.

In fairness it needs to be noted that the numbers of scholars investigating domestic American problems were great enough to establish a substantial scholarly community which made possible both specialization and the development of precision in communications, two prerequisites for the scientific enterprise. (Indeed, in the history of the social sciences there was a phase when it was probably essential for the building of this sense of a professional community to employ, to an otherwise excessive degree, jargon; but once the community was established it was possible to allow the level of jargon to decline to a point essential for necessary precision.) As long as there were only a handful of scholars dealing with distant places, each in communicating his research had to begin at the beginning and provide a general context for his results, which meant that the area specialist did have to engage in more descriptive writing. Thus the differences in the problems of communication helped contribute to a sense of major differences in approach: those working at home had to communicate with other specialists and focus on precision while those working abroad lacked an audience of specialists and had to reach for a more diversified public; the first adopted a style that suggested greater scientific specialization, while the latter tended to employ a style that down-played the rigor or precision of their work.

During the last two decades these and other issues in the confrontation between disciplines and area studies have had many consequences on graduate education in the social sciences. Students choosing to specialize in a foreign area have had to assume additional burdens in their education. At the most elementary level they must generally spend considerable time learning foreign, and at times esoteric, languages. Often undergraduate preparation for specialization has been less complete than for the regular graduate student in the discipline and therefore supplementary course work becomes necessary. Furthermore, in order to gain perspective and background students have usually felt it necessary to take additional courses in other disciplines relating to the country or region of their interest. Consequently, area specialization generally demands a longer period devoted to classroom study.

From these initial experiences students with area interests often developed uncertainties and even anxieties about their professional identity. At the undergraduate level many universities did institute regional area "committees," composed of faculty members in different departments, authorized to administer a "major," which usually emphasized language training and a choice of courses among the social sciences. Often students in such programs find that they must balance the lack of the institutional or formal support of an official department with the pleasure of having individual professors with great enthusiasm for some foreign culture displaying uncommon interest in them. At times undergraduates have been confused as to whether they were getting a formal education or being won over to a cause.

The confusion of self-identity has tended, however, to be much more serious with graduate students. Uncertainty about what they are becoming is often heightened by the practice of first passing through a master's degree program in an area field before shifting to a discipline for their doctorate. The fact that American universities have universally agreed that after the master's degree all advanced work must be associated with a degree in a traditional discipline is generally translated in the minds of students to mean that disciplinary work is intellectually superior to area-oriented work. Therefore, some students fear that if they are overly tainted with an area specialization it may suggest to others that they are academically inferior to the regular student. During the last two decades many graduate students have wrestled with their self-doubts as they have tried to balance personal preferences and academic self-images in deciding whether they should be area specialists with a discipline competence or discipline specialists with an added area competence.

Although ultimately academic careers have been overwhelmingly defined by the ladders of advancement located in the separate disciplines, many other factors have generally entered into the decisions of graduate students about how they should personally balance and mix area and discipline specialization. Some have enjoyed, and learned to exploit, the ambiguity of their situation, while others have conceived of themselves as second-class citizens. As with so many circumstances of marginality, the individuals involved experience privately both benefits and liabilities.

The experience of gaining background knowledge from courses in other disciplines has possibly left those with a foreign area interest less intimidated by disciplinary boundaries and more willing to absorb the skills and knowledge of related disciplines than those whose professional identities are limited to disciplinary concerns. Indeed a plausible case can be made that the trend in political science toward importing ideas and techniques from related social science disciplines was significantly facilitated by the young political scientists in the postwar period who became interested in political development in the non-Western world. In dealing with new problems in new social contexts political scientists were compelled to examine the work of cultural anthropologists, social psychologists, economists, historians, and other nonpolitical science specialists. The expansion of political science to include more of the globe also encouraged borrowing from other disciplines. Furthermore, as the diversity and the scope of the universe of political science became large enough to employ statistical manipulations and various indices of aggregate data the discipline had to reach beyond the limits of Western culture.

The intellectual confusion which graduate students specializing in area work have experienced has possibly been balanced by the exhilaration of finding competence in new intellectual fields and being knowledgeable about developments in a variety of disciplines. Instead of being outcasts in political science, these area specialists could assume the comforting role of being lonely but visible spokesmen for their discipline among intellectual strangers. Whereas in the eyes of some political scientists they might have been marginal members of their disciplines, they were taken by other social scientists as being models of political science; and thus rather than being pariahs they achieved their identity as honored representatives of their profession as they consorted with other social scientists.

The situation on various campuses has differed but generally the greater the availability of research funds, the stronger the tendency to establish area centers or institutes. The emergence of such centers has gone hand in hand with the decision of the major foundations that the best way to stimulate growth of knowledge about foreign affairs and distant cultures was to arrange to bring together within universities all who shared a common interest in a country or region regardless of discipline. Even before World War II the Rockefeller Foundation supported the first generalized institutions of international relations, as for example, the Yale Institute of International Studies. Shortly after the war, the Carnegie Corporation funded the Russian Research Center at Harvard, and in seeking to play a comparable role in advancing the study of Communist China the same foundations established the Universities Service Centre in Hong Kong in order to provide facilities for all students and established scholars affiliated with any university anywhere in the world who were interested in studying Communist China.

It has, of course, been the Ford Foundation which has had the greatest impact in funding area centers across the country. From 1950 through 1973 the Ford Foundation gave $278 million for international studies. Of this total, some $37 million went to Asian studies; $31 million to European, including Soviet, studies; $13 million to African and Middle East studies; $11 million to Latin American studies; and $4 million to comparative studies. Of the $176.6 million which the Foundation classified as grants to International Training and Research, a considerable proportion went to work which we are here speaking of as "area studies." Much of this flow of money to the universities went to individual projects but by far the larger proportion went to build and strengthen area centers or programs which cut across disciplines.

Unquestionably, the existence of such centers has greatly facilitated research, both on the campus and overseas. Often such centers provided desirable office space, more generous secretarial assistance for staff members, and a congenial atmosphere for both students and senior scholars who might otherwise be lonely figures in their separate departmental locations. These and other benefits from special budgets often were more than adequate compensation for the professional ambivalences and anxieties over discipline versus area identities.

Recognition of the legitimacy of area studies was furthered by the availability of fellowships for overseas field work which became such an important part of the American graduate school scene with the establishment in 1952 of the Foreign Area Fellowship Program through Ford Foundation funding. It is not unlikely that this program has been the most influential single formal institution in helping to reduce the confrontation between the disciplines and area studies. The Foreign Area Fellowship Program's grants became one of the most prestigious scholarships based on national competitions. The program significantly changed the debate between discipline and area work by strictly adhering to a policy of insisting that all candidates have excellence in both. Candidates with strong area backgrounds had to convince panels that they were potential leaders in their disciplines, and those with more extensive disciplinary backgrounds had to demonstrate their qualification in a foreign language and their personal interest in, and career commitment to, work on a particular area. Fortunately, the FAFP leaders had the wisdom from the outset not to allow the program to become merely a funding source for graduate students who had come mainly from area centers or programs. By insisting upon high disciplinary qualifications and treating on equal terms students from universities without area centers, the FAFP helped to establish the image of the new scholar who was capable of being an innovator in his discipline while fully in command of esoteric knowledge and the language of a non-Western country.

During the two decades from 1952 to 1972, the FAFP awarded 2,050 fellowships to students in 40 different disciplines; the largest number, 605, went to historians, and the second largest was in political science with 439 grants. (If international relations is included in political science the total would be 498.) The distribution of grants to political scientists reveals that Soviet specialists received the most with 25.51 per cent, followed by East Asia with 12.30 per cent, Africa with 17.31 per cent, Latin America 11.39 percent, South Asia 9.11 per cent, Southeast Asia 7.74 per cent, Near East 7.74 per cent, and Western Europe 6.61 per cent. This distribution pattern for political science is very much the same as the general distribution of all the awards, which suggests that the attraction of different regions was pretty much the same to all graduate students and the commitment to a discipline had little effect on preference for area specialization.

Although the initiation of area specialization came largely from the contributions of the foundations, the stabilization of area programs came only with federal funding, largely in the form of the National Defense Education Act. From 1958 to 1973, the NDEA Title VI provided some $206 million, of which $68.5 million went to language and area centers, which for many of those years totaled 107.[1] The centers funded by NDEA have produced 35,500 B.A.s, 14,700 M.A.s, and over 5,000 Ph.Ds. Over 17,000 students have received grants because of commitments to study selected foreign languages. The full funding for the NDEA contribution to area and language training was about $14 million a year, all of which has greatly contributed to the rise in respectability of area studies throughout the country.

The massive investment in area specialization in American

universities did influence academic developments elsewhere in the West. The British, for example, sensed early the need for some additional forms of area training as their empire contracted and new powers emerged in the world. In 1947 the Foreign Office through a commission headed by Lord Scarbrough recommended that special grants be made to ensure the adequate training of people in Oriental and Slavonic studies.[2] By 1959, however, the mushrooming developments in America and the awareness of a crisis in the training of specialists caused the University Grants Committee to appoint a new commission, chaired by Sir William Hayter, which recommended that British universities should focus more on contemporary problems in foreign areas and produce more area specialists on Asia, Russia, Eastern Europe, and Africa. The Hayter Commission investigated American area studies developments and suggested that Britain could learn much from what was happening across the Atlantic.[3]

Returning to the American scene, a dramatic indicator of the impact of the various forms of support for area studies by foundations and the federal government was the rise in doctoral dissertations in comparative politics with foreign area focus. In 1948 less than 10 per cent of all dissertations were in the subfield of comparative politics; by 1958 over 25 per cent were in comparative politics; by 1968 the figure was slightly over 35 per cent, and by then the next largest subfield was barely over 15 per cent.[4] (This spectacular growth of comparative politics coincided with a decline in international relations, which in 1948 was the producer of the largest number of dissertations of any subfield in political science.)

The fact that this dramatic growth in comparative politics was in part related to the impact of area studies on political science can be seen from the pattern of changes of interest in different regions. For example, in 1949 and 1959 there were no dissertations on Africa, but in 1969 there were 17, the following year 24, and in 1971 there were 46. On Latin America only 3 theses were completed in 1959, but 39 by 1969 and 57 by 1972. The growth rate was much slower, on the other hand, in the more established area of East Asia. As early as 1948 there were 11 dissertations in preparation on East Asian subjects, 9 dissertations finished in 1966, 33 in 1970, and 32 in 1972. In contrast to this more gradual pattern of growth for East Asian specialists, there was a rapid growth of South and

Southeast Asian interest. In 1959 only 9 dissertations dealt with South Asian matters, but by 1966 there were 17, and 23 in 1971. There were 3 on Southeast Asia in 1966 and 17 in 1972. Specialization on the Middle East and Western Europe, which like East Asian studies had to incorporate an earlier tradition, has had a more stable pattern of growth. In 1958 there were 27 theses on Western European subjects, 37 in 1968, and 55 by 1972. On Middle Eastern matters there were 15 theses in 1959, the same number in 1970, and 18 in 1972.

African and South Asian research could expand at a quicker pace than research on China and Japan in part because there was less need to learn difficult foreign languages. Similarly, the difference between learning Spanish and Russian may help to explain the more rapid expansion of dissertations on Latin American matters than on the Soviet Union. Paradoxically, however, the research on those regions for which the learning of a foreign language either was not called for or was not a major hurdle generally employed more of the most advanced method-ological techniques of the discipline, while the more established area specializations have been generally slower in adopting more quantitative procedures. The use of systematic interviews and sample surveys became early a fixed feature of research in Africa and South and Southeast Asia, while such methods have remained the exception in East Asian and Middle East studies.

This development points to the fact that the late expanding area programs, even when fueled by generous funding, did not encourage a sense of divorce from the discipline. Those who chose to work in the former colonial territories have generally been spared the heavy demands of learning esoteric and difficult foreign languages, and hence their claim to having any distinctive research capabilities has had to be built up on their skills as general political scientists engaged in empirical research.

Indeed, the former colonial countries offered inviting opportu-nities for political scientists with a minimum of area specialization to engage in overseas research on political development. The emergence of the subfield of political modernization and develop-ment also provided a form of area-relevant specialization which did not always necessitate the full costs of language and culture training. During the 1960s when the first generation of nationalist leaders in the developing countries were stressing their national goals of change and modernization, and often denying the details of their cultural heritage, it was particularly easy for political scientists with little historical background knowledge of the various cultures to analyze contemporary problems of development. In contrast to the sense of conflict between discipline and area specialization, there was, for a brief period with respect to such countries, a view that discipline skills could serve as a passport to knowledgeability about esoteric countries. In societies in which much was being made of plans for development, academics who were perceived to be generalists in matters of development were often welcomed, while ironically foreign scholars with deep knowledge of the indigenous languages and cultural traits were distrusted. Those who knew the past performances of the society were suspect because they tended to doubt the current rhetoric of development.

The record of relations between developing countries and Western scholars, whether discipline or area specialists, has not been a steady or an easy one. As disillusionment about the prospects for rapid development spread among the leaders and the intellectuals of such societies they came increasingly to resent the presence of foreign scholars, particularly those engaged in empirical investigations. Often there was a reversal in attitudes and foreign researchers were denounced for not knowing the local languages and cultural patterns. Scholars interested in earlier times and "safer" subjects became more acceptable, while those concerned with contemporary and emerging trends were suddenly suspect and questions were often raised as to their possible political motivations. By the early 1970s events in much of the ex-colonial and developing world pointed to a closing down of research possibilities.

As the problem of access for research in foreign areas has become more acute, new issues have emerged in the relationship of discipline to area specialists. Most of the new problems relate to the politicizing of research and the question of the extent to which it is possible to have professional standards in political science which both scholars and governments should respect. Once the issue of access is raised by governments then the question of what are the boundaries of legitimate research becomes a basic matter for scholars.

Concern over access is immediately related to the delicate matter of scholarly objectivity being corroded by an inclination to be the friendly advocate of the country being studied. Scholars are often attracted to studying particular countries because they find that they are fond of the cultures involved, and consequently they develop quite human attachments to their subjects. At times, this leads them to be missionaries in reverse, defending "their peoples" against all criticisms. In some cases this defensive posture is extended to include the government and the particular regimes of the countries. Unquestionably the extent to which area specialists tend to become sympathetic "friends" or sharp critics depends considerably upon the country of specialization. Soviet specialists have tended to be critical and students of Communist China more sympathetic. African specialists have tried to be "understanding" to the point often of explaining away all manner of authoritarian practices, while Latin Americanists have been somewhat more critical of military regimes in their region.

Along with the problems of the appropriateness of identification with foreign societies and governments there has, of course, been the issue of the scholar's relationship to his own government. In many developing countries the influx of foreign researchers, funded by foundation and government grants, has been seen as a threat, and suspicions were often raised as to distinctions between research and spying. In such an atmosphere scholars often wonder about the correctness of their own behavior, and frequently seek to disassociate themselves from their own governments. Even before Vietnam there was a strong antigovernment feeling among many American scholars working abroad.

Traditionally country specialists have always had to confront these problems of political and emotional identification with both the subjects of their intellectual study and their own cultures. Historically scholars resolved their dilemmas by siding with either the foreign or their own society or by seeking a neutral, disinterested position separate from both. For the latter the goal was the dispassionate posture of scholarly objectivity. In the post-World War II period this position of scholarship often took the form of identifying objectively with the tradition of the social sciences. Many scholars working abroad felt that they could avoid all issues of political motivation and personal preferences by giving their allegiance to the "scientific" basis of their discipline.

Thus as political tensions rose in many developing areas and problems of access for research became more acute the relationship between discipline and area studies also changed. Some area specialists felt the need to assert more than before their role as social scientists and this may have contributed to a significant drawing together of discipline and area studies. Other scholars, however, have felt so strongly about the political issues that they have questioned the propriety of even describing the social sciences as being objective and value-neutral. Thus the confrontation between the discipline and area studies has become increasingly blurred by a new division which finds discipline and area specialists allied on each side.

On the side of the first group are those who believe that the role of the scholar should move toward ever more explicit standards of professionalization. With respect to foreign research this would mean that all governments should be expected to recognize and respect the professionalism of scholars just as they now recognize the professional role of, say, journalists. Scholars of this inclination feel that it is a disgrace that throughout the world there is more general acceptance of the legitimacy of international journalism than of international research. Historically it is true that scholars have been less successful in obtaining recognition for the professional independence of their work, and thus governments often feel that they can attempt to politicize the work of researchers and apply forms of pressure on scholars which they would not risk doing to journalists.

At the other extreme are those discipline and area specialists who, highly sensitive to the problems of value biases in scholarship, tend to accept to some degree the charge of public figures that pretensions of professionalism only mask the reality that all research must reflect the values of the analyst. Needless to say the issue of the objectivity and the value-free character of the social sciences goes far beyond the problem of foreign area research and probably would have become a more general issue in the early 1970s without the emergence of the problem of access. Yet it is significant that at the time in history when the social sciences were confronted with the choice of becoming more an international and interdisciplinary enterprise or becoming more nationalistic, a wave of doubt about the objectivity and value-neutrality of the social sciences should have swept through all the disciplines. The impetus behind this wave was, of course, the essentially domestic pressures of the late 1960s to politicize academic life. The effect on many scholars working in foreign areas was to heighten self-doubts, for if they were not practicing skills according to universal standards then maybe they were in effect acting, either consciously or unconsciously, in a political manner.[5]

The pressure toward politicizing both discipline and area studies has therefore eased the earlier confrontation between the two while creating new tensions that cross-cut both. The ideological attacks on the "scientific" character of the social sciences by "radical" scholars know no boundaries and are manifest in all fields. Area specialists are to be found on both sides of the new issue of how far the study of man and society can be divorced from political values. In contrast to the earlier debate over the appropriateness of the scientific method, which dwelt on the importance of precision, rigor, and quantitative measurement and which therefore did tend to single out the various area studies because of the inherent difficulty of achieving exacting standards in uncongenial settings, the current debate is more related to basic philosophical values and assumptions which apply equally to discipline and area-oriented work. What has happened is that as the historical confrontation between discipline and area approaches was gradually being resolved, with area specialists becoming more skilled in social science methods and discipline specialists becoming more experienced in foreign research, a new crisis emerged as the principal paradigms of political science were challenged from new sources.

In this new situation of confusion in the social science disciplines, area specialists may have a special role to play since generally they have had considerable experience with issues of basic concept formation. Area specialists have long had to grapple with such elusive concepts as "development" and "modernization" and with such abstract models of political systems as "totalitarianism" for Soviet specialists, "corporatism" for Latin Americanists,

and in the "area studies" that are nearer at home, the Americanists
have had their struggles with the pluralist versus the power elite
models, and the Western Europeanists have been conceptualizing
the outlines of "postindustrial societies."

What we are suggesting is that at present the task of the social
sciences in seeking advancement lies less in a quest for seeking
greater precision, which preoccupied the early decades of quantitative social science and which exacerbated the division between
discipline and area studies, and more with the task of defining,
elaborating, and checking the utility of a wide variety of analytical
concepts. In this new phase of political science it should be possible
for area specialists to work closely with generalists.

Since it is difficult to foresee all the configurations of the next
stage of political science, it may be appropriate to cease speculation
here and to summarize the history we have just been reviewing. If
we now step back from this history of intellectual, institutional, and
research funding developments, it is possible to see certain basic
trends which have heralded the coming of age of area studies and
the resolution of the first confrontation with the disciplines.
Initially, it was necessary for area specialists to seek acceptability
in the disciplines and to exorcise the traditional, and essentially
humanistic and linguistic, approaches associated with the study of
distant civilizations. Students of China, for example, had to break
with classical Sinology, which was done organizationally in 1948,
when the modern historians and social scientists concerned with
both China and Japan founded the Far Eastern Association (now
the Association of Asian Studies, with the addition of scholars
concerned with South and Southeast Asia). The creation of this
new organization reflected in part dissatisfaction with the long-es-
tablished American Oriental Society, which emphasized philology
and philosophy and the classical Sinological tradition. In 1966 the
Middle East Studies Association was founded, again as the result
of a break from the American Oriental Society, as students of that
region with an interest in more contemporary matters and methods
felt a need for professional identities more congenial to the social
sciences. The African Studies Association was established in 1956
with a view to facilitating communications among Africanists in all
the social sciences.

All these new professional associations had in common a

concern with strengthening the social science component of studies of their regions. In general they sought a sense of profession based on more than just the ability to use an esoteric, or at least a non-Western, language. The emergence of these professional associations also greatly facilitated interdisciplinary contacts, for at their conventions political scientists, sociologists, economists, geographers, and other social scientists share panels and participate in more extensive interdisciplinary dialogues than is possible at the professional association meetings of the separate disciplines.

The rise in interest in "political development" further strengthened the professional esteem of area specialists: first, because the non-Western world attracted for a time the attention of leading theorists in most of the social science disciplines; and later because when disillusionment over rapid development took place the area specialists generally had the most convincing explanations for why the deeper character of politics in Asia and Africa inhibited the emulation of Western development. Thus as the discipline of political science expanded, the area specialists discovered that, rather than standing at the margins of the field, the discipline had reached out to incorporate their areas of interest. This process ultimately changed their status within the profession.

There have thus been some significant zigzags in the relationship of area and discipline specialists over theories of political development. On the initial tack it was the area specialist who sought to gain skills and concepts from the disciplines. During this phase increasing numbers of area specialists combined in their own research advanced theories, sophisticated methods, and cultural knowledge, and this brought to an end the view that there should be a division of labor between high status general theorists and lower status data collectors. Once the area specialists gained confidence as social scientists they shifted their tack and began to question more and more the general utility of concepts developed in the disciplines and especially from the study of Western societies and more particularly American politics.

At this stage when area specialists were rejecting Western concepts they frequently ran into new difficulties because they at the time accepted the rhetoric of politics in their region, which often turned out to be as self-serving to the political classes of these foreign countries as the Western language of politics was to actors in the American and liberal Western systems. Justification of foreign practices often went hand in hand with the de-idealization of Western norms. Confusion often reigned because inadequate distinctions were made between analytical concepts and normative models. Ultimately there was a clear need for new paradigms. The crisis in both values and analytical rigor was dramatized when scholars simultaneously questioned the appropriateness of the pluralist model for American politics while defending the concept of one-party or even military rule for Africa. To criticize the rule of an elite in the United States while justifying authoritarianism abroad represented a bankrupt form of ethnocentrism which inevitably challenged the integrity of political science. By the early 1970s the discipline was in crisis as it sought to untangle its normative and analytical perspectives.

So we find that as the division of labor between general theorists and area specialists eroded, normative and larger conceptual questions have become more important. In a sense this volume of essays represents both the coming of age of area specialization and the search of the discipline of political science for new theoretical underpinnings. The election of Robert E. Ward in 1973 as President of both the American Political Science Association and the Association of Asian Studies symbolizes the co-equal status of discipline and area specialization. It was the occasion of his presidency which made it appropriate to review the relationship of discipline to area studies; this in turn led to the series of papers which were delivered at the annual meeting of the American Political Science Association and which now in revised form are collected in this volume. It is striking that the authors of the papers generally reflect strong sympathy for area specialization, a perspective which certainly would not have dominated the annual meetings of the American Political Science Association even a few years ago. If the same theme had been chosen for attention only five to ten years earlier, the prevailing view would unquestionably have been that area specialists need to take their cues from generalists in the discipline and that there is a natural division of labor between theorists who develop ideas and methods, and country specialists who collect data.

The essays which follow will reveal the end of any such historical relationship. This can certainly be taken as a positive development, for it suggests that an artificial division is being broken down in the scholarly community and more and more people are engaged in a collective enterprise. Unfortunately, the essays will also reveal deep uncertainty over what now should be the direction of political science. As the confrontation between discipline and area studies disappears there is confusion as to what should constitute professionalism in the social sciences. What is certain is that this new search for professionalism will be a quest in which all political scientists, whether or not they have any area specialization, will have to engage on equal terms.

NOTES

1. The rest of the funds were divided with $71.6 million going to language and area fellowships, $32.7 million to research, and the rest to teacher training, the preparation of teaching materials (in 145 different languages) and 35 intensive summer language programs or institutes.

2. Foreign Office *Report of the Interdepartmental Commission of Enquiry on Oriental, Slavonic, East European and African Studies* (London: His Majesty's Stationery Office, 1947).

3. University Grants Committee *Report of the Sub-Committee on Oriental, Slavonic, Eastern Europe and African Studies* (London: Her Majesty's Stationery Office, 1961).

4. These, and the figures which appear in the following paragraphs, are taken from Steve Blank, "Survey of Western European Studies in the United States," mimeographed manuscript, Council of European Studies, University of Pittsburgh, 1973.

5. With respect to the comparison of the professionalization of journalists and social scientists, there are several troublesome paradoxes which deserve attention as social scientists have become more self-doubting. We have already noted the initial paradox that scholars, in spite of their presumed greater social prestige, are often treated by foreign governments with less regard than foreign journalists—many governments insist upon reviewing research plans and will casually deny visas to scholars while accepting foreign journalists on their own terms. Undeniably the power of the press is greater, but by that same reasoning it might seem hardly worth troubling about the politically inconsequential work of scholars. Therefore, it is puzzling that governments trouble themselves to harass scholars. It is more self-evident why scholars should inflate their own significance and call for self-disciplining codes of conduct.

Culture and the Comparative Study of Politics

Robert E. Ward

STANFORD UNIVERSITY

It may well be that presidential addresses are seldom read and, for the most part, deserve this fate. There are, of course, exceptions to this rule and, in my estimation, one of the most notable is an address delivered to the Southern Political Science Association by Jasper Shannon in 1950. It was entitled "An Obituary of a Political Scientist." [1] Its style is literate, its wit well-honed, and its message compelling if not comforting.

Dr. Shannon's address was an allegory—poignant, mocking, bitter and yet funny, exaggerated but possessed of a discomforting core of truth. It consisted of autobiographical fragments from the writings of Caspar Don Quixote Milquetoast, a recently deceased and not altogether mythical professor of political science.

These, in microcosm, trace Dr. Milquetoast's own career and shifting professional commitments and, in macrocosm, reflect the "development" of the discipline between 1917 and 1950, a dark and prescientific age known to most of us only by dim repute.

A different version of this paper appeared as "Culture and the Comparative Study of Politics, or the Constipated Dialectic," *American Political Science Review*, vol. LXVIII, no. 1, March 1974, pp. 190–201.

Professor Milquetoast has an impressive albeit dwindling capacity for enthusiastic and wholehearted commitment to the reigning professional passions of the discipline. The flavor is well conveyed by a passage from his writings dated April 10, 1917:

> Political Science is a new study, one whose frontiers are scarcely clear. Reflection and investigations reveal certain laws of politics as clear and definite as those of physics. First of all, it cannot be disputed that the whole trend and tendency of human relations is towards more democracy. Man is an incurable political animal. The evils which have crept into democratic governments are the result of too little democracy. Without question the cure for the evils of democracy is more democracy. The rebirth of American democracy is on its way with the introduction of the initiative and referendum, the development of proportional representation in cities, the movement for the short ballot and the growth of the direct primary, together with federal control of Big Business monopolies. As we look back to the dark days of the last half of the nineteenth century it is evident that the vision of democracy held by Jefferson and Lincoln was only temporarily obscured. La Follette, Bryan, Theodore Roosevelt, and now one of our own professors of political science, Woodrow Wilson, have made clear the truth which Rousseau undertook to demonstrate a century and a half ago; namely, that human nature is basically and fundamentally good though it has been temporarily corrupted by political institutions. It is true that some critics have wanted to know who created these institutions if not men, and if men were good why did they create them? This is unworthy of the true student of government for we have simple and conclusive evidence of the contrary in our contemporary world. The present war in which we are now unfortunately engaged is showing once more the inevitable progress towards the perfection of democracy.
>
> When this war is over, undoubtedly some kind of world organization will arise and, with American Democracy in the lead, we will move towards a fuller and more complete freedom. The triumph of democracy is only a question of time.

A marginal notation added in December 1923 indicates that: "This chapter needs revision in the light of subsequent developments in the Harding Administration."

The entry for 1925 reads:

> It is more and more clear that governmental problems must be solved at the grassroots. The principal issues of government are essentially

those of administration. Government is not only a police agency, but it is a service agency as well. The trend of the time is towards urbanization and centralization. The census returns show that rural America is passing. We must make our cities more healthful, more beautiful, more livable. This demands the integration of power in the hands of one man who can give us better city government. The invention of the city manager plan combined with the employment of a merit system in government is what is essential to sound local government. Efficient business practice must be applied in city government even as it has been in our well-run corporations. Businessmen must play a larger role in government so that their organizing and administrative talents may be brought to the solution of political problems, just as they have so competently improved our standard of living.

This, too, bore a subsequent annotation dated November 1929: "My confidence in business efficiency is somewhat shaken."

A note of doubt and discontent creeps into our now unemployed hero's credo in 1933:

In previous chapters I have neglected the importance of economics for politics. A perusal of Charles A. Beard's the *Economic Interpretation of the Constitution*, his *Economic Basis of Politics*, or his more recent volumes, *The Rise of American Civilization*, will convince the most stubborn mind that economics is the clue to politics. The only trouble is the way economics is taught. Professors of economics are generally as dismal as their subject and are creatures of little imagination who have become slavish idolators of the capitalist system. They are proof of Plato's contention that we become like that which we study. Congressional investigations have showed that much of the economic order is wrong. It will have to be turned upside down. We need to study the Russian system more closely. They have solved the problem of unemployment while millions here are near starvation.

But then after four years as a public administrator with WPA, Caspar concluded in 1937:

. . . I confess my feelings are somewhat contradictory. . . . I have always been an opponent of monopoly, but I had thought only of business monopoly. My experiences in government lead me to question the total monopoly of government as much as the partial monopoly of business. I suspect my senses are now more keenly

attuned to the doctrine of the separation of powers than formerly. . . .
Bureaucracy really exists and is not solely a chimera of the Republican National Committee. . . . Why I never saw the close relationship
of the welfare and police state I do not know. . . . It is really tragic
what we political scientists do not know. I think I will turn to
psychology for help. . . .

Needless to say he did and by 1939 found that:

> All they [the psychologists] have told me is that life is a dream and a
> bad one at that. . . . Psychoanalysis has told me little about political
> science but much about political scientists.

Thereafter our hero staggered on toward 1950, death, and final
repose, insatiable in his quest for the Holy Grail of professional
truth. At points en route he concluded variously. In August 1945:

> . . . My life, everything, is now dependent upon the ability of a
> Missouri ex-necktie salesman in Washington and an ex-divinity
> student in Moscow. Not even the gremlins could have created such a
> condition. . . . Honestly I am beginning to have a nostalgia for Calvin
> Coolidge.

And, finally, in August 1950:

> Occasionally I feel an urge to be an historian, a mortician of the past,
> for hindsight is so much more helpful than foresight. Thirty years ago
> I mounted my good horse and rode off to war against politicians. Now
> I pray for more and better politicians. I seek not uniformity and
> efficiency, but cohesion and peace. These can come only through
> compromise. . . . I am tempted to say, "Blessed are the politicians for
> they are the architects of peace. Oh, Lord, save us from preachers,
> generals, idealists, educators, and administrators."

The fragments end with an injunction to his wife: "Please
destroy this manuscript. . . ."

I

Dr. Shannon brings perspective and humor as well as irony to
bear on a question that too seldom engages our systematic
attention: "How over time the discipline changes?"—against such

a background, I dare not say "develops." In an immediate sense we are all in varying degrees aware of and sensitive to the disciplinary fads, fancies, and feuds of the moment. But memory is a selective faculty—perhaps mercifully so—and we seldom reflect on these sometimes painful matters in deeper perspective or in much detail. Were we to do so, I suspect that we would discover a phenomenon that I hereby denominate as "the constipated dialectic." It has theses and antitheses aplenty, but whether it leads to synthesis remains questionable.

Let us consider a particular instance of just such a "constipated dialectic" and do so with cathartic ends in mind. The context is that of comparative politics, the general topic is the practical implications and consequences of cultural differences for the comparative study of politics, and the specific thesis and antithesis involved are the oft-alleged incompatibility of what, for shorthand purposes, I will call respectively the area and the behavioral approaches to the comparative study of political systems.

What is the nature of the problem? As best I can tell and reduced to its simplest and most basic elements it seems to be as follows.

Many behavioralists allege that something called "the Area Approach" lacks rigor and scientific potentiality. It is viewed as descriptive and relativistic, often historical or institutional rather than behavioral in focus, and normally idiosyncratic in terms of its findings. In current professional parlance these are not terms of praise.

A few so-called "area types" respond with countercharges of cultural illiteracy, gross ethnocentrism, uncritical scientism, and scornful characterizations of those members of the opposition who venture abroad as "itinerant methodologists" or worse.

And thus thesis confronts antithesis and battle is joined.

The fray is a strange one, however, which is explicable more in psychoanalytical than objective terms. To begin with the area camp is in considerable disarray. Even in a physical sense it is by no means a unitary force. There really is no single area movement, approach, or method comparable in any sense to even so diffuse a phenomenon as the behavioral movement or approach. What actually exist are very loose congeries of academics united only by a common interest in particular areas such as Japan, China, India,

Slavic Europe, or Latin America and lacking any common identity or organization that transcends such specific regions or cultural areas. They certainly do not share anything so pretentious as a methodology or a theory.

Secondly, the area group, despite truly remarkable accomplishments, is not at all complacent about its own scholarly performance. Everywhere in area circles one encounters fervent injunctions about going beyond traditional area studies, of escaping from the "area box," as it is frequently put. Considering that a brief twenty-five years ago the universities of the United States possessed the merest handful of scholars fluent in any non-Western languages or competent in such subject matters as the politics, history, economics, literature, or philosophy of any non-Western society and that today its endowment in these respects is not even remotely rivaled anyplace else in the world, such self-abnegation on the part of those responsible for this achievement is, to say the least, remarkable.

These two characteristics—a lack of unity and appreciable intellectual dissatisfaction with their own performance—combine to produce a third relevant phenomenon: the area group is far more aggressed against than aggressing. The charges come largely from the behavioral side and are usually justified as necessary to the effort to convert political science into a more scientific discipline. Occasionally an area proponent replies but, to use the military metaphor, the area tactic has been one of skirmishing rather than pitched battles or frontal attack.

The locus of this anti-area animus in what I have been calling in grossly oversimplified terms "the behavioral camp" is also of interest. It is not shared by many of the founders or leaders of what has been termed the Behavioral Revolution. Any such bias is notably absent—indeed, often specifically disavowed—in the works of such scholars as Almond, Dahl, Deutsch, Eulau, or Truman. In fact it is difficult to trace the evolution of the animus in specific terms. Like Topsy, it just growed, and eventually became a part of the behavioral view, widely shared in many, although not in all, quarters.

If, for the sake of argument, one grants that all this is true, that I am providing an essentially accurate description of an episode of disagreement and strife within the discipline, the question remains:

"Does it really matter? Isn't this just one more tempest in the academic teapot? Why should we care?"

It does matter, and I would like to explain why I believe this to be so. I have three categories of argumentation in mind:

1. The grounds for dissension are mostly spurious.
2. The episode provides important and, we may hope, constructive insights into the processes of intellectual change and commitment within the discipline.
3. It points the way to catharsis and synthesis. The dialectic need not continue constipated.

Allow me to develop these points in sequence.

II

My first point was that the grounds for dissension are largely spurious. I would argue that there really is no such thing as an "area approach."

There are undoubtedly individual political scientists of faculty rank who in their teaching or research specialize to varying degrees in the politics of particular areas such as Japan, Nigeria, India, or Brazil. The forthcoming Lambert survey of area programs estimates that there are probably several thousand of them. As one of their number, I have always found it a bit difficult to understand why this was in any way more remarkable—let alone more questionable—than specialization in the political systems of Great Britain, France, Germany, or the Commonwealth. These latter have been standard parts of the discipline since the nineteenth century.

Logic aside, however, it is true that the large-scale extension of systematic professional interest to non-Western political systems that developed after World War II did entail both stress and change within the discipline. Those involved in this intellectual Diaspora were faced with at least three critical problems: 1) an unusually formidable language barrier—few American scholars spoke or read such languages as Chinese, Arabic, or Hindi; 2) the manifest inadequacy of the traditional categories of comparative political analysis, which were largely legal and institutional in nature and had been developed with only the Western European and American experiences in mind; and 3) the problem of devising alternative categories of analysis of sufficient amplitude and precision to incorporate both the traditional Western political systems and a variety of quite different non-Western polities.

The shared characteristics of what some have called "the area approach" derive from this particular set of problems, which are common to all scholars working in non-Western settings. These characteristics are basically commonsensical. First such so-called area specialists place great emphasis on the importance of learning at least the major language of the society concerned. Communication is prerequisite to effective study or learning. Our most common languages—English, French, German, or Spanish—are usually not adequate for this purpose. Therefore one must learn to speak and read the languages that are. It is that simple.

Second, area specialists are apt to be unusually sensitive to the impact of culture on politics. The postwar study of comparative politics in non-Western settings began with a recognition of the sterility of trying to analyze these polities in terms of their constitutions, laws, and executive, legislative, and judicial systems. Political institutions that bore familiar Western names simply did not perform functions analogous to those of their Euro-American namesakes. The obvious question was: "Why?"—the equally obvious answer: cultural difference.

From this rather elementary perception stemmed a much more detailed and sophisticated search for the cultural determinants of particular non-Western political institutions, events, attitudes, and behaviors. The questions asked were not basically different from those involved in a similar analysis of the American or British political system. They differed primarily with respect to the investigator's point of departure—and, I might add, that of his audience. One started more or less from scratch. Little or no prior research that was directly relevant existed; the basic data in currently useful forms had literally to be created. Lacking were the enormous advantages of operating in the culturally familiar settings of developed Western societies with scholarly traditions that are both compatible and, in important degree, cumulative. The result was that political scientists working under these circumstances shortly became very sensitive—perhaps overly so—to the total cultural matrix in which politics is set and felt obliged to write and teach about the societal setting and determinants of politics to a degree that is uncommon in professional writings about the American political system, where both author and readers usually share so much more of the contextual knowledge concerned, or at least think that they do. It is only in this limited sense that an area specialization may be said to be interdisciplinary. While sensitized to the relevant theories and findings of other disciplines, area specialization in political science is still basically monodisciplinary.

A final characteristic that area specialists tend to share is a high regard for the importance and relevance of history as a determinant of political outcomes. This is really a subcategory and a consequence of their concern with the cultural context of politics. One does not study culture in an historical vacuum. The same should be true of politics. It is a conceit born of the Enlightenment and reinforced by certain trends in current social science theorizing that political attitudes, behavior, or institutions can be explained or understood in terms that do not involve a substantial historical element. Professional exposure to societies where the so-called premodern stages of history are chronologically so much closer to the present, where nation states have emerged well within the reach of living memories, and where people still live and strive to cope with problems that seem by our standards archaic imbues one with a particularly keen sense of the contemporary relevance of history.

This set of characteristics—a concern with language, with culture, and with history—is really all the "theoretical" or "meth-odological" baggage that area specialists possess in common. I personally do not find it a very impressive endowment. It is basically commonsensical, wholly predictable, and, I should say, inevitable given the nature of their professional subject-matter. It is certainly not of an order of complexity, precision, interrelatedness, or pretentiousness that would justify labeling it as a methodology or even a technique. Where then is "the area approach"?

The matter does not stop at this point. Richard Lambert of the University of Pennsylvania has recently completed a massive and most impressive review of language and area programs in the United States. In the course of his activities he tried not only to identify area specialists but also to determine what they actually do. The results are interesting. For example, among the more than four thousand college and university teachers in Lambert's sample

with area specializations, 73.6 per cent taught at least one course
that had no area-specific required reading material.

The same group were asked to rate themselves on a seven-point
scale as to the degree to which their teaching, research, and other
professional activities were concerned with their area rather than
their disciplinary interests, a rating of seven indicating complete
area orientation. The mean scores were 4.1 for teaching activities,
5.3 for research, and 4.8 for other professional activities. Only a
minority (14.6 per cent for teaching, 33.2 per cent for research, and
24.3 per cent for other professional activities) regarded themselves
as completely area rather than disciplinary in their orientations. It
should also be noted that these figures represent results for all area
specialists regardless of discipline and are seriously skewed toward
the area pole by large numbers of historians and humanists whose
disciplines are traditionally organized along area lines. They would
be far lower for political scientists with area specializations.

In the light of these findings I would submit that not only is
there no shared body of theory or methodology that can legiti-
mately be labeled an "area approach," but also there are relatively
few political scientists who see themselves as more area than
disciplinary in their professional activities and orientations. It is in
this sense that I view the grounds for dissension between the
behavioral and area camps as well as the concomitant charges
against area specialists within the discipline as largely spurious. To
revert to the symbolism implicit in the name of Professor Shannon's antihero, they remind one of Don Quixote's famous tilt with
the windmills—sincere, energetic, and zestful to be sure, but sadly
ill-informed.

III

But the windmills were there! The valiant but myopic Don was
right in at least this respect. And in a sense the windmills of the
mind at which some of our colleagues have been tilting are also
there. Which brings me to my second point: This episode that pits
some behaviorally-inclined members of the profession against some
area-inclined members provides potentially important insights into
the processes of intellectual change and commitment within the
discipline.

What has actually been going on?

In my estimation we have here a case of parallel development leading to intra-disciplinary hostilities. Permit me to explain. In doing so I will ignore the pre-1945 antecedents of both area studies and behavioralism. They are significant in both cases, but isolated and small in scale and disciplinary prominence.

In their early modern stages area studies were a newborn phenomenon in the sense that our vastly expanded national relations and concern with Japan, China, and the U.S.S.R. in particular—although not necessarily friendly—produced a widespread awareness of our abysmal ignorance of these major societies and their cultures. The postwar world was really new in this sense. It expanded enormously our national spheres of interest, concern, involvement, and responsibility. A sort of communications revolution ensued and brought with it a demand for specialized higher education in the languages, histories, cultures, and politics of the non-Western peoples involved. In the event, the interest and response generated in academic circles were genuinely academic and professional in nature. The early area programs were financed by the universities themselves with substantial assistance from the Rockefeller Foundation and the Carnegie Corporation of New York. Government funds were not involved.

The oldest organized area programs date from about 1947 and relate primarily to Japan, the U.S.S.R., and China. For the most part programs specializing in other areas—South or Southeast Asia, the Near and Middle East, Latin America, Africa, or Eastern Europe—are of considerably later vintage. Most have been established since 1959. The ages of area programs range, therefore, from about twenty-six years down to ten or eleven years. The average is probably around fourteen.

Their organizational form varies widely from the loosest type of committee structure to full-fledged centers and institutes and occasional departments. So does their leadership. Most directors are historians or humanists. Practically all area programs are interdisciplinary in the sense that the staff includes representatives of two or more—occasionally as many as ten or twelve—different academic disciplines ranging widely over the humanities and social sciences. Relatively few of them, however, have separate staffs. The individuals concerned are mostly on loan from departments and thus professionally dependent primarily on their disciplinary rather than their area connection for such basic matters as appointment, pay, and promotion. This is important.

Important also are certain aspects of the developmental history of area programs. There was a certain mystique about them in the early days and some rather ill-considered and exaggerated claims were made about areas as a basic mode or unit of scholarly organization alternative to the standard disciplines. In practice such claims were seldom taken very seriously, however, and far more significant was the sense of excitement aroused by being involved in an activity that was simultaneously pioneering in character, calculated to redress the older ethnocentric biases of the profession, and operating along lines that promised substantial achievement in both humane and disciplinary terms.

Such circumstances inevitably fostered group loyalties and a mild sort of academic nationalism. It is noteworthy, however, that these loyalties were parochial in nature and focused not on the area approach or movement as such, but on the particular country or region with which a given scholar was involved, to wit, Japan, China, India, etc. What bound these groups together was not shared theory or methodology but a common interest and stake in studying and interpreting the language, literature, history, economy, or politics of the area concerned. Note also that in the early days at least this specific area focus tended to rule out any more general comparative interests. The tendency was to study and explicate the political systems of these non-Western areas for their own sake as major and neglected political artifacts about which very little was known. For the most part these early investigations were not guided by theory partially because there were then—as now—no very persuasive universal models of political systems, and partially because from a scholarly standpoint the most impressive and demanding aspect of the societies concerned was our almost total ignorance of their workings. Practically speaking, it was felt that some measure of basic information-gathering had to precede the construction of grand theory.

This did not, however, connote a total absence of theoretical or methodological concerns. The political scientists involved tended to share a profound dissatisfaction with the traditional forms of political analysis developed in Western settings. Their search for alternative modes of analysis had a great deal to do with the emergence of the structural-functional approach and the new emphasis on process rather than form in the study of foreign political systems, as well as with the renaming and restructuring of the field that we now call comparative politics rather than comparative government. They were also among the first to use systematic interview techniques in societies other than our own and thus to add a new dimension of life and realism to what had been a decidedly documentary if not dreary tradition.

What I would like particularly to emphasize, however, is not so much the state of the area art in its earliest stages—exciting, innovative, parochial, mildly cliquish, descriptive, and but marginally concerned with theory and methodology—as the subsequent processes of change which are common to its later stages and are in a number of cases still emergent. I will do so with specific reference to political scientists who have area specializations and largely ignore the other disciplines and specialists involved in the area endeavor.

The important thing to note is that nothing stays the same; everything changes. If one's prime concern is with the scholarly quality of this area-oriented product in terms of teaching and research, a number of factors besides the competence of the individual scholar must be taken into account. Among them are the age and stage of scholarly development of the particular area group concerned, the state of indigenous scholarship in that area and thus of the native resources upon which the area specialist may draw, the ease or difficulty of access to the area for purposes of study or research, and the availability of funds for research and training purposes. All of these factors are subject to change and, as they change, so does the area field concerned.

Several aspects of this process of change are of particular importance. First, the professional loyalties of the political scientist who is also an area specialist have always been bifurcated. He may participate actively in an area program, but usually his career interests lie basically with the discipline. He is, therefore, impelled to keep abreast of changes in the discipline and is apt to be affected by them in very much the same fashion as are his non-area-oriented colleagues. Second, the mild cliquishness that characterizes the early stages of area organization does not normally persist.

With the passage of time the initial mystique of both the language and the culture diminishes, particularly for the social science members of an area program. They tend to become less absorbed with the particularities of the area and progressively more concerned with how their area knowledge fits into such more general frameworks as political development or comparative politics. Finally and most important of all, the process of generational change has time to operate. New cohorts of political scientists trained along newer disciplinary lines infiltrate the ranks of the older first-generation area specialists and bring with them all of the theoretical and methodological apparatus of their day in graduate school.

The result of this joint process of attrition and development is an area field that differs greatly from what it was five, ten, or twenty years ago. Its practitioners are trained primarily as political scientists. Their professional interests and skills reflect quite faithfully those of the discipline at large. They differ mostly in the sense that they have spent an additional year or two in graduate school or abroad acquiring language skills and general area competence.

This then is the first of the two processes of development that I set out to explain. It is also the thesis in the dialectic that I am positing. The parallel development of the behavioral movement constitutes the antithesis.

The reader does not need still another account of the rise within the political science profession of that composite of theories, methods, and techniques that is loosely subsumed under the title of behavioralism. Permit me, however, to dwell briefly on those aspects of the movement that are in my opinion responsible for engendering its antipathy to area studies and area specialists.

First, the life spans of the two movements—area studies and behavioralism—largely coincide, with area studies being somewhat the older of the two, having started in organized fashion about 1947 rather than in the early 1950s. This overlap facilitated several kinds of rivalry, both real and fancied. To begin with there was obviously a potential for conflict between a creed that proclaimed: "The root is man," to borrow Eulau's famous phrase, and one that at least seemed to be saying "The root is area cum culture." That in fact few area specialists in social science fields really upheld such a tenet did not much matter. They could with some superficial validity be portrayed as doing so.

At a more mundane level some behavioralists also felt that they were in competition with area specialists for scarce foundation funds. In the 1950s and for much of the 1960s behavioralism was a young and struggling movement. Some of its most characteristic techniques, in particular survey research, were uniquely expensive and the dollars were hard to come by. This was precisely the period when the major foundations were providing relatively handsome support for a selection of area programs and, given the adverse opinion of area studies held by many behavioralists, it was natural that they should both envy and resent what they perceived as a regrettable misallocation of scarce funds.

There was also some rivalry at the campus level. At the major universities in particular area specialists were usually organized in centers or programs which were externally funded in substantial part and which enjoyed a peripheral status in the contentious hierarchy of their colleges of liberal arts. The behavioralists on the other hand were apt to be based either in the Department of Political Science or in research institutes. In either event they tended to view the area centers and personnel as rivals for both support and status within the university community. This, too, was not conducive to amiable relationships.

In the 1950s and early 1960s in particular there were also strong contrasts between the professional working styles, methods, and products of behavioralists and area specialists that could only accentuate what other causes for dissension existed. The behavioralists in those days worked almost exclusively in the field of domestic American politics. By so doing they inherited the fruits of the richest storehouse of social science data and findings in the world. To this they brought new approaches, greater rigor, important discoveries, and, ultimately, an impressive increment of new knowledge. Their work was characterized by a predominant concern with methodology, theory building, and canons of proof, by the emphasis placed on mathematical and statistical techniques, and, ultimately, by their attempts to achieve for the discipline a more truly scientific status.

The area specialists on the other hand were at this time

contemplating the legacy of social science data and findings that awaited them in such places as China, India, Bolivia, or Kenya. It varied enormously in quantity, quality, and accessibility. In some cases—China and Russia for example—the borders were physically closed to meaningful social science research and it was necessary to observe from a distance and to develop the black arts of Kremlinology and Pekinology. In others the borders were open but the social science cupboard was bare. Practically no one had ever seriously studied the political systems concerned in terms that had contemporary utility. In still others one encountered rich and ancient traditions of indigenous scholarship that had in varying degree been modernized. But the prime emphasis of such scholarly communities was apt to be historical, literary, or philosophical and, where they addressed themselves to contemporary politics, there was a high probability that they did so in descriptive, legal, and institutional terms. In few of these cases was there much cause for rejoicing among American-trained political scientists and area specialists confronting these scenes with the sorts of questions engendered by their own recent revolt against legal and institutional analysis at home.

The professional consequences of circumstances such as these are not well understood by those who have not confronted them in person. Practically speaking, one never really starts quite from scratch. There is always some sort of pre-existing literature or lore to be discovered and assayed for its ore content. Thereafter, if one has any sound sense of the impact of cultural difference on the shape, content, and interrelations of political institutions, attitudes, and behavior, it is not wise to plunge right into the sort of rigorously and compatibly defined microstudies of political attitudes and behavior that are the norm at home. You may not be measuring the same thing at all when you are dealing with concepts so shifting and elusive as party identification, leadership styles, or sense of personal political competence or efficacy. Some prior sense of overall cultural form and style and of the interrelations of particular political institutions, attitudes, and behaviors therewith is a functional prerequisite to more refined ventures. So is the collecting and evaluating of basic political data that is simply taken for granted in this country.

This type of scholarly inquiry has, in my opinion, very

appreciable value in its own right. Ideally it need not preclude a growing attention to more scientific modes of inquiry but, in fact, in the early years of an area venture it often tends to do so. For the most part this has been the predominant style in what I characterize as the initial stage of the development of a given area field. This has been particularly true of the older area fields such as the Japanese or Russian. It is probably less so in the case of the newer fields such as Africa where the relative youth and recentness of academic training of the individuals involved acts as a countervailing variable. In any event it is easy to see how in the 1950s and early 1960s the American-oriented, scientifically-fixated behavioralist element in the discipline came to look askance at their foreign-oriented, culturally-fixated area colleagues on grounds of incompatibility of working styles, methods, and scholarly products. The practice of the time largely substantiated such a judgment and few on either side really understood or took the trouble to investigate what the other group actually did and why they did it.

More fundamental, and also more lopsided, than this, however, is what I can only define as the ideological element in the behavioral versus area confrontation. I have made the point earlier that the level of ideological—or, if you will, methodological and theoretical—commitment to an "area approach" was never very high in area circles and that it has diminished in later years, especially for the social science contingent involved. The typical attitude is one of concern about the so-called "area box" and whether or not the work of area specialists is contributing appropriately to something often described as the main stream of innovation in the discipline. A modicum of ideological ardor or arrogance is involved.

The situation is different with many of the behavioralist group—with numerous notable exceptions, particularly among the intellectual leaders of the movement. I find the phenomenon fascinating, especially against the background so admirably depicted in Dr. Shannon's "Obituary of a Political Scientist." Like Caspar Milquetoast, the discipline has to an extent seldom acknowledged lurched from one ruling obsession to another. In the space of thirty-three years (1917-1950)—slightly more than the classic definition of a single generation—Caspar's career embodies at least five such movements, impressive in scale if not in duration:

evolutionary democracy, efficiency in government via city managers and business methods, economic determinism and socialist politics, the merit system, and psychological determinism. But whereas Caspar's capacities for enthusiastic commitment dwindled with time and progressive disillusionment, those of the profession show little sign of doing likewise. They are more reminiscent of the valiant Don Quixote, untouched by repeated rebuffs, ever ready to pick himself up from the dust, mount his staunch Rosinante, and ride off to new and more glorious quests and combats.

It is not that the discipline lacks a solid underpinning of impressive accomplishments that have added enormously and cumulatively to its sophistication and to the understanding of political phenomena since the early years of the century. It is rather the undiminished ardor with which, against such a background, it embraces new causes and panaceas. What a truly stupendous "forgettery" must be involved! What a magnificent, if short-sighted, capacity for emotional as well as for intellectual commitment! What price a cultivated and cautious skepticism toward all professional nostrums? Perhaps this is a subconscious reason for the recent aversion to historical inquiry?

It must be added that, if Caspar Milquetoast's successive intellectual idols have been able to mobilize even briefly an impressive following and degree of commitment within the profession, their potency pales before the totems of behavioralism. No magic—unless that of religion or of nationalism—has proven as strong or as energizing as that of science. A social scientist who is really convinced of the scientific quality of his methodology and findings is reminiscent in several respects of the legendary Presbyterian rising from his knees to do the will of God. Not infrequently such apocalyptic zeal carries over into professional relations with colleagues of less faith or different persuasion. This would seem sometimes to have been the case where attitudes toward area specialists are concerned. It has inevitably rendered more difficult their relations with behavioralists.

It is sad to think that the process I have described may be all that lends substance to this particular controversy within the discipline. If the diagnosis is accurate, the estrangement is compounded largely of ignorance, misunderstanding, and misplaced zeal. Insofar as it has substance, this is found in circumstances which prevailed in the earlier stages of development of both area specialization and behavioralism and then probably only in marginal degree insofar as the social science contingent of area specialists is concerned. Despite this, the animosity has been real and has had unfortunate consequences in terms of the training, staffing, and funding of political scientists. Most important of all, fruitful professional relations between behavioralists and area specialists within the discipline have been impeded and rendered unnecessarily difficult.

IV

The third and final point that I want to address relates to the possibility of synthesis and catharsis. Must the relation between behavioralists and area specialists continue to be estranged and barren? I think not—and I would like to offer a few observations and speculations on this score.

Fundamentally, two emerging and, let us hope, reinforcing trends are involved in this possibility of synthesis. On the one hand, the area specialists in political science have for the reasons stated earlier long been subject to professional influences that have moved them steadily away from idiosyncratic area orientations in the direction of far greater interest in the sorts of methodological, theoretical, and comparative concerns that are central in the discipline. Even a cursory examination of the research designs of work in progress in most area fields will demonstrate the extent to which this is true in practice. The trend is, of course, not universal, but it is certainly impressive and growing.

On the other hand, as you are all aware, the interests of many behavioralists have been shifting to the international and comparative scenes in recent years. This is a development of major significance. In its origins and for most of its brief history behavioralism in the discipline of political science was almost wholly an American movement. Although gradually it has acquired foreign converts, including some very distinguished ones, it began in this country, its leaders have almost always been Americans, and its data base and findings were long geared almost exclusively to the American scene. The results were, of course, impressive but the degree to which they may in fact be culture-bound has never been adequately explored.

The problems involved are numerous and serious. For example, no behavioral field is better developed, more sophisticated, or more mature than that of electoral attitudes and behavior. And, I would assume, since the American Voter series no concept has been more seminal or central to the conduct of scholarly research in this field than that of "party identification." But unless I misread him completely, Donald Stokes, a principal author of the American Voter series, was suggesting in his 1972 paper before this Annual Meeting that the role of party identification or partisan self-images in electoral change is significantly different in Great Britain and the United States.[2] I am practically certain on the basis of my own experience in Japan that the concept lacks any very close cognitive equivalent in that quite different cultural milieu. One does not have to go far to uncover comparable problems of equivalence in such popular fields as elite studies or political socialization. Apparently cultural variations can make a critical difference with respect to the validity or, perhaps, even the relevance of some of our more cherished conceptual units of analysis and comparison. If so, this cuts very close to the heart of the entire comparative endeavor insofar as it is couched in cross-cultural terms.

Lest anyone think that the problem is limited to this particular level, let me recall to your memories Frederick Frey's splendid essay on "Cross-Cultural Survey Research in Political Science."[3] There he sets forth in impressive and appalling detail the sorts of problems that await the scholar who seeks to optimize the accuracy and reliability of data obtained through a given survey instrument administered in several different cultures. If not sufficiently dismayed by Frey's account, I would suggest that you go on to peruse Dell Hymes' equally prescient and pioneering but even more basic essay in the same volume entitled "Linguistic Aspects of Comparative Political Research."[4]

I point out these difficulties not to discourage further cross-cultural and comparative research by political scientists but to suggest that the profession has yet to face effectively the problems of training and research strategy that are involved. If it is true that cultural difference is this critical a variable in the entire comparative enterprise and if the attendant problems can be as severe between cultures as similar as those of Great Britain and the United States as Stokes suggests, we are in very serious trouble. If our research abroad, particularly in non-Western settings, is to acquire a respectable behavioral dimension, distressingly few of our behaviorally-inclined colleagues have been adequately trained for this purpose. For the most part they really don't know enough about the languages and cultures involved to be able to cope effectively with the scholarly problems posed by cultural difference. Methodology alone is not enough.

I see two long-term solutions to this problem. The first lies in a synthesis of behavioral and area training. Fortunately, this is already under way, but the initiative comes more from the area than from the behavioral side. Increasingly at a selection of our major universities a Ph.D. in political science with area specialization differs in only one significant respect from a straight disciplinary doctorate. The individual concerned meets the same requirements, receives the same training in statistics, methodology, and theory, and is distinguishable from his other colleagues only by reason of the fact that he has invested an additional eighteen months to two years in language and area work in order to secure his degree. As the entry requirements became more difficult and the better universities cut down still further on the size of their entering graduate classes, this tendency has become even more pronounced. From the profession's standpoint this is a most satisfactory solution. It results in the implantation of what a colleague of mine used to refer to as: "Two skills in one skull"—an ideal synthesis.

The only real problem with this solution is cultural lag within the discipline. Both graduate students and faculty with area specializations are still viewed with suspicion in many behavioral quarters. They are not infrequently regarded as a different breed, inherently inferior in quality, and of dubious loyalty to the cause—not true believers. The result is a subtle but effective form of discrimination which tends to steer individuals who are not really dedicated to an area interest along other and more orthodox career paths.

I submit that this is not in the long-term best interests of either the profession as a whole or, for that matter, the future development and enrichment of the behavioral approach. We have spoken for years of the comparative mode as the only truly scientific approach to the study of politics. If we really believe this, we must equip ourselves and train our successors to understand and deal far more effectively with the problem that is fundamental to all cross-national and much domestic research—cultural difference. One does not do this by exalting methodology at the expense of language and area training. Both are essential to the future of comparative politics.

I indicated a moment ago that I could envisage two long-term solutions to this problem. Actually they are symbiotic, not mutually exclusive. One is the "two skills in one skull" technique just described. The second has a better-known rubric—"the internationalization of social science."

It sometimes seems to me that there are curious and little-remarked parallels between the postwar course of world politics on the one hand and the global social science scene on the other. I would not press this analogy too far but let me mention a few of the similarities I see.

In both spheres the period from 1945 to about the mid-1960s is at least mildly reminiscent of the attitudes, values, and performance characteristics implicit in the phrase "The American Century." If American foreign policy may be said to have been characterized during this period by global pre-eminence; by either monopoly or supremacy in nuclear weaponry; by worldwide involvements and engagements; by a more or less general acceptance of the superior wisdom, virtue, and efficacy of its own motivations, policies, and acts; by what on balance can only be termed its "good intentions"; and by enough explicit or tacit acceptance of these views in some foreign circles to facilitate their acceptance at home, do not certain analogies suggest themselves with respect to the postwar record of American social science in general and political science in particular?

It was not only the cities and the political and economic institutions of the ancient civilizations of Europe and Asia that were decimated by the war. Their scholarly institutions suffered equally, thus creating what—to pursue the initial metaphor—we may call a "vacuum" into which American intellectual and academic aid, prestige, ideas, training, and influence flowed or pushed. The domestic immunity of the United States to the physical consequences of the war plus its unprecedented affluence and the fervor and energy of some of its social scientists resulted in a species of worldwide scholarly penetration and colonization that was certainly unprecedented in so short a space of historical time. This was particularly the case in the field we call the social sciences.

The reception of this enhanced American presence abroad, of course, varied but the aid was accepted and in time enough converts were made to the views and methods of American social science so that new currents of scholarship were set in motion throughout the world. The entire process was undoubtedly much helped by the fact that during most of this period the United States was in the throes of the so-called Behavioral Revolution and that this seemed to many at home and not a few abroad the newest, most vital, exciting, and promising development in the field of the social sciences to be found anywhere. The result has certainly not been a mass capitulation of foreign systems of higher education in the social sciences to the American persuasion, but it has resulted in a vastly expanded American presence, and a degree of activity, ferment, and influence that has never before characterized the external reach of American social science.

The result is that in postwar times American social scientists have been concerned, involved, and active abroad in both the West and the non-West to a completely unprecedented extent. Whatever the underlying assumptions and short-term consequences of this American social science Diaspora, a great deal of contact of academic subcultures across national boundaries ensued and one began to hear talk of something called rather vaguely "the internationalization of social science."

This is not the occasion to discuss the manifold problems and pitfalls of such an endeavor. I merely want to point out the physical and intellectual improbability of long-term progress in the study and understanding of comparative politics so long as the endeavor is based largely on American money, personnel, methods, and theories. The cultural and intellectual arrogance and the degree of ethnocentrism that underlie any such assumption should be obvious. However, such can be our passion for the cause of social science and our unquestioning acceptance of the rectitude and value of our own professional endeavors that the question may never be raised in these terms. It should be routine! There is no day-in and day-out equivalent for the cultural sensitivity and understanding of a talented scholar native to the society concerned who has also been trained in a social science tradition that is in working terms at least compatible, if not identical, with our own. There is also a real function and need for the perspective and objectivity of the foreign observer, particularly if he adds to his linguistic and area skills the perceptiveness of a de Tocqueville or a Bryce, but such individuals cannot really replace native scholarship. Among other things, there is simply too much to be done and far too few qualified foreign scholars to do it.

It is curious how seldom we discuss this question of the role of non-Americans in the advancement of comparative social science. If we did, it would never occur to most of us to think that this was really an American monopoly. Yet we often act as if this were the case, especially where the other cultures concerned are non-Western. In any long-run sense it should be obvious that the bulk of the data-gathering and of the scholarship with respect to any society is going to be done by its own scholars, if it is done at all. There is a role for Americans, as there is for all other foreign scholars of comparative bent and appropriate training, but this is apt ultimately to be supplementary and, eventually, derivative in the sense that it builds upon and critiques the products of local scholarship.

In the interim pending the advent of a time when particular societies have produced conditions in which such fruitful interaction across national lines by social scientists is possible, there are problems of a scope, complexity, and virulence that sometimes surpass belief. I do not underestimate these. There will undoubtedly be more instances of governments that choose to regard the raw data of social science as national possessions akin to oil deposits or classified military intelligence. In such aggravated cases the only remedy is time; the only effective prescription—continued effort plus patience. This type of denial of access, while worrisome and inconvenient, is not fatal and is often partial or temporary. The Chinese and Russian cases demonstrate what can be accomplished even in the face of extreme difficulties.

Granting the problems involved, our long-term interest clearly lies in supporting more general freedom of access to the data of social science by all responsible and objective scholars, providing training and other forms of professional assistance to foreign communities of political scientists where this is both feasible and desired, and seeking to extend opportunities for collaborative research with foreign political scientists both at home and abroad where the nature of the project involved renders this both efficient and practicable. A program of this sort lends substance to that otherwise undefined phrase "the internationalization of social science." It is also calculated to add an invaluable second dimension to the profession's capacity to carry out effective cross-cultural research in comparative politics—the first dimension being the aforementioned combination of behavioral and area training that I have referred to as "Two skills in one skull."

This is the type of synthesis that in my opinion the discipline of comparative politics really needs. Given the developments already in process in both the behavioral and area camps, it seems to me that the time is ripe for its realization. By this I mean that in an increasing number of individual cases behavioral training and skills have already been combined with their area counterparts. All that remains to be done is to acknowledge openly the utility, indeed the essentiality, of both the area and behavioral traditions to the further progress of the discipline and to expand the numbers receiving such dual training. At that point synthesis will at last have been achieved and the dialectic consummated. I venture to predict that so glorious a dénouement would rejoice the shade of the late Professor Caspar Don Quixote Milquetoast.

NOTES

1. *Journal of Politics*, vol. 13, no. 1 (Feb. 1951), pp. 3–18. Quoted by permission of the author and the *Journal of Politics*.

2. "Some Comparative Reflections on Electoral Cleavages in Britain," unpublished paper, pp. 2–10.

3. In Robert T. Holt and John E. Turner, eds., *The Methodology of Comparative Research* (New York: The Free Press, 1970), pp. 173–294.

4. Ibid., pp. 295–341.

Political Science, American Area Studies, and Their Paradigms of American Politics

Samuel P. Huntington

HARVARD UNIVERSITY

EDITOR'S NOTE

To begin a review of area studies and political science with American studies may seem perverse and even embarrassingly ethnocentric. Even to include American studies in a discussion of what is usually thought of as "foreign" area studies is to stretch the topic to an unnatural limit. Yet there is an important intellectual consideration for not only including but more importantly starting with America. The reason lies in the historical character of political science: this is the social science discipline which grew and flourished in America, and in countless ways the field reflects inordinate influences of perceptions of the American political system.

In his presidential address to the American Political Science Association (1966), Gabriel A. Almond* pointed out the extent to which political science is an American discipline: from Plato to the founding of the American Political Science Association only a few hundred political

* Gabriel A. Almond, "Political Theory and Political Science," *American Political Science Review*, vol. LX, no. 4 (Dec. 1966), p. 869.

A somewhat different version of this paper appeared in the *Political Science Quarterly*, 89 (March 1974), 1–26.

theorists and philosophers contributed to systematic speculation and study of politics; today there are nearly 20,000 professional political scientists who are Americans and furthermore nine out of ten political scientists in the world are Americans. By sheer might of numbers Americans have dominated the discipline, and quite inevitably they have allowed their understanding of their own political system to color their theoretical views about politics in general.

Explicitly or implicitly the American system and the issues of American politics have thus had a greater influence on the norms, models, and problems of political science than any other political system. The importance of Samuel P. Huntington's contribution is that he illuminates the unique characteristics of the American system, which should have disqualified it in the age of empiricists for consideration as the prime model of politics in any universal terms. Yet Huntington also notes paradoxically that the peculiarities of the American system make it an attractive subject for intellectuals and thus a strongly congenial archetype for political theorists. This is because America has produced a politics of idealisms in which the basic divisions and conflicts revolve around issues not of class, traditions, or history, but rather of how specific ideals are or should be achieved. In American politics, normative and empirical statements are hardly distinguishable, and descriptions of processes are normally seen as either justifications or condemnations.

Political science has thus been oddly contaminated by the American tendency in politics to confuse values and facts and to vacillate between idealization and cynicism. The intellectual history of the discipline has been so shaped by such characteristics of American politics that it becomes in fact necessary to begin with American studies before it is possible to go on to other areas and their relations to a field that is so American.

I. Paradigms of American Politics

"In American social studies," Louis Hartz observed eighteen years ago, "we still live in the shadow of the Progressive era." [1] The book in which he wrote these words played a major and, in some respects, decisive role in dissipating that shadow and moving the study of American society into the bright, warm, soothing sunlight of the consensus era. For a decade thereafter, the dominant image of American society among scholars and intellectuals was that formulated and expressed in the works of Boorstin, Hofstadter, Parsons, Potter, Bell, Lipset, Hartz himself, and many others. The consensus theory was the product of a new scholarly concern with what was "different" about American society and, indeed, "American civilization." In the years after World War II, this concern rapidly became institutionalized in various graduate and undergraduate programs, committees, and departments of American "area studies." The consensus theory also marked not only a rejection of the earlier progressive* paradigm of American politics; it also differed from, although it was not entirely incompatible with, the pluralistic model, which, from the early decades of the century, had been the most popular paradigmatic child of the American political science profession. The progressive theory stressed class conflict; the pluralist model stressed the competition among a multiplicity of groups; and the consensus view, the absence of serious ideological or class conflict and the presence of a fundamental agreement on values. Could American politics best be understood in terms of one consensus, two classes, or many groups? Such was the issue dividing the paradigms.

Even in the 1950s the consensus theory had its critics,[2] but the critics were themselves only additional evidence of its intellectual dominance. For they were in fact *critics,* and in scholarly debate to criticize a theory is to testify to its importance and perhaps to its persuasiveness. A paradigm is threatened not when it is criticized, but when it is ignored, when people find a different paradigm a more compelling and useful way of organizing their thoughts. In the rather turbulent latter half of the 1960s, the criticism of the consensus model intensified, and there were frequent expressions of the need to move "beyond consensus" in interpreting American society and politics. But just what one was to move to remained rather vague. Did going beyond consensus mean going back to the progressive or pluralist models? If American politics were not thought of in terms of either the one, or the two, or the many, how

* When capitalized, Progressive refers to the intellectual and political currents generally dominant in the first decade of this century; when in lower case, it refers to the particular ideas and approaches of the "progressive" historians, especially Smith, Turner, Beard, and Parrington.

could it be thought of? Didn't these just about exhaust the possibilities? If consensus was largely the product of American area studies, could political science come up with a newer and better model? The purpose of this paper is to review the role of political science and of area studies in developing paradigms of American politics, to analyze sketchily the advantages and disadvantages of these paradigms, and to take a quick look at American politics in the perspective of comparative politics, suggesting some alternatives to the tyranny of the one, the two, and the many in the study of American politics.

II. Progressivism, Pluralism, and Political Science

The progressive theory to which Hartz referred was, of course, that reflected in the works of Beard, Parrington, J. Allen Smith, Turner, and other social scientists, primarily historians, at the turn of the century. The two key elements distinguishing the progressive approach were, first, a stress on the significance of economic interests, as distinguished from idealistic purposes, as the motive moving men in history, and second, an emphasis on the extent to which American history could be interpreted in terms of the clash between two contenders for power: the popular party and the elite party. Over time the particular groups in this conflict might change, but the struggle itself continued. The essence of the progressive paradigm was well summed up by Parrington in some notes which he wrote for but did not use in *Main Currents in American Thought*:

> From the first we have been divided into two main parties. Names and battle cries and strategies have often changed repeatedly, but the broad party division has remained. On one side has been the party of the current aristocracy—of church, of gentry, of merchant, of slave holder, of manufacturer—and on the other the party of the commonalty—of farmer, villager, small tradesman, mechanic, proletariat. The one has persistently sought to check and limit the popular power, to keep the control of the government in the hands of the few in order to serve special interest, whereas the other has sought to augment the popular power, to make government more responsive to the will of the majority, to further the democratic rather than the republican ideal—let one discover this and new light is shed on our cultural tendencies.[3]

In stressing the continuing cleavage in American society between elite and mass, the progressive historians were, as Hartz noted, reacting in large part against the earlier "Patriotic" historians, who had celebrated the unity of the country and the beneficence of its founders. They were also echoing a viewpoint which was not, however, unknown among the founders. What the progressives saw as a parochial dialectic of American history, the federalists had earlier seen as a common characteristic of all societies. "All communities divide themselves into the few and the many," said Alexander Hamilton. "The first are the rich and well born, the other the mass of the people." John Adams similarly argued that "The people, in all nations, are naturally divided into two sorts, the gentlemen and the simplemen. . . . The great and perpetual distinction in civilized societies has been between the rich, who are few, and the poor, who are many." [4] The difference between progressives and federalists, of course, lay in their evaluations of this conflict. For Hamilton the rich were good; for Adams both were bad (or, at least, could not be trusted); while for the progressives, of course, the poor were good. The federalists accepted the elite-mass division as an inevitable feature of any society, including American society, which was not in any way unique: "There is no special providence for Americans," as Adams said, "and their nature is the same with that of others." Governmental institutions, consequently, had to reflect this division. For the progressives, on the other hand, the division was bad because one of the parties was bad, and hence governmental institutions should promote the victory of the popular party over the elitist party. Until that victory was achieved, however, American history would be a continuing conflict between the good guys and the bad guys, and, as Hartz pointed out, one of the comforting aspects of the progressives' theory was that it "always had an American hero available to match any American villain they found, a Jefferson for every Hamilton." [5]

At almost the same time that the new historians were setting forth the progressive paradigm, other scholars, primarily political scientists, were delineating a related but also different image of American politics. This pluralist paradigm stemmed from the coming of age of the new discipline of political science. The American science of politics, to use Bernard Crick's challenging but accurate label, was fundamentally a product of the Progressive period in American history. Before the 1890s, the first steps had, of course, been taken toward a more systematic study of politics and government. American students had attended the German universities, absorbed the standards of scholarship and concepts of *Staatswissenschaft*, and returned home to attempt in some measure to duplicate and to apply them. John W. Burgess founded the Columbia School of Political Science in 1880; Johns Hopkins also developed a significant graduate program before the end of the century; Woolsey, Burgess, and Willoughby produced *Political Science* (1877), *Political Science and Comparative Constitutional Law* (1890), and *The Nature of the State* (1896). These and other studies were general, comparative, formalistic, and, in part, historical. This was, as it were, the period in which the preconditions for the scholarly take-off of the science of politics were being laid.

That take-off occurred during the first decade of the twentieth century. Political science as it developed during these years became realistic rather than formalistic, reformist rather than conservative, and parochial rather than comparative. The development of the discipline was one element in the Progressive movement. This take-off involved, in the first place, a shift from a sympathy for conservatism to a commitment to reform. This was reflected, in part, in the breaking away from the stress on moralism and natural law and a greater emphasis on a pragmatic approach to political life. "To call the roll of the distinguished social scientists of the Progressive era," Hofstadter has argued, "is to read a list of men prominent in their criticism of vested interests or in their support for reform causes. . . ." [6] The means of promoting reform was the exposure of the inequities, vested interests, corruption, and attendant evils which were interwoven into the dominant pattern of political and social life. Hence the emphasis on realism—how people in politics actually behave—rather than upon the description and analysis of formal institutions. The student of politics, as Woodrow Wilson put it, "must frequent the street, the counting-houses, the halls—yes, and the lobbies—of legislatures." He must study "the life, not the texts, of constitutions." [7] He must investigate his subject in much the way the superior journalist does. He must, in short, become a muckraker, and that, indeed, was precisely what the American political scientist at the turn of the century did become. No clear line separated the journalistic muckraker from the scholarly one. In both, the emphasis was on the exposure of facts—facts, which simply by virtue of their exposure would serve to generate demands for reform. "The documentation of the muckraking journalism and its alleged objectivity makes it only in style and published location different from the empirical studies in city government that the sociologists and the new political scientists were beginning to interest themselves in. . . . Facts, once put before the people, would do their own work." [8]

In addition to being reformist and realistic, the political science of the first decade was also increasingly parochial. These were the years of the " 'Americanization' of Political Science," in which American scholars less frequently studied in Europe and less frequently read or used European sources. In 1896, for example, 40 per cent of the books reviewed in the *Political Science Quarterly* were published in languages other than English; in 1915 and 1920, these figures had dropped to 14 and 4 per cent respectively. The proportion of references to foreign language sources in articles published in American political science journals similarly declined and American government supplanted comparative government as the most widely offered undergraduate course.[9] The progressive historians, epitomized in Beard and Turner, were, of course, almost totally preoccupied with the American historical experience to the exclusion of any significant comparisons of it with Europe. American political scientists similarly became almost totally preoccupied with American politics; the reality which they studied was an American reality. As the "emerging political science," in Crick's words, "tried to become more scientific, it in fact became more parochial." [10] The study of comparative politics in both Europe and America declined; in the United States the decline was more marked, but it was also associated with what can only be termed a more healthy emphasis on the realistic analysis of political behavior, which soon came to the fore in the Chicago work of Merriam, Gosnell, and Lasswell. "The narrow notion of science in politics concerned with the extension of 'hard data' techniques to trends in behavior was the American answer to European theory, but it remained almost exclusively concerned with American problems. There remains a paucity of materials using behavioral methods and dealing with governments and institutions of countries other than our own." [11]

The reformism, realism, and parochialism of American political science led eventually and naturally to a stress on the pluralistic character of American politics and the critical role of groups, particularly organized groups, in shaping the course of public life. The group approach received its most explicit formulation, of course, in Bentley's *Process of Government*, published in 1908. In Bentley the emphasis was analytical; it stressed the utility of the group concept as a category for political analysis. In others, the approach became more descriptive; the stress was on the multiplicity of groups as the distinguishing characteristic of American politics. The American pluralists were not, however, pro-group like the English normative pluralists such as Laski and Cole. If anything, the thrust was in the opposite direction. If the progressive historians harked back to an inverted Hamilton, the pluralist political scientists harked back to a semi-inverted Madison. The group concept was hailed as a scientific and realistic category for analysis, but the role of groups in politics was seldom viewed as better than ambiguous and was often viewed as nefarious. The machinations of interest groups were exposed. The extent to which organized groups threatened the rights of the individual and the power of the majority was emphasized.

At times the analytical and descriptive elements of the model were tangled together. The usefulness of the concept when applied to American politics often led to the assumption, not generally tested until much later, that it would be equally appropriate to the study of other politics, an assumption which could be far from the truth. "Had the disciples of Bentley," as Hartz observes, "tried to apply his analysis to the Dreyfus Affair as they did to the Smoot-Hawley Tariff, they would hardly have found the procedure so easy. . . ." [12] The pluralist political scientists were thus using a category of limited territorial applicability to analyze American politics, often implicitly assuming that that category and analysis could also be applied equally well to other political systems. The progressive historians, on the other hand, were using categories of much more general applicability (elite-mass; class) and implicitly assuming that they were useful and relevant to the analysis of the American political system.

The emergence of political science was thus part of a broad movement of Progressive reform in American intellectual and political life. The nature and focus of the discipline plus the critical role of the pluralist paradigm also reflected the extent to which political science in some measure was a substitute for political theory in America. The discipline's empiricism and realism and the assumption that facts exposed became evils reformed were themselves evidence of the extent to which, despite the progressive and pluralist paradigms, there did indeed exist a consensus on basic political values. In its scope, sophistication, and general scholarly achievement, American political science soon easily exceeded the much more primitive levels which continued to prevail in Europe. American political theory, on the other hand, remained as underdeveloped and primitive as European political science. Political theory is most likely to develop where there is a need to rationalize some forms of authority and to invalidate others; it normally flourishes during periods of intense conflict and controversy over fundamental issues of political and social organization. If, however, there is a relatively broad-gauged consensus on basic political values, there is little need for political theory. There is, however, a need for an empirically oriented political science to analyze and to expose the extent to which political institutions and practices in the society are in fact congruent with its political values. This process of exposure, of establishing the gap between ideal and reality, is also both a cause and a consequence of the low status which politics itself has in such a society. In this context, to study politics is almost necessarily to criticize it.

III. Consensus, Pluralism, and American Studies

Until World War II, the progressive paradigm was thus pre-eminent among historians and the pluralistic paradigm among political scientists. The years after World War II saw the rise of American studies as a major field of scholarly research and teaching in the United States. Before 1940 there were only about half a dozen programs in American studies in American colleges and universities. By 1948 there were over 60, by 1955 93, and by 1969 165. In 1951 the American Studies Association was founded; in 1973 it had over three thousand members and regularly published the *American Quarterly* five times a year. By 1969 there were 20 M.A. programs and 26 Ph.D. programs in American studies.[13] Hand in hand with the development of American studies as a scholarly field came the rise of the consensus paradigm as an intellectual construct. There may or may not have been a direct causal link between these two phenomena, but even if there was not, both certainly expressed in their different ways a new concern with the nature and meaning of the American experience as compared with that of other societies and cultures. They reflected a focus on issues which had been almost totally absent from the intellectual world prior to World War II: How unique is the American experience? How relevant is the American experience?

The consensus interpretation of American politics was a product of the absence of social revolution in the 1930s, the success of the New Deal, and the development of the Cold War. If Hamilton was the devil figure for the progressive historians and Madison the patron saint of the pluralists, de Tocqueville was, of course, the prophet of the consensualists. The central thesis of the consensus argument was advanced in most blatant form in Boorstin's *The Genius of American Politics* (1953) and in its most sophisticated form in Hartz's *The Liberal Tradition in America* (1955). The latter remains probably the most significant interpretation of American experience written since World War II. Hartz's analysis is outstanding among the consensus writings for three reasons.

First, while the consensus theorists were generally much more comparatively inclined than either the progressive or pluralist theorists, Hartz made the comparison with Europe the central theme of his analysis. He viewed the American experience from a European vantage point and argued, persuasively, that from that vantage point the dualism which had been the central theme of the progressives shrank almost to insignificance. Unlike Europe, America lacked both feudalism and socialism. The controversies of American history were simply between different variants of liberalism. Subsequently, Hartz elaborated his concept of the "fragment" to view the United States not just in comparison with Europe but also in comparison with the other societies created by European colonization and settlement.[14]

Second, Hartz married Marx to Tocqueville. His basic categories of analysis were Marxist, much more explicitly so, indeed, than those of the progressives. Viewed in class terms, the United States, except in the South, had lacked an aristocracy; because of this, it also lacked a class-conscious proletariat. Instead the middle class had from the first predominated; liberalism, the political philosophy of the middle class, had been unchallenged. In a brilliant manner, Hartz thus used Marxist categories to arrive at Tocquevillian conclusions. Hofstadter once called Calhoun "the Marx of the Master Class"; Hartz could equally well be described as "the Marx of the middle class."

Third, unlike many other consensus writers, Hartz also saw that consensus was not simply a cause for celebration; it was an ambivalent legacy. The absence of class conflict might be a blessing, but it was gained at the price of liberalism turning in and shadow boxing against itself. Unchallenged liberalism became irrational liberalism. America's "colossal liberal absolutism," Hartz concluded, "hampers creative action abroad by identifying the alien with the unintelligible, and it inspires hysteria at home by generating the anxiety that unintelligible things produce." [15]

Probably the most important contribution of the consensus theorists was to place the American experience in some form of comparative perspective. The issue of "American exceptionalism," of what's different or the same about American life and thought, was at the heart of this theory and of the American studies movement with which it was so closely associated. In American studies, as Marcus Cunliffe has argued, "the assumption that the Americans were set apart from other peoples was taken as almost axiomatic." [16] In a sense, the consensus theorists took the dichotomy which the progressive historians saw within American experience and transformed it into a dichotomy between America and Europe. America was defined as the antithesis of Europe; the theme was, of course, an old one which could be formulated in a variety of ways to serve a variety of purposes. In the years after World War II, the scope of the argument was also broadened to encompass not just the difference between America and Europe but the uniqueness of America with respect to all the rest of the world. Was the American Revolution a real revolution or something different from those of Europe, Asia, and Latin America? Was the United States the "first new nation," whose experience had parallels with and lessons for the new nations of the twentieth century? Could Americans transcend their limited experience to understand and to act effectively with people of other societies and cultures? If the American experience was unique, it was irrelevant to the rest of the world; if it was relevant, it could not be unique. The preoccupation with this set of issues implied that there was indeed something different about the United States. In how many other countries did scholars and intellectuals debate the historical experience of their societies in terms of its uniqueness or relevance? The very fact that this issue was debated was, in some measure, evidence if not of American uniqueness at least of American hubris. Implicit in the argument for uniqueness was the assumption that no other society was as good as the United States; implicit in the argument for relevance was the assumption that every other society should be like the United States. Each side of the argument had its own form of national pride. Lost in the debate was the chastening possibility—which, I would suggest, was closer to actuality—that the United States could well be neither unique nor relevant.

The consensus interpretation of American politics was elaborated and developed in a variety of ways by historians and sociologists. Within the historical fraternity, the progressives and their disciples had "pushed polarized conflict as a principle of historical interpretation so far that no one could go further in that direction without risking self-caricature." [17] There was a need for a fresh start. While historians rode off in a variety of directions after abandoning the progressive interpretation, the major stream, insofar as there was one, clearly flowed from the springs of consensus. In sociology the end-of-ideology school plus the popularity of structural-functionalism and equilibrium models all tended to parallel, supplement, and reinforce from other methodological directions the message of the consensus school.

Within the discipline of political science, consensus did not play quite the same role as it did within sociology and history. It did not lead to the displacement of the earlier pluralist paradigm; rather it led to its reformulation and redefinition in conservative rather than radical terms. In history, Hofstadter argues, the last two major works clearly in the progressive tradition were Schlesinger's *The Age of Jackson* (1945) and Jensen's *The New Nation*

(1950). In political science, however, the main stream of pluralist analysis, which had flowered earlier in the writings of Bentley, Merriam, Herring, Holcombe, and Schattschneider, was carried forward and given a new lease on life in the works of Key, Truman, Dahl, and many others. Earlier the "discovery" of pluralism in American politics had been "shocking" in that it meant that American politics was not contained simply in the concepts of majority rule and individual rights. Organized groups, not popular majorities or individual citizens, were the hard reality of American politics. By the 1950s, however, pluralism was redefined from a bad thing to a good thing: it was a way of dispersing power and of insuring (through cross-cutting cleavages) moderation in politics. In the first decade of the century, the pluralist paradigm had been born of the same impulse to exposure and reform which produced the progressive interpretation: Beard could be indulgent toward Bentley.[18] In the 1950s, on the other hand, the pluralist interpretation became a corollary of the consensus model: Hartz could be indulgent toward Truman.[19] Within the basic ideological consensus of American politics, the only conflicts which could take place were the relatively minor ones among interest groups over their marginal shares in the economic pie. The pluralist interpretation was used to defend American politics against the C. Wright Millses and Floyd Hunters who argued that power was concentrated at the national and local levels. Its political and ideological functions shifted from the exposure of the evils of American politics to the celebration of its virtues. In due course, of course, this pluralistic celebration itself came under attack with the familiar arguments, first, that not all sectors of the population are equally represented in the group process and hence the interaction of groups produces a skewed and biased result in public policy, and secondly, that there are public interests which transcend group interests and which do not receive appropriate recognition in the group process.[20]

To be accepted and useful, a paradigm has to meet two tests. First, in one way or another it has to be meaningful and relevant, that is, it has to make sense to people in terms of what they see about them and what they feel they need. The progressive and then the pluralist paradigm met these tests during the reformist years of the early part of the century; the consensus and the redefined conservative pluralism paradigm met them in the Cold War years of the mid-twentieth century. During the late 1960s and early 1970s, domestic upheaval—racial conflict, student unrest, political controversy—combined with subsequent international détente to make consensus make less political sense than it did a decade earlier. Second, every paradigm also has to "make sense" in terms of the historical and political experience it purports to explain. It cannot be way off the scholarly mark no matter how useful it may be politically and ideologically. More specifically, in terms of explaining the principal characteristics of politics in a society, a paradigm should do three things. (a) It should highlight some aspect of social reality; it should distinguish what is of critical importance in the political experience of the society from what is of peripheral significance. (b) It should be comparative; it should call attention to the principal similarities and differences between the politics of the society and those of other societies. (c) It should be dynamic, in the sense that it should account for change (and continuities) in the political experience of the society.

As they have been developed by historians, political scientists, and American civilizationists, the three paradigms we are considering differ considerably in the extent to which they meet these criteria. The progressive paradigm makes somewhat more provision than the others for change: it is rooted in a theory of conflict which, like the Marxist class struggle, can be interpreted as looking forward to the progressive victory of one party over the other. On the other hand, the sandwiching of the complexity of American political struggle into a dualistic framework scarcely did justice to the complexity of that struggle, and the progressive theory had virtually nothing to say about the similarities and differences between American politics and other politics. The pluralist paradigm, on the other hand, came to grips with a critical reality of American politics, but had no theory of change (except in terms of the replacement of one interest group by another) and also shed little light on the comparisons and contrasts between American politics and that of other societies. Finally, the consensus theory was very much a product of an explicit comparison of the American experience with Europe but also had little to say about change and obviously failed to account for the conflict and violence which had taken place in American history. In this respect the Marxist categories of the consensus theory, at least as it was formulated by Hartz, became blinders. Implicitly it was assumed that the only real conflict was class conflict, and hence the absence of class conflict meant the presence of consensus. The United States, however, may well have had less class conflict but also more social and political violence than many European countries. "Americans," as Hofstadter neatly put it, "do not *need* ideological conflict to shed blood on a large scale." And, as Dahl has argued, the case can be made that the United States has experienced relatively severe conflict about once every twenty years.[21]

While the paradigms of the one, the two, and the many differ in their particular strengths and weaknesses, they also have one important characteristic in common. Each explains politics in terms of social structure. The decisive influence on the nature of American politics is held to be the nature of the American society: it is not political values, or institutions, or practices, or the nature of development and change. It is whether American society can best be understood in terms of one consensus, two classes, or many groups. The social structure also shapes the nature of the values, interests, and ideologies which are manifest in politics. There is a presumption of congruence between social unit and political outlook. The consensus is liberal; the classes are conservative and progressive; the groups are materialistically self-interested. In addition, the picture of society and hence of politics is, by and large, a static one. The progressive interpretation does hold open the possibility of the eventual victory of the popular party, but even with it and to a much greater extent with the consensus and pluralist schools, there is little provision for change. How will American society and politics in the future differ from what they have been in the past? At best, consensualists, progressives, and pluralists all suggest more of the same.

IV. The Comparative Context of Modernization

For a good part of this century American political science was political science of America. The strand of parochialism which developed in the 1890s remained strong; it coincided with the noncomparative, if not isolationist, inclinations of the progressive and pluralist paradigms. With a few exceptions comparative government (which, in any event, meant European government) was not at the center of the discipline. Even in the late 1930s, the two outstanding texts on comparative government were the products of two recent migrants: Carl Friedrich and Herman Finer. After World War II, however, the expansion of American influence throughout the world created the environment and the impetus to develop area studies programs and to attract political scientists to the analysis of what had been rather esoteric regions of the world. For political scientists, this work was originally and in larger part the study of foreign governments and then subsequently and in smaller part the study of comparative government. Comparative government, in turn, came to be defined as a subfield within the discipline distinct from American government. While the American studies programs were looking at the American political, intellectual, social, and literary experience increasingly in a comparative perspective, the dominant tendency within political science tended to separate comparative politics from American politics.

This tendency was in some measure tempered by the fact that the study of comparative politics requires typologies for the classification of political systems. In the years after World War II, two such typologies successively played critical roles. The first, the distinction between constitutional and totalitarian regimes, was an obvious product of World War II and the early Cold War. It provided a neat way of collapsing two enemies, Hitler's Germany and Stalin's Russia, into one intellectual pigeonhole. It also, however, meant that the United States itself had to be categorized. While American studies programs tended to draw the contrast between the United States and Western Europe, the categories used by political scientists brought the United States together with Western Europe, minimizing the differences in political institutions and practices between the two. In a sense, by stressing the contrast between America and Europe the American studies programs provided an intellectual rationale for pre-World War II foreign policy, while the political science categories in emphasizing the similarities provided a rationale for post-World War II foreign policy.

In the late 1950s the distinction between constitutionalism and totalitarianism in the study of comparative politics was supplemented and, in large part, supplanted by the distinction between modern and traditional societies and developed and underdeveloped political systems. "The field of comparative politics," as Lucian Pye observed, "has suddenly stopped being merely the study of the major European powers and has become the analysis of political development, one of the most youthful and vigorous subfields of the entire discipline of political science." [22] As the central concerns in the study of comparative politics, modernization and political development provided a more or less common intellectual framework for analyzing and comparing the politics of Asian, African, and Latin American countries. In due course, they also were seen to provide a framework within which the earlier experience of Western Europe and North America might be compared with the contemporary experience of Third World countries. Political scientists studying developing countries developed concepts, hypotheses, and theoretical frameworks which could be applied back to the historical analysis of more familiar societies.

Inasmuch as the United States was clearly the most modern society in the world and inasmuch as, in many dimensions, it was also one of the most politically developed, did it not make great good sense to look at American politics in terms of a paradigm of modernization? Such a paradigm would clearly provide the basis for the comparative analysis of similarities and differences with other societies, as, for instance, in Lipset's *The First New Nation*,[23] and it also clearly would provide a framework for analyzing continuity and change within American society. Why could we not learn a lot more about American politics by looking at it within a modernization framework and in comparison with the experience of other countries? The "modernization" and "political development" of America seemed to offer fertile fields for scholarly exploration.

Alas, it has not exactly worked out that way. To the best of my knowledge only one recent volume has been written with this goal explicitly in mind, and that, Clinton Rossiter's last book, *The American Quest* (1971)[24] leaves one with the undeniable feeling that the concepts of modernization and the experience of America do not really fit together. The reason is a familiar one which flows in part from the valid insights of the consensus theory. The United States was in many critical senses "born modern" as well as "born equal." Consequently, it has not had to modernize in the way in which most European and Third World societies have had to and hence the concepts and themes of modernization are not all that relevant to its history. In other societies, the critical issues have been whether, how, and under whose leadership modernization occurs; how the traditional elites take the leadership in the process or attempt to oppose it. The central feature is the conflict between old and new values, leaders, social forces. It is, however, precisely this sort of conflict which has, with one notable exception, been almost entirely absent from American history. It has generally lacked the tensions and traumas of modernization which have been central to the experience of other societies.

At its most fundamental level, modernization involves changes in human attitudes, which, in turn, requires conflicts within men and among men over traditional versus modern values. The modern syndrome of attitudes has perhaps been well summed up by Alex Inkeles in his "OM" scale, which includes: openness to innovation and change; wide-ranging interests and empathy; a tolerance of differences of opinion; present and future rather than past orientation; a belief in planning and organization; a sense of efficacy, that is, a belief that men can learn from and dominate their physical environment; a freedom from fatalism; an awareness of the dignity of others and a willingness to respect that dignity; a faith in science and technology; and a faith in distributive justice, that is, to each according to his contribution or work.[25] Traditional man would have just the opposite views. But the question then is: When were there traditional men in America? One cannot administer questionnaires to an eighteenth-century sample of Americans, but all the descriptions of American attitudes in the eighteenth and early nineteenth centuries highlight precisely those attitudes which Inkeles has defined as modern. When Crevecoeur asks who is this American, this new man, the answer is Alex Inkeles's "OM" man. The central problem of modernization, that of making men modern, was never much of a problem on these shores, and hence theories which see that as the central problem of development are of only dubious relevance.[26]

What is true of man is also in large part true, as Hartz has argued, of society. And as I have pointed out elsewhere, because there were no traditional or feudal institutions to be overthrown there was no need to create a modern system of government to carry out that purpose.[27] Modernization theories are thus irrelevant because American society was born modern without having to be modernized and American government could be left as it was because its society was modern. The concept of modernization has, however, had a demonstrated usefulness in the analysis of the one segment of American society, the South, where there was something which could be called a fully developed traditional social order. The actors in Southern history clearly have their counterparts in eighteenth- and nineteenth-century Europe and in twentieth-century Latin America. There is a landowning aristocracy, commercial oligarchs, foreign capital; a poor peasantry, slaves, politico-economic entrepreneurs, and populist demagogues. (To understand Huey Long, as Arthur Schlesinger has said, think of him as a Latin American populist dictator.[28]) Modernization concepts illuminate Southern experience precisely because it is different from other American experience, and hence H. Douglas Price, Lester Salamon, and others have been able to analyze aspects of Southern development in much the same way as other social scientists have analyzed development in the Middle East, Latin America, and Asia.[29]

V. The Conflict of Ideas vs. Institutions

The problem then remains. How to capture the valid elements of the unity, dualism, and diversity of the American experience embodied in the consensus, progressive, and pluralist paradigms and also take into account the changes and continuities within the American political system and the similarities and differences between that system and other systems? No one approach can provide a full answer. It does seem, however, that new concepts of American politics are more likely to evolve out of American political science than out of American area studies. The latter movement seems to have lost considerable momentum, if not to have burnt itself out. The Europe-America contrast which has played such a central role in its development is a relatively limited framework in comparison to those which could be adopted from comparative politics. While the concept of modernization generally is not of much help in understanding American development, other more specific, functional concepts and theories may be drawn from the comparative study of political development and applied usefully to the American experience. The need here is to reintegrate American politics into comparative politics, which was where it was in the 1880s, and from which it was dislodged by the parochialism of the Progressive movement.

More fundamentally there is the whole question of the relation between socioeconomic interests and politics. All three familiar paradigms rested on the assumption that political behavior and political ideas were outgrowths of socioeconomic interests. That this is often and, indeed, generally the case is clearly true. But the assumption of the correspondence between economic interests and political behavior—so dramatically reflected in their different ways in Beard, Bentley, and Hartz—also may leave much of politics unaccounted for.

This paper presents no paradigmatic panacea, but it does seem to make some sense to suggest at least two other lines of approach to American politics which may in some small way supplement those of the one, the two, and the many. The first involves the relation between political ideas and political institutions in the United States. All three familiar paradigms tend to minimize the autonomy of politics and particularly the independent role which political ideas may play as a stimulus, guide, and shaper of political action. They have generally, and correctly, assumed that political theory has been relatively underdeveloped in comparison with Europe. The highly systematized ideologies rooted in social classes have been notably absent from the American scene. But it is a mistake to move from this truth to the assumption that political ideas have played a less important role in the United States than in Europe. In fact just the reverse may be true. American politics has been characterized by less sophisticated political theory and more intense political beliefs than that of most other societies.

Political ideas have played a critical role in the American experience in two ways. First, more than in any other major society apart from the Soviet Union, political ideas have been the source of national identity. In Europe political ideology and nationalism crossed each other. Ideologies expressed and shaped the interests of "horizontal" units, social classes, while nationalism, in its various manifestations, expressed and shaped the interests of "vertical" units, ethnic and linguistic communities. This produced a system of cross-cutting cleavages. In nineteenth-century Europe, it was not immediately clear who had more in common: two aristocrats (or two bourgeois or two socialists), one of whom was a Frenchman; or two Frenchmen, one of whom was an aristocrat (or bourgeois or socialist). This interplay between nationalism and ideology led each to be expressed in more extreme form but also meant that each exercised a restraining effect on the political manifestations of the other. In the United States, on the other hand, nationalism was defined in terms of a set of political beliefs, a political creed, which formulated in imprecise but highly meaningful fashion the basic ideals of the American way of life. From Crevecoeur to de Tocqueville to Bryce to Myrdal to Brogan, foreign observers, as well as domestic ones, have not failed to comment on this striking phenomenon. A society produced by immigration needed such a way of defining its identity just as much as a society produced by revolution. If it were not for the "American creed," what, indeed, would Americans have in common?

Political beliefs thus played a necessary and positive role with respect to national identity and integration. They reinforced American nationalism and yet also in some respects moderated it. And in this respect there was an American consensus. The consensus theorists, however, tended to emphasize the *extent* of consensus over the *substance* of the consensus. The substance of that consensus was basically liberal, egalitarian, individualistic, populist. In 1889 Bryce summed it up in words which de Tocqueville might have used fifty years earlier and which Myrdal did, for all intents and purposes, use fifty years later. The key dogmas of American thinking, according to Bryce, were: (1) the individual has sacred rights; (2) the source of political power is the people; (3) all government is limited by law and the people; (4) local government is to be preferred to national government; (5) the majority is wiser than the minority; and (6) the less government the better.[30] The distinctive thing about the substance of the liberal consensus or American creed was its antigovernmental character. Populism, individualism, egalitarianism formed the basis for a standing indictment of any political institutions including American ones. The political creed which formed the basis of national identity was also the threat to governmental legitimacy. The more intensely Americans committed themselves to their national political beliefs, the more hostile and cynical they became about their political institutions. The legitimacy of American government varied inversely with belief in American ideals.

The extent to which people take those ideals seriously changes from time to time and from group to group. Commitment to political beliefs will be particularly strong during periods of rapid social and economic change, when the relations between social forces are changing, new groups are emerging on the scene, and old ones are fading. Certainly at times substantial groups of Americans have rededicated themselves to the creed, have been appalled at the gap between their ideals of how government should operate and the ways in which it actually does operate, and have made vigorous efforts to bring reality into conformity with the ideal. At other times, Americans have mouthed the rhetoric and clichés of the creed but have not been intensely concerned about the extent to which political practice measured up to these political ideals. Americans take pride in their governmental institutions only when they do not believe very deeply in American political ideals.

In this sense the dualism of American politics between American political ideas and American political institutions is rooted in the broad consensus on political ideas which has existed in America. This consensus has, in turn, furnished the basis for alternating periods of institutional stability, on the one hand, and ideological renewal, on the other. Until the present, the reaffirmation of American political ideas has taken place in four major historical instances: the Revolution against British imperial institutions; the Jacksonian movement against the undemocratic and elitist aspects of the established political and economic order; the struggle culminating in the Civil War to restrict and eventually to eliminate the "peculiar institution" of slavery in the South; and the Populist and Progressive movement at the turn of the century to impose limits on the emerging concentrations of corporate economic power. In these invocations, American ideas of equality, individualism, and popular sovereignty have been used for anti-imperial, anti-elitist, anti-slavery, and anti-big-business purposes. The principal invokers of the creed have been the spokesmen for yeoman farmers and independent entrepreneurial and professional types. Their relative success in challenging hierarchical institutions has declined steadily with each successive invocation. British imperial rule was effectively eliminated in the 1770s and 1780s. The existing political and economic system was in large part but not entirely democratized in the 1820s and 1830s. In the 1860s and 1870s the legal basis of slavery was eliminated, but the social, economic, political, and even legal basis for a caste system in the South remained for almost another century. Finally, the Populist-Progressive effort to curtail and break up corporate power had, in many respects, the air of a movement reacting against the mainstream of historical development; it was a partial success at best.

Political ideas have thus had a role in America, albeit a purgative role which is not characteristic of other societies. In countries in which there are a variety of ideologies and belief systems, there are a variety of sources of challenge to governmental institutions but also almost invariably a variety of defenses for major institutions. Tradition and social structure furnish a basis for the legitimacy of some institutions and particular ideologies and political theories can be utilized to legitimize individual institutions. Attacks on one set of institutions from the perspective of one ideology generate equally intense defenses of that institution from the perspective of other ideologies. In the United States, on the other hand, the consensus is basically antigovernmental. What justification is there for government, for hierarchy, discipline, secrecy, coercion, the suppression of the claims of individuals and groups, within the American context? In terms of American beliefs, government is supposed to be egalitarian, participatory, open, noncoercive, and responsive to the demands of individuals and groups. Yet no government can be these things in any whole-hearted way and still remain a government.

The ideological challenge to American government thus comes not from abroad but from at home, not from the conspiracies of anarchists but from the idealism of liberals. To the extent that Americans become carried away by their political ideas, they are in danger of doing away with their political institutions. It is in this conflict and interaction between ideas and institutions, between the invocation of the former by some social forces for an attack on the latter, that there lies a critical dimension of American politics which reflects its consensual, dualistic, and pluralistic quality, distinguishes it from most other political systems, and throws some light on both the cyclical and secular trends in American political evolution.

VI. The Conflict of Generations

American society has been distinguished by an unusual degree of consensus. It has also been characterized by an unusual amount of social and economic change. Change, however, usually involves conflict. How can large amounts of change coexist with large amounts of consensus? Part of the answer, of course, lies in the extent to which the opportunities for mobility and expansion have permitted social-economic change to be carried out apart from the political realm. But another part of the picture concerns the relative pre-eminence of a type of group cleavage in America which is closely associated with the tensions between political ideas and political institutions.

Conflict and change in Europe have normally been analyzed in terms of the rise and fall of social classes. Class analysis clearly has some relevance to the American experience, but also considerably less than to the European experience. Much more important in America than in Europe has been the role of generations and generational differences. In this sense, one can argue that a consensus has existed in the United States and its fundamentals have remained relatively stable, but its particular manifestations in attitudinal outlooks and public priorities and policies have changed from one generation to another. In Great Britain, for instance, the middle-class ethos and the working-class ethos (including in each social values, life styles, political attitudes, speech) are relative constants of the social structure. In the United States, on the other hand, classes are less sharply differentiated and generations more sharply differentiated than they are in Europe. This is true both in terms of the leading elements of particular age groups—those who articulate and express the group's values in literature, art, politics—and even, in a different way, for the mass of the public as a whole. The massive swings of public opinion from the progressivism of 1912 to the stand-pattism of 1920 to the reformism of 1932 clearly cut across class lines and while the evidence is inconclusive, are yet susceptible of interpretation in terms of generational changes. More recently, survey data have revealed marked differences in outlook among generations which can, in varying degrees, be explained in terms of the maturation, interaction, and experiential theories of generational differences.[31]

"Among democratic nations," de Tocqueville argued, "each generation is a new people." [32] In some measure, American history is divisible into phases, or "peoples," which more or less coincide with different generations: the Founding Fathers; the new generation of Western political leaders which emerged in and after 1810; the generation focused on sectionalism and slavery which emerged in and after 1840; the post-Civil War generation of politician-plutocrats; the Populist-Progressive generation; the stand-patters of the 1920s; the New Deal generation; and the Cold War generation which emerged after World War II. During each phase leaders sprang from a different age cohort and embodied a different set of values and policies which came to reflect a high degree of popular consensus. The major political struggles took place between the advance guard of the new generation and the rear guard of its predecessor. The extent to which conflict has been intergenerational also explains why conflict in the United States has so often had such a fleeting quality. By its very nature, intergenerational conflict tends to be intense but brief, as in due course the consensus of one generation supersedes that of the earlier generation.[33] The shift in consensus pioneered by one generation, however, often means an abrupt and vicious turning on those associated with the consensus of the earlier generation. In the 1940s the Red scare and McCarthyism produced the capture of some Soviet spies but also the pillorying of many well-meaning liberals of the New Deal generation as security risks and subversives. By 1970, the latter (in almost classic Soviet fashion) were being resurrected and rehabilitated as heroes and martyrs, while a new generation was, in turn, denouncing the foreign policy leaders of the intervening years as imperialists and war criminals.

The relevance of generations to American politics is also underscored by the extent to which various aspects of American experience have been interpreted in terms of cycles which normally approximate a generation in longevity: Schlesinger's liberal and conservative tides, Klingberg's introversion and extroversion moods, Burnham's party realignments, and Harris's oscillations in social mobility serve as examples.[34] Has the history of any other modern society been so frequently interpreted in such generational cycles? In addition, of course, the generational notion has been explicitly applied to the differences between first, second, and third generation immigrants; to the nature of the leadership during the Revolution by Elkins and McKitrick; and to the Populist-Progressive era by Hofstadter.[35]

Like classes, generations have objective and subjective existences. Objective existence exists in part simply from age differences, but also from the facts of generational interaction and differences in generational experience. Generational consciousness, however, is a rarer phenomenon and it is only such consciousness which turns the generation from a categoric group into an interaction group and a meaningful political actor. Generational consciousness is not constant; some age cohorts in some places are much more conscious of themselves as a cohesive unit than are others. The generation as a source of political action is also one whose interests cannot normally be defined in familiar economic terms. The generation is an experiential and attitudinal group, not an economic interest group. And, as we have suggested, one of the most significant differences which can exist between generations is precisely the extent to which they have serious commitments to American political ideals. In addition to the other phases and cycles in terms of which American history can be interpreted along generational lines, the cycle of political idealism and institutional stability clearly plays a major role.

VII. Beyond the One, the Two, and the Many

Contrary to the implications of the consensus thesis, conflict has played a significant role in American political development. Contrary to the images of the pluralist and progressive paradigms, the most significant forms of conflict have not been simply between upper and lower classes or among economic interest groups. They have instead been the product of differing degrees of intensity of belief in American political ideas and of commitment to American political institutions. They have also reflected the differing experiences and priorities of successive generations. The predominant role of these types of conflict helps to differentiate American politics from those of other societies. It also helps to explain some of the patterns of continuity and change which have characterized American politics. In the development and refinement of other comparative, dynamic, and realistic concepts, of which these are only limited specific examples, new paradigms of American politics may eventually emerge which will be more illuminating, useful, and relevant than those of the one, the two, and the many.

NOTES

1. Louis Hartz, *The Liberal Tradition in America* (New York: Harcourt, Brace, 1955), p. 27.

2. For the first major attack, see John Higham, "The Cult of the 'American Consensus': Homogenizing Our History," *Commentary*, 27 (Feb. 1959), pp. 93ff.

3. Quoted in Richard Hofstadter, *The Progressive Historians: Turner, Beard, Parrington* (New York: Vintage Books, 1970), p. 438.

4. Alexander Hamilton, in Max Farrand, ed., *The Records of the Federal Convention* (New Haven: Yale University Press, 1911), I, 299; John Adams, *Works*, ed. by Charles Francis Adams (Boston: Little Brown, 1850–56), VI, 185; IX, 570.

5. Hartz, *Liberal Tradition*, p. 31.

6. Richard Hofstadter, *The Age of Reform* (New York: Alfred A. Knopf, 1956), p. 154.

7. Quoted in Albert Somit and Joseph Tanenhaus, *The Development of American Political Science* (Boston: Allyn and Bacon, 1967), p. 32.

8. Bernard Crick, *The American Science of Politics* (Berkeley and Los Angeles: University of California Press, 1959), p. 84.

9. Somit and Tanenhaus, *American Political Science*, pp. 61–62.

10. Crick, *American Science*, pp. 111–12.

11. David E. Apter, "Comparative Politics and Political Thought: Past Influences and Future Development," in Harry Eckstein and David E. Apter, eds., *Comparative Politics: A Reader* (Glencoe: The Free Press, 1963), p. 730.

12. Hartz, *Liberal Tradition*, p. 30.

13. See Tremaine McDowell, *American Studies* (Minneapolis: University of Minnesota Press, 1948), pp. 26ff.; Marshall W. Fishwick, ed., *American Studies in Transition* (Philadelphia: University of Pennsylvania Press, 1964), p. 7; David W. Marcell, "Recent Trends in American Studies in the United States," *American Studies*, 8 (Spring 1970), p. 5ff.

14. Louis Hartz and others, *The Founding of New Societies* (New York: Harcourt, Brace, 1964).

15. Hartz, *Liberal Tradition*, p. 285.

16. Marcus Cunliffe, "New World, Old World: The Historical Antithesis," in Richard Rose, ed., *Lessons from America* (London: Macmillan, 1974).

17. Hofstadter, *Progressive Historians*, p. 439.

18. Beard praised Bentley for his efforts "to put politics on a basis of realism where it belongs" and for making "effective use of the idea of 'group interests,' as distinct from class interests in the Marxian sense." *Political Science Quarterly*, 23 (1908), 739–41, quoted in Hofstadter, *Progressive Historians*, p. 186n.

19. In Hartz's words, "Bentley went deeper than Beard, for the free and easy play of pressure groups was a real characteristic of the American liberal world, inspired by the moral settlement which underlay it and hence obscured class lines." *Liberal Tradition*, p. 250.

20. See Henry S. Kariel, *The Decline of American Pluralism* (Stanford: Stanford University Press, 1961); Grant McConnell, *Private Power and American Democracy* (New York: Alfred A. Knopf, 1966); Theodore J. Lowi, *The End of Liberalism* (New York: W. W. Norton, 1969).

21. Hofstadter, *Progressive Historians*, p. 461; Robert A. Dahl, *Pluralist Democracy in the United States: Conflict and Consent* (Chicago: Rand McNally, 1967), pp. 283ff.

22. Lucian W. Pye, "Advances and Frustrations in Comparative Politics," in Fred W. Riggs, ed., *International Studies: Present Status and Future Prospects* (Philadelphia: American Academy of Political and Social Science, Monograph No. 12, Oct. 1971), p. 94.

23. Seymour Martin Lipset, *The First New Nation* (New York: Basic Books, 1963).

24. Clinton Rossiter, *The American Quest, 1790–1860: An Emerging Nation in Search of Identity, Unity, and Modernity* (New York: Harcourt Brace Jovanovich, 1971).

25. Alex Inkeles, "The Modernization of Man," in Myron Weiner, ed., *Modernization* (New York: Basic Books, 1966), pp. 138ff.; and David Norton Smith and Alex Inkeles, "The OM Scale: A Comparative Socio-Psychological Measure of Individual Modernity," *Sociometry*, 29 (Dec. 1966), 353ff.

26. That is, they are of limited relevance so far as understanding the American past is concerned. They may be considerably more useful in understanding the transition which appears to be taking place in America and some other affluent societies from industrialism to post-industrialism. The parallels of this transition with the earlier transition from agrarianism to industrialism are at times rather striking. See my "Post-Industrial Politics: How Benign Will It Be?," *Comparative Politics*, vol. VI, no. 2 (Jan. 1974), 163–91.

27. *Political Order in Changing Societies* (New Haven: Yale University Press, 1968), pp. 125ff.

28. Arthur M. Schlesinger, Jr., *The Politics of Upheaval* (Boston: Houghton Mifflin, 1960), p. 68: "At bottom, Huey Long resembled, not a Hitler or a Mussolini, but a Latin American dictator, a Vargas or a Perón. Louisiana was in many respects a colonial region, an underdeveloped area; its Creole traditions gave it an almost Latin American character. Like Vargas and Perón, Long was in revolt against economic colonialism, against the oligarchy, against the smug and antiquated past; like them, he stood in a muddled way for economic modernization and social justice; like them, he was most threatened by his own arrogance and cupidity, his weakness for soft living and his rage for personal power. And, like them, he could never stop."

29. See H. Douglas Price, "Southern Politics in the Sixties: Notes on Economic Development and Political Modernization" (paper presented at the Annual Meeting, American Political Science Association, September 1964); Lester Salamon, "Protest, Politics, and Modernization in the American South: Mississippi as a 'Developing Society'" (Ph.D. diss., Harvard University, 1972); and idem, "Leadership and Modernization: The Emerging Black Political Elite in the American South," *Journal of Politics*, 35 (August 1973), 615–646.

30. James Bryce, *The American Commonwealth* (London: Macmillan, 1891), I, 417–418.

31. The *maturation* theory holds that intergenerational differences are the result of differing positions in the life cycle, and that each generation in effect repeats the cycle of earlier generations (e.g., each moves from youthful liberalism to elderly conservatism). The *interaction* theory holds that the outlook of a later generation is a reaction to that of the earlier generation (e.g., if one generation values economic success, the next generation will assign low priority to that value and instead pursue cultural achievement). The *experiential* theory holds that a generation is produced by a shared historical experience at a formative time in its development (late teens or early twenties) which shapes its outlook and distinguishes it from earlier and later age cohorts whose views were the product of different experiences (e.g., Munich and Pearl Harbor shaped the outlook on foreign policy of one American generation which remained dominant until an equally traumatic event—Vietnam—generated a different outlook in another generation). On the role of generations in political analysis, see Karl Mannheim, "The Problem of Generations," *Essays on the Sociology of Knowledge* (New York: Oxford University Press, 1952), pp. 276–322; Marvin Rintala, "A Generation in Politics: A Definition," *Review of Politics*, 25 (1963), 509–522; Norman B. Ryder, "The Cohort as a Concept in the Study of Social Change," *American Sociological Review*, 30 (1965), 509–522; Philip E. Converse, "Of Time and Partisan Stability," *Comparative Political Studies*, 2 (1969), 139–171; Neal E. Cutler, "Generation, Maturation, and Party Affiliation: A Cohort Analysis," *Public Opinion*

Quarterly, 33 (1969–70), 583–588, and "Generational Analysis in Political Science" (paper presented at the Annual Meeting, American Political Science Association, September 1971).

32. De Tocqueville, *Democracy in America* (New York: Vintage Books, 1955), 2, p. 62.

33. For a striking recent illustration of this point, see Graham Allison, "Cool It: The Foreign Policy of Young America," *Foreign Policy* (Winter 1970–71), pp. 144–160. Allison contrasts ten "axioms of the postwar era" of foreign policy with their opposites which were the "axioms of elite young Americans" under thirty and argues that there is a fundamental generational difference on foreign policy. And, indeed, there was—for all of about five years in the 1960s. It is quite clear that an overwhelming consensus exists now among elite Americans in their fifties on the validity of Allison's "axioms of young Americans."

34. Arthur M. Schlesinger, *The Tides of National Politics, Paths to the Present* (Boston: Houghton Mifflin, 1964), pp. 89–103; Frank L. Klingberg, "The Historical Alternation of Moods in American Foreign Policy," *World Politics*, 4 (January 1952), 239–273; and Samuel P. Huntington, *Military Intervention, Political Involvement, and the Unlessons of Vietnam* (Chicago: Adlai E. Stevenson Institute of International Affairs, 1968); Walter Dean Burnham, *Critical Elections and the Mainsprings of American Politics* (New York: W. W. Norton, 1970); P. M. G. Harris, "The Social Origins of American Leaders: The Demographic Foundations," *Perspectives in American History*, 3 (1969), 159–344.

35. Margaret Mead, *And Keep Your Powder Dry* (New York: William Morrow, 1943); Stanley Elkins and Eric McKitrick, "The Founding Fathers: Young Men of the Revolution," *Political Science Quarterly*, 76 (June 1961), 181–217; Hofstadter, *The Age of Reform*, pp. 165–168.

Political Science and East Asian Area Studies

Chalmers Johnson

UNIVERSITY OF CALIFORNIA, BERKELEY

EDITOR'S NOTE

Historically, scholars of East Asia contributed to the popular Western belief in the mysterious East, cutting themselves off from the mainstreams of scholarship and escaping into their own esoteric traditions. Rather than facilitating general understanding, the pioneers of Chinese and Japanese studies joined in exaggerating the complexities of understanding languages based on ideographs, and thus they tended to set themselves apart from all other traditions of scholarship.

This tendency was further heightened before World War II because the elite centers of Sinology and Japanology were in Paris and Berlin at the heart of the most refined and rarefied academic environment of the European continent.* Young Americans anxious to specialize in China or Japan paradoxically went to Europe first rather than to Asia, and there they were initiated into a most select society. The code of this fraternity demanded years of study before publication should be tried, and one

* An earlier version of this paper appeared in *World Politics*, vol. XXVI, no. 4, July, 1974, pp. 560–75.

always guarded against any suggestion of rude boldness by exaggerated modesty and the use of titles which suggested one's effort was not more than a preliminary note, a first step, and more was customarily promised for the future than was ever delivered. In contrast to physical scientists, who are impatient to communicate their findings long before digesting their significance, the Sinologists tended to hold their knowledge close to their chests, and like poker players only revealed one card at a time, or what was necessary to surpass a competitor. The established authorities frequently achieved their eminence through word of mouth, weighty lectures, and devastating reviews of any scholar foolish enough to practice publication. The discipline was like an iceberg, what showed was assumed to be trivial, and everyone cooperated in conspiring to suggest that the knowledge possessed by the initiated far exceeded anything that could be learned from merely reading in any Western language.

Possibly, it required a shock as severe as World War II to break down this tradition. In any case, the requirements of rapidly training language specialists and the spectacular increase in the numbers of young Americans with first-hand experiences in Asia dramatically altered the nature of Chinese and Japanese studies. As Chalmers Johnson's chapter indicates, an entirely new breed of East Asian specialists has emerged in the past two decades. Instead of being cut off from the rest of academia, the new tradition of scholarship on China and Japan demands that the student not only employ the newest techniques of social research but that he also make a substantial contribution to the advance of concepts and findings in the mainstream of social sciences. Chalmers Johnson has carefully weighed the quality of this new body of social science literature, which has only just appeared but which already displays marked signs of maturity and sophistication.

Political science "area studies," or what the American Political Science Association calls "foreign and comparative government and politics" in order to insure that they not be confused with the biggest area study of them all, United States government and politics, have always posed difficulties for the Emily Posts of the discipline. Not a year goes by without a guardian of the method-ological flame writing an article bemoaning the "atheoretical" quality of area studies or issuing a warning that "The immersion in local materials may cast the researcher adrift far from any theoretical shore." [1] Strangely enough, despite these strictures, area studies continue to meet all kinds of market tests: publishers much prefer them to other forms of political science writing (they sell), and students write more dissertations in this field than in any other of the eight categories of political science recognized by the A.P.S.A.[2] In Chinese studies alone, between 1945 and 1970, Americans wrote some 1,401 dissertations in all fields, while at least 2,217 were written in the various Western languages, including Russian.[3] This is a rather large number of drifters away from the theoretical shore (perhaps they were merely heeding Chairman Mao's dictum, "We learn to swim by swimming"). Equally astonishing, given the hostility of political science tastemakers to area studies, between 1946 and 1970 the Ford Foundation alone spent $26.8 million on Chinese studies in the United States, while the U.S. government contributed an additional $15.0 million.[4] It is of course possible that the China specialists were merely adrift in a sea of money.

There have been defenders of area studies, but their defenses usually tend to sustain rather than weaken the case that area studies are not quite respectable, even if they are profitable and popular. The two most common defenses are (1) area studies, of East Asia, for example, are important to the United States as a matter of national interest (our last three wars started there, we trade a lot with Japan, etc.); and (2) East Asia embodies one of the world's three or four great civilizations (much of our social science is culture-bound, we need to offer students a well-rounded education, etc.).[5] I tend to agree with both of these views, but neither constitutes an intellectual defense, and the first has become a virtual anathema in many of our "liberal" institutions of learning.

One criticism of East Asian area studies is irrefutable: the field is dominated by historians. And history, although undoubtedly basic to social science, is at the same time antithetical to social science for the simple reason that "explaining what a thing is . . . is just not the same enterprise at all as explaining why it . . . happened." [6] The domination of historians has inhibited, if not intimidated, social scientists, so that as Richard Wilson has pointed out, there is "a frequently articulated need on the part of many scholars of China to be intellectually acceptable to the non-social science reference group within Chinese studies." [7] Although I agree with this observation, it is not so much a criticism of political science area studies as it is a plea for more of them and fewer historical studies.

The area specialist is, of course, granted a role within the discipline. He is regarded as a supplier of raw materials, rather like a Bantu miner, chipping away at the cliff face of a South African mine, who is supposed to ship the unrefined ore off to the master goldsmiths living elsewhere—in this case, to "generalists," or "theorists," or "comparativists" toiling away at New Haven, Cambridge, Ann Arbor, or the Stanford "think tank," where the data will be processed. Even Dankwart Rustow acknowledges, "There is no question that without the solid empirical foundation laid by such studies [area studies], past and future, no intelligent theorizing about political modernization would be possible." [8] However, rather like the Third World itself, a good many nationalizations are going on: the theorists have not been sending back very good theories to the field, and some of the commodity suppliers are going into manufacturing for themselves. This is a point we shall illustrate later.

A few political science theorists do take area studies seriously, in an intellectual sense. Arend Lijphart, in what is probably the best recent article on the comparative method, finds that "The area approach appears to lend itself quite well to . . . the comparative method because of the cluster of characteristics that areas tend to have in common and that can, therefore, be used as controls. . . . By means of an inductive process—a factor analysis of 54 social and cultural variables on 82 countries—Bruce M. Russett discovered socio-culturally similar groupings of countries, which correspond closely to areas or regions of the world as usually defined. Comparability is indeed not inherent in any given area, but it is more likely within an area than in a randomly selected set of countries." [9]

On this score East Asia seems to form a natural laboratory for comparative analysis: contemporary China and Japan—controllable for a range of factors including relative ethnic homogeneity, influence of classical Sinitic civilization, closure to foreign intercourse from the seventeenth to the nineteenth centuries, and primary challenges from Western imperialism within a fifteen-year period—today constitute the two most important archetypes of the "revolutionary" and the "reformist" strategies of national development.[10] In addition to the use of areas to solve the control problem, Lijphart recommends "diachronic," or "era," studies of a single country—for example, the comparison of the Weimar and Bonn republics in Germany in order to analyze a range of German political problems. This is of course possible and has been undertaken in East Asian area studies,[11] but an equally good opportunity for the kind of control suggested by Lijphart can be found by comparing the halves of divided countries, of which two important examples exist in the East Asian area—North and South Korea, and North and South Vietnam. Relatively little research has actually been done utilizing the Sino-Japanese or divided nation comparisons, but at least the pretheoretical foundations for the latter have been laid by the monumental two-volume work, *Communism in Korea*, by Robert Scalapino and Chong-sik Lee (Berkeley, 1973).

In addition to proposing area and era studies, Lijphart believes that the comparative method (here understood as one of a triumvirate of fundamental strategies of scientific research, the other two being the experimental and the statistical methods) can be carried out through the case study. He distinguishes six ideal types of case study, and an exploration of them affords us the opportunity both to review the intellectual place of area studies in social science and to survey some of the recent reports of research in the East Asian field.

Lijphart's first type is the "atheoretical case study." At first glance, this category seems to be nonexistent, since even the purest forms of description still depend upon theoretical concepts. "Only a totally mystical experience," writes Leonard B. Meyer, "is entirely nonanalytic, and it cannot be conceptualized or even adequately described—since the act of description is itself a distortion. Those who seek to savor the singularity of their own psyches must, therefore, abandon all hope of rational discourse or intelligible communication. The only valid response to unmediated experience is silence. As Tom Lehrer has said: 'If you can't communicate, the least you can do is shut up!' " [12]

Perhaps the only widespread form of supposedly "pure" description in the political field is that of an intelligence estimate made by a national government, in which the analyst attempts to avoid every impulse toward the theoretical or conceptual because it may prove as easily a source of error as of insight. Needless to say, however, no intelligence estimate is ever *purely* descriptive; that is why they are so often intensely controversial.[13] What Lijphart seems to mean by the "atheoretical case study" is one in which the writer is wholly innocent of, or unselfconscious about, the concepts and theoretical notions that influence his descriptions. The value of such books is that they offer their descriptions uncluttered by jargon or the pretensions of the author. The reader must, of course, exercise his judgment about the distortions implicit in an atheoretical description, but then he must also do this with selfconsciously theoretical books, where the bias may be greater simply because the theorist is under the impression that he has eliminated it through the use of his, perhaps worthless, methodology. Examples of outstanding atheoretical descriptive works in East Asian area studies include Edward E. Rice, *Mao's Way* (Berkeley, 1972), and Ezra Vogel, *Canton under Communism* (Cambridge, 1969).

Lijphart's second category, the "interpretive case study," is according to him an exercise in "applied science." "In these studies," he writes, "a generalization is applied to a specific case with the aim of throwing light on the case rather than of improving the generalization in any way." Works in this category are of the type that are said to fulfill the alleged national interest function of area studies: they utilize the best of social science theory in order to explain the politics of an area of concern or attention. It is sometimes forgotten that the purpose of empirical theory, or of science itself, is to make precisely such interpretive case studies possible—that is, to allow the perception of pattern and structure in the world and to permit the making of choices.

Lijphart makes this point, but in suggesting that the essence of the interpretive case study is the application of theory to the problem, he greatly oversimplifies "applied science." As Leonard B. Meyer has argued with regard to the field of explaining music: "Because specific musical events are the result of nonrecurring concatenations of conditions and variables, no set of general laws can adequately explain the particular relationships embodied in an actual composition. In other words, no matter how refined and inclusive the laws of music theory become, their use in the explanation of particular musical events will have to depend in part upon the *ad hoc* hypotheses of common sense. . . . A theory which covered every possible interaction of all possible variables would be useless because it would lack precisely what any theory must have—namely, generality." [14] Many of the controversies in political science over the alleged "inadequacies" of theoretical formulations derive from a misplaced belief that a theory can or should explain everything about a concrete case—for example, the often lamented inadequacy of theories of revolution and political violence, a subfield of direct relevance to East Asian area studies.[15] This is a problem to which we shall return. The following works in the East Asian field constitute, in my opinion, interpretive case studies, but only in the sense that they are instances of "applied science" as described by Meyer: A. D. Barnett, *Cadres, Bureaucracy, and Political Power in Communist China* (New York, 1967); Ruth Benedict, *The Chrysanthemum and the Sword* (Boston, 1946); John Lewis, *Leadership in Communist China* (Ithaca, 1963); William W. Lockwood, ed., *The State and Economic Enterprise in Modern Japan* (Princeton, 1965); Roberta Wohlstetter, *Pearl Harbor: Warning and Decision* (Stanford, 1962); and the work mentioned earlier by Scalapino and Lee on Korean Communism.

The next category, "Hypothesis-generating case studies," is one of the types, according to Lijphart, that is most conducive to theory-building. They begin, in his words, "with a more or less vague notion of possible hypotheses to be tested subsequently among a larger number of cases. Their objective is to develop theoretical generalizations in areas where no theory exists yet." The East Asian field has produced a rather large number of these case studies, suggesting that the area offers many forms of politics that are as yet unexplained by political science and that political science theory is not as "general" as some of its authors think. Examples include Nobutaka Ike, *Japanese Politics* (New York, second edition, 1972), on the theory of stable patron-client democracy; Chalmers Johnson, *Peasant Nationalism and Communist Power* (Stanford, 1962), on the processes and motivational bases of the wartime mobilization of the peasantry in China and Yugoslavia; Robert Lifton, *Thought Reform and the Psychology of Totalism* (New York, 1961), on the way Chinese culture is conducive to Chinese Communist psychic engineering; Chie Nakane, *Japanese*

Society (Berkeley, 1970), on "vertical stratification" and its consequences for social organization and politics; Lucian W. Pye, *The
Spirit of Chinese Politics* (Cambridge, 1968), on the psychocultural
foundations of authority in China; Benjamin Schwartz, *Chinese
Communism and the Rise of Mao* (Cambridge, second edition,
1958), on "ideological degeneration" in the migration of Marxism
eastward; William Skinner and Edwin Winckler, in A. Etzioni, ed.,
Complex Organizations (New York, 1969), on cycles of compliance
in Chinese Communist policy implementation; Frederic Wakeman,
Jr., *History and Will* (Berkeley, 1973), on the nature and implications of the synthesis of Chinese and Western philosophical
traditions in the thought of Mao Tse-tung; and K. A. Wittfogel,
Oriental Despotism (New Haven, 1957), on the socioeconomic bases
of authoritarianism in traditional and modern China.

Lijphart lists fourth what he calls "theory-confirming case
studies," that is, "analyses of single cases within the framework of
established generalizations." Such studies seem to resemble interpretive case studies, and therefore the same reservations apply to
them as to the second category regarding Lijphart's somewhat
jejune understanding of "applied science." Actually, very few
studies are undertaken solely to test a proposition, and his
contention that "the demonstration that one more case fits does not
strengthen [the proposition] a great deal" underestimates the value
of such work. These case studies are comparable to "normal
science" in the puzzle-solving sense described by Thomas Kuhn in
his *Structure of Scientific Revolutions.* Puzzle-solving is omitted in
Lijphart's division of the work of science into "theorizing" and
"applied science," thereby overlooking the fact that it is usually in
the interstices between the two where theory actually becomes
operational and anomalies are discovered. A few examples of work
in the East Asian field that seem to belong to the theory-confirming
category are: Robert Bellah, *Tokugawa Religion* (Glencoe, 1957), a
test of the Weberian theory of entrepreneurial motivation in a
Japanese context; G. DeVos and H. Wagatsuma, eds., *Japan's
Invisible Race* (Berkeley, 1966), a test of the theory of caste in a
context in which race is not the primary stigma; Glenn Paige, *The
Korean Decision* (New York, 1968), a test of decision-making
theory in the context of the first week of the Korean War; Richard
Solomon, *Mao's Revolution and the Chinese Political Culture*

(Berkeley, 1971), a test of much of the psychocultural theory of politics, including the hypotheses of Lucian Pye mentioned earlier; Robert Ward and Dankwart Rustow, eds., *Political Modernization in Japan and Turkey* (Princeton, 1964), an attempt to apply the theory of "political modernization"; Max Weber, *The Religion of China* (Glencoe, 1951), a "negative proof" of Weber's own theory of the relationship between religion and economic enterprise; and James W. White, *The Sōkagakkai and Mass Society* (Stanford, 1970), an explicit test of Kornhauser's and others' theories of the genesis and nature of mass society, using the explosive development of a religiopolitical movement in Japan as a case study.

The next category in Lijphart's list is "theory-infirming case studies," which are said to be similar to theory-confirming case studies in terms of their low theoretical import. This is because, "assuming that the proposition [being tested] is solidly based on a large number of cases, . . . theory-infirming case studies merely weaken the generalization marginally." The assumption here, however, seems inconsistent with Lijphart's overall analysis of the comparative method, since there is "no clear dividing line between the statistical and comparative methods; the difference depends on the number of cases," and with the principal problems facing the comparative method being "many variables, small number of cases." [16] It would seem that while a theory-infirming case might have only a marginal effect on a statistically-derived proposition, it could have a major effect on a proposition derived via the comparative method, given the small number of cases on which it is based. Whatever effect infirming studies have on the theory under test, the same reservations apply to Lijphart's belief that they, like interpretive and theory-confirming studies, involve merely applying a theory to some "data." Examples that come to mind from the East Asian area include: Chalmers Johnson, *Conspiracy at Matsukawa* (Berkeley, 1972), a challenge to the proposition that during the Allied occupation Japan internalized American procedures in the criminal law field; Jack M. Potter, *Capitalism and the Chinese Peasant* (Berkeley, 1968), a challenge to the theory that imperialist treaty ports led to the impoverishment of the Chinese peasantry and to the polarization of Chinese society; Mark Selden, *The Yenan Way* (Cambridge, 1971), a challenge to the theory of a politically-based mobilization of the Chinese peasantry during the Communist revolution in favor of a theory of economically-based mobilization; and James R. Townsend, *Political Participation in Communist China* (Berkeley, 1967), an explicit challenge to the theory that increased political participation increases popular influence on political decisions.

Finally, Lijphart cites the "deviant case study," which together with hypothesis-generating studies is said to contribute most to the development of theory. These are "studies of single cases that are known to deviate from established generalizations. They are selected in order to reveal why the cases are deviant." In the East Asian field, even though most case studies might be fitted into this category given the Western bias of much theory, we might mention: Robert E. Cole, *Japanese Blue Collar* (Berkeley, 1971), on the extent to which the behavior of the Japanese industrial working class can be explained using Western-derived generalizations; Ronald P. Dore, *English Factory: Japanese Factory* (Berkeley, 1973), on the same subject but employing a direct comparison between a factory of the English Electric Corporation and one of the Hitachi Electrical Manufacturing Company; Donald C. Hellmann, *Japan and East Asia* (New York, 1972), on the anomaly of Japan's relatively weak state but great economic power; Franz Schurmann, *Ideology and Organization in Communist China* (Berkeley, 1966), on the characteristics of the Chinese Communist revolutionary system in light of the Soviet model; and Donald W. Treadgold, ed., *Soviet and Chinese Communism, Similarities and Differences* (Seattle, 1967), on the same subject as Schurmann.

As this typology of case studies and list of illustrative works indicate, an intellectual defense of area studies more serious than the "national interest," "exotic cultures," and "raw materials supplier" defenses can be made and sustained. It must be said, however, that very few of the works listed above were actually written as case studies, and the idea that they should be so regarded is only slightly less misleading than calling them raw data for the "generalists." There is, in fact, a defense to be made of area studies that goes beyond any possible roles they may have to play as various kinds of case studies. It is a perspective that reveals a logical foundation and contribution to social science (not to mention fascination for the political researcher) that is every bit as indispensable to true scientific thought about politics as any other style or mode of analysis. The case I have in mind for area studies, not necessarily as they are taught and practiced in area studies institutes, is similar to what Verba has identified as the "disciplined configurative approach," but I prefer to present it here in terms of some ideas borrowed from the "critical analysis" of music.[17]

In his 1971 Ernest Bloch lectures on music, Leonard B. Meyer of the University of Chicago sought to distinguish three interrelated forms of music scholarship that, it seems to me, are relevant to political science scholarship. The first is "style analysis," a normative (as distinct from idiosyncratic) activity, and one that is

> . . . concerned with discovering and describing those attributes of a composition which are common to a group of works—usually ones which are similar in style, form, or genre. It [style analysis] asks, for instance, about the characteristic features of late Baroque music—its typical textures, harmonic procedures, and formal organization; or it inquires into the features common to diverse movements in sonata form or different types of operas. Style analysis, in its pure form, ignores the idiosyncratic in favor of generalization and typology. Consequently statistical methods are as a rule more appropriate in style analysis than in criticism. For style analysis, a particular composition is an instance of a technique, a form, or a genre.[18]

With a proper substitution of terms, this strikes me as a perfect description of what is loosely called "theory" in contemporary political science. Political science "theory" seeks to discover the typical patterns of political behavior, the procedures, and the formal organization of diverse social groups or movements, and it ignores the idiosyncratic in favor of generalizations and typologies. While music scholars are interested in diverse movements in sonata form, political scholars are interested in diverse movements in "revolutionary," or "national integration," or "international cooperation" form. Statistical and comparative methods are employed, and particular cases are considered important only as instances of a technique, form, or genre (for example, of a "parochial," "subject," or "participant" political culture, or, in different language, of a "traditional," "authoritarian," or "democratic" polity). Lijphart contends that such activities are theoretical in nature and add up to science, which he defines (quoting Meehan) in these terms: "Science seeks to establish relationships; science . . . is empirical; science is a generalizing activity." [19] Meyer would not agree with this narrow a definition of science, nor would I. Science does attempt to do these things, but scientific theory, Meyer's second category, certainly attempts to do much more.

"An authentic theory of music . . . ," writes Meyer, "endeavors, where possible, to discover the principles governing the formation of the typical procedures and schemata described in style analysis." Music theory must try to find explanations in terms of general laws. "We might, for instance, cite the Gestalt law of completeness, which asserts that the human mind, searching for stable shapes, wants patterns as complete as possible." One might have to go further and "explain that because human behavior is not for the most part genetically determined, men must envisage the consequences of choices in order to know how to act in the present; and they can envisage and choose only in terms of patterns and processes which are regular and complete." In sum, "We endeavor to go beyond descriptive or statistical norms to the simplest explanation which takes the form of a general principle. The goal of music theory is to discover such principles."

It is commonly asserted that in political science we have very few theoretical principles of the sort mentioned by Meyer (the "iron law of oligarchy" is usually the one cited whenever a layman asks). What we do have is "style analysis," in the form of participation rates in various democracies, majoritarian and consensual processes of political decision-making, comparative Communist studies, instances of and typical procedures for military intervention in the politics of new nations, "theories" (styles) of representation, reformist and revolutionary modes of mobilization, and so forth. These tools and correlations are very valuable, but they are not theory. Yet it is this "theory," actually style analysis, that the area specialist is expected to apply if he wants to gain professional recognition for his work. This is not to say that there is *no* general theory in the social sciences; rather, there is no widespread agreement about its theoretical status (which is also true in music scholarship). In behaviorism, structural-functionalism, organization theory, game theory, strategic analysis, and parts of classical political philosophy, political science has a rich heritage of general principles.[20] But those who advocate a greater role of theory in area studies should be reminded that what they are calling theory is, in the main, political style analysis.

Meyer's third category he calls "critical analysis," and it is this genre that I suggest should be taken as the model toward which serious area studies ought to aspire. As a matter of basic definition, Meyer writes,

> Critical analysis seeks to understand and explain what is idiosyncratic about a particular composition: how is this piece different from all other pieces—even those in the same style and of the same genre? . . . Criticism tries to discover the secret of the singular—to explain in what ways the pattern and processes peculiar to a particular work are related to one another and to the hierarchic structure of which they form a part.

This commitment to explaining the singular should come as no surprise to political scientists: it is the obvious but unstated first principle in the field of United States government and politics. The difference between the American politics specialist and the music critic is simply that the latter knows, and acknowledges, that he is trying to explain the secrets of a single case—for example, what distinguishes Mozart's 39th symphony from the 40th, both of them being masterpieces.

In studying the singular, "Critical analysis uses the laws formulated by music theory—and . . . the normative categories of style analysis—in order to explain how and why the particular events within a specific composition are related to one another. Theory gives us the general principles governing, say, the processes of melodic implication and closure, while criticism is concerned with the ways in which these principles are actualized—or perhaps evaded—in the case of a specific motive, theme, or section in a particular work." To offer a political example, the theory of supranational functionalism (say, in the work of Ernst Haas) reveals to us the complementarities, spillovers, and processes that may allow a regional grouping to transcend the nation states of which it is composed; critical analysis reveals to us how a single leader, say de Gaulle, may inhibit such general processes from working, or how another single leader, say Nasser, may promote a supranational grouping, the U.A.R., even when the functional complementarities do not exist.

Critical analysis is indispensable to the study of music or politics for the simple reason that the way a general principle, or theory, is actualized depends upon the choices of composers or political actors. Lijphart's conception of social science, quoted earlier, is deficient because a political actor can, and often does, observe the same correlations that are made by political scientists, and he can act to enhance or avoid their likely consequences. Strategic, or policy, analysis—probably the single most distinguished theoretical achievement of postwar political science—lies at the heart of critical analysis and is the indispensable complement to theory and style analysis in the explanation of politics.[21] In music, writes Meyer:

> Psychological constants such as the principles of pattern organization, the syntax of particular styles, and typical schemata such as triadic holons constitute the *rules of the game*. Their actualization as specific musical events is the realization of what Koestler [in *The Ghost in the Machine*, 1968] calls *flexible strategy*. For any given musical repertory the "rules" determine the kinds of patterns that can be employed in a composition. They are the province of style criticism. Strategies, which are variable and nonrecurring, give rise to particular instances of some general class or type. The task of critical analysis is to explain why a general rule was actualized in the way it was. . . . Because rules do not determine strategies, commonsense reasons are necessary to explain specific musical events. They bridge the gap between rule and strategy. . . . Because they depend upon particular circumstances, strategy reasons are generally eclectic. Sometimes they will be drawn from established disciplines such as acoustics or psychology; at other times they will be based on common sense. Rule reasons, too, at least for the present, will from time to time be eclectic. This, because music theory is still rudimentary and style analysis only somewhat less so.

One way to illustrate Meyer's point is to cite some of the recent literature from East Asian studies—books that resemble Meyer's conception of a critical analysis and that were not mentioned earlier. The following works are neither purely descriptive nor case studies in Lijphart's sense; they draw upon theory, style analysis, and *ad hoc* hypotheses of the authors in order to offer scientific explanations of significant strategic or policy choices and their consequences: N. R. Chen and Walter Galenson, *The Chinese Economy under Communism* (Chicago, 1969); George R. Packard III, *Protest in Tokyo: The Security Treaty Crisis of 1960* (Princeton, 1966); Dwight Perkins, *Market Control and Planning in Communist China* (Cambridge, 1966); Tang Tsou, *America's Failure in China, 1941–50* (Chicago, 1963); Peter Van Ness, *Revolution and Chinese Foreign Policy* (Berkeley, 1971); and Allen Whiting, *China Crosses the Yalu* (RAND, 1960). It seems to me nonsense to suggest, as some political scientists have, that work of this sort is "atheoretical" or in some sense inferior-grade social science.

The analysis of political strategy or policy requires the use of both theory and style analysis, but it also inevitably involves the use of *ad hoc* (though potentially generalizable) hypotheses. Such analyses are in no sense deterministic, contrary to the implication of Lijphart in his characterization of the interpretive case study as a form of "applied science." As Meyer notes:

> Even in the long run, our most confident surmises about routes and goals may prove wrong. This is because, given the particular style within which he works, the composer is a *free agent*. . . . The implications—the possible consequences of a musical event, of a motive, phrase, or even section—are always plural. A musical event implies a number of alternative actualizations. What the composer [or the political leader, e.g., Mao Tse-tung or Fidel Castro] does is to discover the possibilities implicit in his own musical [or political] ideas. . . . Determinism is a mistaken notion applied to works of art [or of strategy or policy] not only because implications are plural, but also because, within the style he employs, the composer may at any particular point in a piece be absolutely arbitrary [numerous political parallels come to mind, but compare Truman and the atomic bomb, Khrushchev and de-Stalinization, and Mao and the Cultural Revolution[22]]. That is, he may invent and use a musical idea or relationship which has nothing to do with—was in no way implied or dependent upon—preceding events in the piece. Though he is free at any point in a work to do as he likes, a responsible composer will subsequently take such an arbitrary act into account. That is, the relationship between antecedent events and the arbitrary one will, taken together, have consequences later in the composition.

The Sino-Soviet dispute and the extensive analytical literature on it illustrate these points of Meyer's in the political field.[23]

In order to clarify further Meyer's concept of the critical method, two additional issues must be discussed. First, critical analysis of strategic choices does not attempt either to recreate the cognitive processes of the actors or to write a straight history of what occurred. The first is probably impossible and perhaps irrelevant, while the second is relevant but misses the point. As Meyer says, "The critic attempts to understand not the history of the decisions which resulted in a composition, but the 'logical' alternatives presented to the composer given the structure of a particular set of musical circumstances. He is, to paraphrase Aristotle, concerned with what might be called the poetry of creative [or political] choice, not its history."

Second, the methods of the critical analyst are extensive, but the best critical analyses require not simply serviceable tools of the trade but also broad knowledge, experience, judgment, art, and a "good ear." And even then the critic may be wrong. This is because of the idiosyncratic, nonrecurring nature of virtually all significant strategic choices. Meyer comments:

> Critical analysis should in general be as *in*clusive as possible. That is, *all* the methods, theories, and techniques which are relevant to and will illuminate the composition being considered should be brought to bear. . . . [The critical analyst] may refine existing hypotheses, devise quite new ones, or borrow concepts and methods from other disciplines such as linguistics, psychology, or systems analysis. . . . Because its reasons are often *ad hoc* and its explanations eclectic, criticism may at times seem somewhat improvisatory. But this does not mean that it is arbitrary or illogical. Different sorts of arguments from a variety of sources may be employed, but they must be applied *objectively:* rules and techniques, arguments and evidence must be used in the same way in each analysis; and, though not systematized, reasons must be consistent with one another. Criticism must obviously be musically [or politically] persuasive, but this is not enough. For what finally convinces is aural [political] cogency combined with logical coherence.

Political science, to vary slightly a point made recently by Samuel Huntington, is always borrowing ideas from other disciplines—"political development" from an analogy with "economic development" and "political culture" from the anthropologists' key concept.[24] I have here borrowed extensively from one chapter of Leonard B. Meyer's outstanding book on critical analysis in music, perhaps the first modern instance in which that field has been tapped for insights into political science. I am indebted to Meyer because he has made the case for area studies—that is, the "disciplined configurative approach" or "critical analysis"—better than I could and because, since his conception is oriented entirely toward the analysis of music, a subject at some distance from political science, perhaps his case will be persuasive in a way that it would not be if it had been couched in social science practices and mores, given the long-standing confusion over the theoretical import of area studies.

It seems to me that the intellectual case for area studies of the "critical analytical" type is irrefutable and that work of this type will continue to be undertaken and be in demand because of its intellectual challenges and pleasures. However, I do not believe that all, or even most, area studies reach the standard indicated by Meyer, or that run-of-the-mill area studies programs necessarily prepare students to do good area studies work. Nonetheless, instead of attacking or abandoning area studies—an action that in the short run would merely cut the discipline's empirical roots and in the long run prove futile—area studies, perhaps retitled "critical analysis," ought to be upgraded and taught more seriously. If, for example, I were asked to choose only two books from the field of East Asian area studies—one dealing with China and one with Japan—that came close to achieving the highest standards of critical analysis, I would name Etienne Balazs, *Chinese Civilization and Bureaucracy* (New Haven, 1964), and William W. Lockwood, *The Economic Development of Japan* (Princeton, 1954).

Finally, one additional reason why political science seriously needs area studies is the perilously weak state of political science "style analysis"—or what is sometimes called, carelessly, "middle level theory"—and the continuing need for inputs into *it* of critical analyses of real world politics. To mention merely one example, the current state of political development "theory" does not present a picture of great intellectual power and persuasiveness, as several analysts have pointed out.[25] There have been notable advances in conceptualization and method in this and other areas of comparative politics, but there have also been too many instances of style analysis being confused with theory and of arcane methodologies being confused with both. Real area studies constitute the only legitimate road to a genuine theory of political development—as, for example, can be found in two comparative analyses with significant East Asian components: Reinhard Bendix, *Nation-Building and Citizenship* (New York, 1964), and Barrington Moore, Jr., *Social Origins of Dictatorship and Democracy* (Boston, 1966). Even if widespread agreement on the general theory and styles of politics should materialize in the future, area studies, requiring knowledge and experience in addition to the theoretical and stylistic texts, will persist in the form of critical analyses of concrete instances of political activity.

NOTES

1. Dankwart A. Rustow, "Modernization and Comparative Politics, Prospects in Research and Theory," *Comparative Politics*, I (October 1968), 44.

2. My information on publishing trends is based on eight years of membership, two as co-chairman, of the Editorial Committee of the University of California Press. Regarding dissertations in political science, see Peter J. Sackman, "Some Additional Data on Dissertations in Political Science, 1960 and 1970–72," *PS*, IV (Winter 1973), 28, table IV.

3. Leonard H. D. Gordon and Frank J. Shulman, eds., *Doctoral Dissertations on China, A Bibliography of Studies in Western Languages, 1945–1970* (Seattle, 1972), 199.

4. John M. H. Lindbeck, *Understanding China, An Assessment of American Scholarly Resources* (New York, 1971), 79, table III.

5. For two excellent articles defending area studies, see Robert E. Ward, "A Case for Asian Studies," presidential address delivered at the 25th annual meeting of the Association for Asian Studies, March 31, 1973 (Ann Arbor, Mich.: Association for Asian Studies, 1973); and John N. Hazard, "What Future for Communist Area Studies?", *Newsletter on Comparative Studies of Communism*, IV (February 1971), 3–10.

6. William Dray, " 'Explaining What' in History," in Patrick Gardiner, ed., *Theories of History* (Glencoe, 1962), 403, 408.

7. Richard W. Wilson, "Chinese Studies in Crisis," *World Politics*, XXIII (January 1971), 313.

8. Rustow (fn. 1), 44.

9. Arend Lijphart, "Comparative Politics and the Comparative Method," *American Political Science Review*, LXV (September, 1971), 688–89.

10. Cf. Chalmers Johnson, "Reformerische und revolutionäre Durch-bruchstrategien, Zur vergleichenden Untersuchung gesellschaftlicher Ver-änderungen," in Peter Raina, ed., *Internationale Politik in den siebziger Jahren* (Frankfurt a.m., 1973), 217–227.

11. See, e.g., Chalmers Johnson, "Chinese Communist Leadership and Mass Response: The Yenan Period and the Socialist Education Campaign Period," in P. T. Ho and Tang Tsou, eds., *China in Crisis* (Chicago, 1968), I, 397–437.

12. Leonard B. Meyer, *Explaining Music* (Berkeley, 1973), 5.

13. On intelligence estimating, note Klaus Knorr's comment: "One must assume that there exists some sort of operational theory of intelligence, even though most intelligence officers—who, like most other government officials, tend to associate the term 'theory' with 'long hair' and ivory towers—are apt to flinch, if not blanch, at the thought. Any problem-solving organization will evolve premises, analytical procedures, rules of thumb, and other intellectual practices that are based implicitly, if not explicitly, on hypotheses about the reality and about the kinds of events and consequences they must cope with. Such theory is informal rather than formal, apt to be fragmentary rather than integrated, the cumulative sediment of experience rather than the product of self-con-scious endeavor." "Failures in National Intelligence Estimates," *World Politics*, XVI (April, 1964), 465–466.

14. Meyer (fn. 12), 11–13.

15. See, e.g., Chalmers Johnson, *Autopsy on People's War* (Berkeley, 1973); Lawrence Stone, "Theories of Revolution," *World Politics*, XVIII (January, 1966), 159–176; Charles Tilly, "Revolutions and Collective Violence," in Fred I. Greenstein and Nelson W. Polsby, eds., *Handbook of Political Science* (Reading, Mass., forthcoming); and Perez Zagorin, "Theories of Revolution in Contemporary Historiography," *Political Science Quarterly*, 88 (March, 1973), 23–52.

16. Lijphart (fn. 9), 684, 685.

17. Sidney Verba, "Some Dilemmas in Comparative Research," *World Politics*, XX (October, 1967), 114.

18. Meyer (fn. 12), 7.

19. Lijphart (fn. 9), 683, n. 13.

20. For a recent, succinct statement of the truly theoretical concerns of political science, see D. D. Raphael, *Problems of Political Philosophy* (New York, 1970).

21. A few titles, more representative than comprehensive, will illus-trate what I am here calling strategic and policy theory: Raymond A. Bauer and Kenneth J. Gergen, *The Study of Policy Formation* (New York,

1968); Bernard Brodie, *Strategy in the Missile Age* (Princeton, 1959); David Braybrooke and Charles E. Lindblom, *A Strategy of Decision, Policy Evaluation as a Social Process* (New York, 1963); Charles E. Lindblom, *The Policy-Making Process* (Englewood Cliffs, N. J., 1968); Frederick W. Pryor, *Public Expenditures in Communist and Capitalist Nations* (London, 1968); Edward S. Quade, ed., *Analysis for Military Decisions* (Chicago, 1964); George Quester, *Deterrence before Hiroshima* (New York, 1966); Thomas C. Schelling, *The Strategy of Conflict* (Cambridge, 1960); Warner R. Schilling, Paul Y. Hammond, and Glenn H. Snyder, *Strategy, Politics, and Defense Budgets* (New York, 1962); Glenn H. Snyder, *Deterrence and Defense* (Princeton, 1961); and Aaron Wildavsky, *The Politics of the Budgetary Process* (Boston, 1964).

22. On the undetermined nature of strategic choices, see Jeremy R. Azrael, "Varieties of De-Stalinization," in Chalmers Johnson, ed., *Change in Communist Systems* (Stanford, 1970), 135–151.

23. See, e.g., Chalmers Johnson, "The Two Chinese Revolutions," *China Quarterly*, No. 39 (July–September, 1969), 12–29.

24. Samuel P. Huntington, "The Change to Change: Modernization, Development, and Politics," *Comparative Politics*, III (April, 1971), 305.

25. See, e.g., ibid.; Ann Ruth Willner, "The Underdeveloped Study of Political Development," *World Politics*, XVI (April, 1964), 468–482; and Mark Kesselman, "Order or Movement? The Literature of Political Development as Ideology," *World Politics*, XXVI (October, 1973), 139–154.

Comparative Politics and Its Discontent: The Study of the U.S.S.R. and Eastern Europe

Alfred G. Meyer

UNIVERSITY OF MICHIGAN

EDITOR'S NOTE

Like East Asian studies, work on Soviet Russia has been characterized by a sharp break with the past and the emergence of new traditions of scholarship in the postwar period. In contrast, however, to East Asian studies, study of the Soviet Union appears to have passed through a phase of close collaboration with the rest of the social sciences and has now entered a period of profound self-criticism which is extended even to doubts about the inherent capabilities of the social sciences.

Before World War II, the academic focus on Russia was largely through Slavic studies, which stressed history and language, and courses which debated the merits of the "Communist Experiment." After the war, when the United States and the Soviet Union confronted each other as the two superpowers, an entirely new emphasis had to be given to Soviet studies. During the 1950s there was rapid growth in all fields of work on the Communist world as new talent was recruited from the conventional disciplines and large-scale research projects were substantially financed.

Creativity took the form of both detailed empirical studies, based on interviews with refugees or captured archives, and theoretical characterization of the Soviet system, which generally revolved around concepts of totalitarianism. With the passing of the Stalin era, there was decline in the drama and excitement of Soviet studies. The advent of scholarly exchanges between the United States and the Soviet Union was heralded by academic specialists, but opportunities for visiting Russia have not opened the way to empirical research.

At present, the field of Soviet studies seems to be in a state of uncertainty, as Alfred Meyer makes clear in the chapter which follows. The initial excitement has passed, research funds are less available, and there are profound doubts about the quality of past work. Whereas in the 1950s there was widespread agreement among scholars as to what were the appropriate basic assumptions about the Soviet political system, by the 1970s there was uncertainty and debate. Although fewer students of the Soviet Union than of Communist China have become self-appointed spokesmen for and rationalizers of the regime they study, most specialists are plagued by some degree of uncertainty about the validity of their knowledge and the utility of the social science methods. Self-doubts are bound to be compounded in a field in which it is difficult to make precise statements and in which judgments are hard to defend. Scholars who thought that possibly they had exaggerated Soviet realities with their models of totalitarianism have learned from Solzhenitsyn that conditions may have been far worse than they had ever imagined. Those who suspected that Western scholarship had gone too far in making the Soviet system unique have tried to experiment with describing Soviet politics according to models of group competition and pluralistic decision-making employed in liberal democratic societies. The results have not been as enlightening as hoped for, and those who foresaw a liberalization of Soviet politics and expounded an historical trend of congruence between advanced socialist and capitalist systems have found that many of the distinctive features of the Soviet system have persisted. Difficulties in describing precisely current realities or of foreseeing future trends have made many Soviet specialists increasingly distrustful of the claims of the social sciences to be truly scientific. The need for wisdom, maturity in judgment, and historical perspective on the human condition in interpreting Soviet developments has suggested the need for a more reflective approach to knowledge than is exemplified in much of contemporary social science.

Alfred Meyer identifies these problems and the shifting mood in the field of Soviet and comparative Communist studies.

I

Confronted with the question, "political science or area studies?"—for that seems to be implied in the theme set for our discussion—I am tempted to shrug my shoulders, raise my eyebrows, or by some other gesture indicate a mixture of impatience and disbelief. For the reply could surely be nothing else than "Why, both, of course!" All knowledge we can gather about discrete political units, systems, cultures, etc., must be placed within a framework of concepts that are generally understood by specialists in other areas. Area knowledge can be communicated only in the vocabulary of the systematic knowledge we have about politics throughout the world and indeed throughout the ages. Political science must inform the study of Soviet and East European politics if only to guide the students to the most salient or fruitful questions they might ask of the available material. At the same time there can be no political science without area studies. All information in which generalization, hypotheses, models, and other theoretical devices of political science are based comes from the study of various systems and cultures. Moreover, once they have been formulated, all generalizations about politics, all systematic knowledge, must continually be checked and tested against our knowledge of all the unique political formations we can investigate. The globe we are inhabiting is an exceedingly heterogeneous community. All its constituent societies and cultures must be studied carefully if we want to comprehend its politics. Induction and deduction must feed each other. The unique, the particular, the concrete configurations in human relations must be points of departure and of reference in social science.

All this is trite. The fact that it nonetheless merits being reiterated is a symptom of deep malaise in political science. Another symptom of the same malaise is the very question around which this discussion revolves. Area studies versus discipline: how ludicrous it is even to raise that question! A student of mine suggested it was like asking whether one should study biochemistry or cell biology, when obviously one can concentrate on either of these only by knowing a great deal about the other. But that was not a good analogy. A better one would have been to say that the choice between "area studies" and the discipline is more like opting between zoology, on the one hand, and the study of spiders, elephants, or frogs, on the other. If there is a deplorable lack of communication between the generalists and the area specialists in political science—as most of our colleagues doubtless would agree—then that is analogous to a situation in which specialists on frogs (or elephants or spiders) and general zoologists would learn almost nothing from each other. One would not expect either the species specialists or the generalists to be competent.

Yet precisely this seems to be the situation in political science. The relationship between the discipline and the study of Soviet and East European politics has been tenuous. Many area specialists in this field write as if they had no knowledge of the theoretical work in the discipline. In many cases this leads them to do better work than otherwise they might; for the discipline has not offered them many useful theoretical aids—regrettably, because if there were useful theory, the area specialists would profit from it. But if some work of the area specialists suffers from being insufficiently informed by disciplinary skills, I have been even more appalled by some so-called cross-cultural studies by highly respected members of our profession, employing the latest methodological tools, but betraying gross ignorance of historical events, political institutions, the cultures, and the languages of the people they claim to be discussing. As if, somehow, the study of spiders, frogs, and elephants were considered a confusing and misleading input into the study of zoology. Indeed, it often seems as if political scientists were not interested in politics (and knew precious little about it), just as English professors often seem uninterested in novels; and for obtaining a doctorate in linguistics a candidate in some of our leading linguistics departments no longer needs to know any foreign languages. In many fields, a preoccupation with methodology has crowded out all interest in the human activity supposedly under investigation. We no longer know what political science is all about. We produce many Ph.D.s but few scholars. Perhaps we have fallen victims to a mad search for short-cuts to knowledge and wisdom. But in fact there are no short-cuts to knowledge.

I write as a specialist in the study of the Soviet Union and Eastern Europe who has tried valiantly to combine area studies with contemporary political science. What do we mean by area studies? We mean the attempt to gain comprehensive knowledge of some culture or group of cultures found in some portion of our globe. The area specialist must steep himself in a brew of knowledge mixed from very many ingredients. He must familiarize himself as much as possible with the history, economy, social structure, literature, ethnography, of the people in the area, to say nothing about its geography. These aspects of area knowledge are indispensable for anyone wishing to talk meaningfully about their politics. To acquire that kind of knowledge is not an interdisciplinary endeavor, but something much less systematic. One might call it nondisciplinary or predisciplinary. It would, of course, help to have systematic knowledge of methods and tools of enquiry used in anthropology, climatology, soil science, economics, sociology, literary criticism, social psychology, and others. But since few if any of us are all that encyclopedic, area study in practice does not proceed according to the methods of a well-defined discipline. Its scope is too broad for that. Area studies imply ceaseless study; but each scholar has to make arbitrary or haphazard choices about what to include and what to leave out of his purview. Nor can he have disciplined judgment about the validity of what he is learning. To be honest about it, we would have to assert that in area studies a certain artistic license must prevail. Area studies, in fact, are art as much as they are science.

The need to deal with information much too complex and varied to handle competently or with scientific rigor is not the only reason suggesting an artistic perception. This also follows from the attempt we must make to shape this wealth of information into something coherent and to identify what is unique in this special coherence. To express this in terms social scientists will think they understand: the area specialist must identify, comprehend, and describe the *culture* of the area he is investigating. Why the irony of my last statement? It is based on the fact that the concept of culture is not readily understood; in fact, it is one of the most nebulous and controversial terms in social science. As I used it, it refers to that unique configuration of beliefs, attitudes, preconceptions, behavior patterns, traditions, and institutions which members of any nation or group inherit, as it were, from the preceding generations. Culture is that which gives coherence to these various things I have enumerated, or what they have in common—the spirit, if you wish, which all these things share. I am tempted to call culture the *style* of a nation or group. But style is an aesthetic category; and its study partakes of the methods of art. The study of styles requires skills, aptitudes, or even emotional states quite different even from the artistic vision of an Einstein; foremost among them I would mention that mysterious quality of understanding other human beings which we label empathy. To understand a foreign culture requires the ability to listen to people defining their lives and views and problems in their terms rather than in ours. It implies a certain emotional openness to people different from us and a willingness to suspend our own ways of thinking, acting, or even asking questions. Incidentally, the obstacles to this understanding are not only in our own minds, but also in the cultures we wish to study. Every attempt to overcome these obstacles must become an artistic endeavor as much as an employment of rigorous methods of enquiry.

As a political scientist, I have tried, for more than two decades of study, to learn method, approaches, and other theoretical tools from my colleagues in the comparative study of politics; and it may well be that I have learned as much from them as any Sovietologist of my generation. The sum total of what has been useful to me, however, has been meager; and one must state in general that specialists in this area and students of comparative politics have learned precious little from each other. The situation, in this sense, is similar to that prevailing in Latin American studies. As Kalman Silvert has shown in his contribution to this volume, the models of contemporary American political science have never made much sense for students of Latin American politics. They do not explain these politics and do not even provide a suitable framework for describing or classifying them. Silvert could have pointed out that textbooks on comparative politics have generally omitted all references to Latin America. The facts would have disturbed the theoretical models. Hence the Latin American specialists have been quite right in disregarding these models, with few exceptions, such as some studies of discrete political processes, e.g., socialization.

With regard to the study of Soviet and East European politics, matters are slightly more complicated. Here, too, the concepts from American political science could not be applied readily. Words such as "party" and "election" refer to institutions or processes different from those they designate in the United States. Certain phenomena that seem essential to every political system according to our models seem to be missing—legislative processes, interest groups, and public opinion, to name a few. Indeed, almost everything which in the Almond-Coleman model belongs to the input side of the political process either seems to be absent from Soviet and East European politics or is so inaccessible that we have not been able to get more than fleeting and teasing glimpses of it. For these reasons alone the models of American political science are not the most meaningful approach to an understanding of what politics is all about in these countries. Indeed, the two definitions of politics most widely accepted in American political science—Lasswell's phrase about who gets what, when, and how and Easton's formulation of politics as the authoritative distribution of certain values—do not readily apply in these countries; or, if they apply, they do not convey some important societal or national problems with which their politics seeks to deal. It has been tempting, because of this seeming lack of political inputs and the seeming irrelevance of politics as we are used to defining it, to conclude that indeed the Soviet Union and the countries of Eastern Europe do not have political processes at all. And, since the absence of American-style politics must appear unnatural to those committed to such ethnocentric definitions, this alleged absence of politics could be explained only as the result of the total reign of violence or the threat of violence, i.e., of terror.

The discipline of political science obviously has not given many useful tools to the area specialists. In turn, the theoreticians of the discipline have dismissed area specialists with considerable disdain for their unprofessional and unrigorous methods. Contemporary political science is quite self-conscious about its methodology and seeks to promote scientific rigor. It endeavors to make scientific generalizations about political institutions and processes, to discover recurring and, presumably, predictable correlations of selected measurable variables. We teach our students the rules of inference; we encourage them to take a course or two in statistics and to learn a few computer languages. Engaged in the empirical study of human behavior, the discipline eschews all value judgments. It attempts to accomplish its task by breaking human action down into measurable behavior units, and social relations or political processes into behavioral "indicators." Imaginary but, I believe, representative examples of such indicators would be any of the following: participation in elections as an indicator of the system's legitimacy; absenteeism as an indicator of workers' alienation; the election of black officials in Detroit as an indicator of diminishing racial tensions.

Indicators of such crudeness must serve us because they are the only ones we can measure; and things are studied not because they are "interesting" or "relevant"—whatever these terms might mean —but because they are researchable. The search for measurable indicators of things less readily measured (legitimacy, alienation, the degree of racial tension, and the like) shows that political scientists are indeed eager to investigate matters they consider significant. But their need for information that can be quantified and for hypotheses that can be operationalized tends to impoverish the discipline. Somehow the feel for what is human and vital in political processes often gets lost; and trivia are measured and plotted on graphs merely because they are available. In one of the recent issues of the *American Political Science Review*, 162 pages were devoted to articles; about two-thirds of this space dealt with voting, elections, and Congressional representation, even though the profession as a whole is well aware that there are many more significant phenomena. Still, voting behavior can be charted nicely.

The discipline, of course, has its grand theorists who search for predictable patterns and overarching typologies. They offer abstract definitions of politics and comprehensive classificatory schemes for political phenomena throughout the world—a taxonomy of political systems. The discipline's preference for the word "system," which often is totally inappropriate to the messy and murky processes we label politics, indicates its pretensions at scientific rigor, while the recurrent need to define politics shows that we are not even agreed on what we are investigating.

Meanwhile, it is widely acknowledged by now that many of the most widely accepted theoretical models of the political system are but abstractions from our image of American politics—and from an idealized image at that. Area specialists have not found these models very useful. And in the cultural and political crisis we ourselves have experienced in the last decade they have been badly strained even in their application to United States politics. "It must be fun teaching American politics today," I recently remarked to a colleague. "No," he answered grimly, "it is a pain in the neck. Here I teach my models; and every time I have given a lecture something happens in Washington to screw it all up. The system won't hold still!" He is not, alas, the only one for whom the textbook models are more real than reality.

My colleague here was caught in a problem which is even more serious for most other area specialists: the search for patterns that are recurrent and predictable requires models with a presumption of stability and recurrence. The theoretical world of the American political scientist therefore is a relatively static world of regularities and pattern maintenance. This might be of some limited usefulness for describing the politics of the United States up to the Eisenhower era, but it makes no sense for most of the regions of the globe we study in our various area centers. The "areas" are all in states of high instability. Most of them are either about to undergo revolution or recovering from major revolutions if they are not at present in revolutionary turmoil. Political science provides stability models in a revolutionary world, process models in a world of "charismatic" leaders, and system models in a world of communities that are very much at odds with themselves.

I have portrayed social scientists as painfully self-conscious and intensely preoccupied with rules of inference and methodological rigor. In this they seem to be totally different from the natural scientists, and the differences deserve to be brought out sharply. The physicist Poincaré once summarized it nicely by stating that natural scientists discuss their findings, and social scientists their methods.

The methods of science are well established, on the whole, while those of the study of human relations are not. That is the reason for this difference. How can they be well established when we do not even agree on what we ought to investigate? Even the past, the record, the relics, the results which are there, dead and analyzable for the historian's investigation—even the past is re-examined again and again, with new questions asked of the same material each time. The same event, the same great personality, the same period is treated many times, each time from a new perspective; and no study ever is definitive.

The vocabulary of the sciences is a precise language which everyone using it understands. Energy, mass, volume, specific weight, and a thousand other terms each have their precise definitions, their correlation defined in precise mathematical formulas which every high-school student must learn. In our discipline every scholar has to make clear (though many do not) what he wants his terms to mean. I do not know whether there are scientific encyclopedias or what they look like; but I do know the contents of encyclopedias of social science. They are not primarily summaries of what we know. Instead, they are discussions of key words, their histories, their many uses, the idea systems into which they have been fitted, and the difficulties in making them operational.

The scientist deals with a universe the constituent elements of which have not changed substantially since the beginning of human history. In the world of human relations everything is flux. At the outermost frontiers of scientific inquiry there are puzzles, contradictions, and problems of indeterminacy. In the study of human relations problems of indeterminacy are at the very center of every inquiry, not just at the frontier. One could cite many reasons for this indeterminacy, but the most important one seems to be the fact that in the study of human relations the inquirers are investigating themselves. Every reader of this piece will be familiar with some of the other reasons, such as the extraordinarily large (not to say infinite) number of variables entering into our purview, which makes the tracing of causal chains impossible. Nor can we study human beings under laboratory conditions; and, while the number of significant variables is practically infinite, the number of larger systems is too small; indeed, in some fashion every system is unique. Hence we often generalize from a statistical sample of one. To think that our work can be done with anything approaching the rigor of a bubble chamber experiment or of enzyme research therefore is pretense or self-deception. Our work is condemned to remain much more arbitrary and haphazard. We must be artists in part because we cannot ever be scientists. Or, to put it more positively, the attempt to come to terms, intellectually, with the reality of human relations, including politics, is art as much as science, even though from the unaesthetic appearance of most social science one would not readily know that.

Further, all political science is evaluative. With a bit of ingenuity, one can probably detect value orientations even in the most arid and formalistic exercises. Political science deals with human beings and revolves around human concerns, preferably important ones. Already the choice of topics, to say nothing about analysis, evaluation, and prescription, implies the injection of the investigator's values into his scholarly work. There is no escape from that. Hence instead of trying to obscure our value orientation by a pseudoscientific stance, it would be better to acknowledge our moral commitments and to lay them open for examination by ourselves and by others. We would then find that the biases underlying political science often are inconsistent; further, that they usually reflect assumptions and values that are typically American, or bourgeois, or in some other sense culture-specific.

In all disciplines of scholarship, just as in art (as I shall show below) there is a trend toward greater and greater refinement of methodological tools. In political science (as in art) this often seems to be a spurious refinement. Be that as it may, in all areas of inquiry and exposition growing refinement of methods has led to, or been accompanied by, growing specialization, hence to increasing difficulties in cross-disciplinary communication, and an almost total lack of contact or communication with the general public. In political science, this must seem a most astonishing phenomenon once we reflect upon it. Political science supposedly discusses matters of the utmost public concern, specifically, the way in which communities govern themselves. And yet contemporary political science does not have much of a clientele. To be sure, some of us write reports for governmental and private agencies on all levels; and the books of some of us are read by educated lay persons. But, with the refinement of our methodological tools, with the specialized languages we have created, and with the degree of specialization we have cultivated, we write primarily for each other, just as painters today seem mostly to paint, and poets to write poetry, for each other or for the professional critics. The public to which political scientists, on the whole, address themselves consists of their students and their colleagues. Their students go on to become lawyers, salespersons, parents, or communal farmers, so that the training they have received in political science will have little relevance to their professional lives. A few, of course, will become professional political scientists, get their Ph.D.s, teach political science courses, and thus perpetuate the profession. In other words, political scientists have no public except each other and their successors. No wonder they engage in formalistic discussions about esoteric methods. No wonder they divide into tiny cliques, each with its own methods, areas of specialization, journals, students, associations, etc., and one more avant-gardist than the other. Much of contemporary political science is astonishingly surrealist in style.

II

If the application of political science models and methods to the study of Soviet and East European politics makes little sense, the attempt to comprehend it in terms of the understanding of the people in this area presents other difficulties. Until about fifteen years ago one could not even travel in these countries; and even today travel as well as access to the people is severely restricted. Those who are ready to function as informants are, by and large, a very biased sample consisting of official spokespersons of the regime, the literary and artistic intelligentsia of the capital cities, and a handful of daring dissenters. Translated into American terms: we must obtain all our information from the Ron Zieglers, the Lenny Bernsteins, and the Daniel Berrigans of the Communist world. At least this has been the situation for most political scientists until recently. The range of persons open to observation and questioning, however, has now begun to widen.

Much information, of course, has always been available. In presenting it to their readers, American scholars, having decided that the concepts and models of conventional political science were not applicable, have used theoretical constructs devised specifically or primarily for systems of the Communist type. These theories stressed the alleged uniqueness of these systems; and at the same time the exceptional interpretation of these political units was concealed by the theoretical framework used to express this uniqueness. "Communist studies" developed as some sort of subdiscipline within the comparative study of political systems, its theories and models expressly designed to account for Communist politics. By inference, Czechoslovakia and Albania, Cuba and the Soviet Union, became systems of the same type, a highly dubious proposition, if only because of the tremendous differences in size, economic development, and political culture. The subdiscipline of "comparative Communist studies" also applied to Communist parties in those parts of the world where they were not in power. This, too, must be questioned because it can be shown that the Communist parties of Italy, Indonesia, or South Vietnam are fundamentally different from each other and can indeed be understood only within the context of their respective political environments of culture, institutions, and history.

Nonetheless the subdiscipline has developed and flourished. It has employed a mix of methodological devices all of which the profession has generally considered inapplicable to the study of other political units, especially the United States. The principal theoretical elements of "comparative Communist studies" at first were the following:

1. The concept of national culture or national character. Focusing on this, one could explain Soviet institutions and politics as manifestations of a political culture much older than the Russian revolution and the Bolshevik movement, although its changes and its importation to other countries were harder to explain. Some highly suggestive work has nonetheless been done by scholars steeped in the knowledge of Russian history.[1] Equally suggestive but highly controversial studies also have been based on a strongly Freudian interpretation of Russian national character.[2] Neither approach, however, has become the dominant theme.

2. An emphasis on elite politics, in which the top one, or three, or nine, or twenty, or two hundred party officials were treated as the only political actors in the country. The politics in which this political Mafia—a caricature of Mills' power elite and of Mosca's political class—engaged was a deadly game in which supreme power was at stake. Whoever was the Number One was seen as a person regarding all his colleagues as potential enemies; and in the more comprehensive model the entire power elite regarded the people as its enemies. All politics therefore revolved around *power* for those who did not possess it, around *control* for those who did, and around *survival* for those who despaired of ever possessing it. This model of Soviet politics, of which Fainsod's magistral work is

the classical statement, was pitifully one-dimensional.[3] When applied either to individual socialist countries or to the totality of Communist parties in the world, it reduces them all to their top elites and their control organizations and leaves out far too much. Even American political machines have been studied in a more sophisticated manner.

3. Ideological determinism. Never dominant, but always present, this approach interpreted the Soviet and East European governments as institutionalizations of Marxism or Marxism-Leninism, making clear always that this was an evil or a mad ideology.[4] Of all theories of politics, ideological determinism (the term is my own) probably is the most naive and the most easily refuted. I list it in order to show that, again, in the study of Communist politics we have been prone to apply theoretical constructs generally spurned in the discipline. Who in general political science theory takes ideology very seriously?

4. Totalitarianism. The one-dimensionality of ideological determinism and of the pop-Paretism adduced above was seemingly obviated in the totalitarian model of Soviet and East European politics, which did, however, absorb and incorporate them.[5] Enough has been written about this model in the last ten years to show its inadequacies.[6] It has not been able to provide adequate explanations of Soviet politics even under Stalin, much less in the last twenty years, either in the U.S.S.R. or in Eastern Europe, to say nothing about nonruling Communist parties. Moreover, by lumping the Third Reich and Fascism together with the Stalinist system it obscured as much as it explained; and by simultaneously asserting the uniqueness of the totalitarian syndrome it removed the study of Communist politics from the discipline of comparative politics.

As this much too sketchy summary indicates, all the concepts with which Sovietology operated were evaluative, even though at times they pretended to be value-neutral. Indeed, we might just as well call them Cold-War concepts. The respectable members of this association seem to have taken it for granted, at least in the early years of comparative Communist studies, that the Communist regimes were altogether bad. Virtually all work in the field contrasted the evils of their politics with the blessings of ours, comparing our freedom with their dictatorship, our welfare with their poverty, our efficiency with their inefficiency, our humane attitudes with their inhumane ones; ours was an open society, theirs was closed; ours was pluralistic, theirs a monolith. Our intentions and policies in world affairs were peaceful and benign; their system was compulsively aggressive. To maintain this judgment, scholarship tended to disregard all evidence to the contrary. Being totalitarian, these systems are totally illegitimate. That they might confer satisfactions and benefits was literally unthinkable for many of us. Some scholars fiercely denied that they could contain interest groups or other elements of pluralism, social mobility, or even a social structure, or that they might be promoting the general welfare.

In a mockery of the truly comparative approach, societies of the Soviet type often were evaluated on the basis of their performance, while the United States was evaluated on the basis of its ideology or its rhetoric. But, as I have tried to point out, even their performance was seen through distorting glasses. That there might be participation, acceptance of the system, some consensus, many satisfactions, and a good deal of legitimacy did not, apparently, occur to American Sovietologists in the early years of Sovietology. (That our Soviet colleagues engage in the identical kind of biased comparison does not excuse us.) Of the many concerns, issues, discussions, and conflicts that feed political processes in the Soviet Union and Eastern Europe only relatively few were ever singled out for study; and the treatment of political actors centered much too narrowly on top elites.

This biased evaluation can be explained to a large extent by the Cold War atmosphere of American politics and scholarship in the 1940s and 1950s. But it was a function also of the personal background of many scholars prominent in the field. The first generation of Soviet and East European specialists included a very large proportion of émigrés and exiles who brought with them not only their knowledge but also their political bitterness. Equally prominent in the field have been repentant Communists from all parts of the world. The specialist on Communism, if he was not a former diplomat, was very often a former Communist or a political refugee. Hence he was more often than not a person with an axe to grind. The loathing for the regimes these writers denounced doubtless was justified, and by expressing it they provided enlightenment. But whether that was the kind of enlightenment most needed by their American readers is to be questioned. For the public in any one country, and therefore also for the political scientists addressing that public, the evils and malfunctionings of their own political processes deserve attention foremost. Moral indignation, if not charity, should begin at home. Directing it primarily at others deflects our attention from what ought to be of greatest importance to us.

Within the last ten to twenty years, students of Soviet and East European politics have reacted to these developments in their field. Their reaction has taken a variety of forms. One of these was a turn toward "behavioralism" or, to put it in the terms of our current discussion, an attempt to integrate Communist studies with political science. It was, at least in part, a search for value-neutral models and paradigms. It was also, in part, an attempt to demonstrate, if only by implication, that the differences between Communist and "Western" political systems had been exaggerated. Ideologically, it could be termed a manifestation of anti-anti-Communism. Thus in my own book on the Soviet Union I have at least suggested that all of the major functions of the Almond-Coleman model of political systems are carried out, somehow, somewhere, in Soviet politics. In this effort, the vocabulary of American political science does get strained at times, indicating that it is an attempt to adjust reality to the model. The theoretical construct has turned into a Procrustean bed. In addition to such exercises, theories of industrial society, technological society, postindustrial society, as well as developmental scenarios leading to them, have been devised or suggested, which would encompass Soviet and American politics in one and the same, or at least similar, rubric. A survey of the many different theories of convergence shows that there are biases hidden behind such attempts as well, and that an exclusive stress on growing or actual similarities at the expense of unique features and "systemic" differences is as false as the opposite. Finally, a great deal of work has been done on Soviet and East European politics studying not the total system but selected institutions or processes, and utilizing methods, concepts, or models taken from the tool kit of contemporary political science: interest group theory, organization theory, communications theory, small group sociology, to name but a few. Most of what has been done in the field during the last ten years falls in this category. While here too the vocabulary at times gets strained and the effort of the area specialist to sound like a bona-fide political scientist may look a bit ridiculous, much of this effort has greatly enriched the study of these societies and their politics.[7]

Another reaction to the cold war bias dominating the field for so long a time has been the attempt—understandable and laudable—to correct the picture of Communist regimes as totally inhuman and inefficient. As examples one might mention the revisionist school of world politics; Berman's book on the Soviet judicial system, which claims that it provides justice cheaply and effectively, on the whole[8]; Hazard's text on Soviet politics[9]; or my own recent essay on the growth of legitimacy in Eastern Europe.[10]

Earlier I alluded to the tendency of Sovietologists to apply a double standard of evaluation, measuring Communist regimes by their performance and ours by its ideals. Occasionally scholars have reacted against this by inverting this double standard. The profession has condemned them as apologists for Communism, though it has been tolerant of apologists for American politics. This is, after all, the *American* Political Science Association; and that the "science" of politics is evaluative I have already asserted. Theories stressing similarities rather than differences between Soviet and American politics, too, come with at least two different value orientations: optimistic ones project the convergence of Communist and Western politics in some highly desirable pattern, be it democratic socialism or some form of the technotronic society; meanwhile the more pessimistic theories foresee a nightmarish development of all highly industrialized nations into authoritarian and bureaucratized Leviathan states.

One startling new attitude toward regimes of the Soviet type deserves to be mentioned. It arises out of the more recent emphasis American political science has placed on stability as the chief measure of worth of a political system—a conservative reaction to the political and cultural crises of most recent times. Among political scientists preoccupied with the problem of stability one can today observe a tendency to view the Soviet Union and East European regimes with great admiration for their ability to build new, viable, stable systems and to do so in the wake of revolutionary upheavals. Just as the theoreticians of counterinsurgency warfare teaching at Fort Benning look to Mao and Giap as their theoretical masters, so Lenin, Stalin, and their East European disciples are now beginning to emerge in the literature of American political science as pioneers and models of contemporary political leadership.

Looking over the total work on Soviet and East European politics that has been done in the past twenty-five years, and picking out what I consider the best research done so far—those books that provide the most enlightenment about the nature of politics in the Soviet Union and Eastern Europe—my vote would go to a few careful and exhaustive descriptions of selective institutions, processes, or elites. The list would include Hough's work on regional party leaders,[11] Berliner's book on industrial management,[12] Daniels' work on the oppositions in the Communist Party,[13] Lewin's account of the collectivization of agriculture,[14] Joravsky's books on the politics of science in the U.S.S.R.,[15] and Jowitt's recent work on nation-building in Romania.[16] Despite occasional glimpses some of their authors may have given of other political systems, these books are not comparative studies at all. Jowitt's book, a real breakthrough in our knowledge of Romanian politics, combines thorough knowledge of the area with high competence in the discipline. By synthesizing these elements he has managed to come up with brilliant hypotheses and arresting models. Again, he helps us understand Romanian politics. But whether any of his knowledge is transferable to other countries, even countries of the Communist world, is questionable. In that sense, the work is not comparative at all. Most of the works I have cited, however, are historical, which means they employ comparisons of a very different kind. Note also that the authors I have singled out include two or three historians and an economist. Must it be left to them to move into concrete research on politics while the professional political scientists polish their theoretical models?

The preoccupation with theoretical models, most of them useless to the area specialist, has left not only much scholarship in Soviet and East European politics to historians, economists, journalists, professional émigrés, and other people outside the discipline. It has deprived the political scientist of another important function as well. I have in mind the task of disseminating our knowledge to the public, which I believe to be a proper function, and an essential one, for the student of comparative politics. It is, in any event, one which in the last twenty-five years the specialist in Soviet and East European politics has not been able to avoid. Now if the best work on the politics of this area was largely uninformed by the theories of political science, the same must be said, by and large, about the information disseminated to the general public and to our political elites, i.e., about the best-sellers on Soviet and East European politics and the counsel (often disastrously misinformed) received by Presidents, Senators, and other policy-makers. The people who advised our top leaders on developments in this area often were neither political scientists nor area specialists but self-appointed experts on Communism or, to put it more provocatively, professional Cold Warriors. The most blatant example of these was perhaps the German physician, Dr. Starlinger, whose knowledge of the U.S.S.R. was based on his long sojourn in Soviet prisoner-of-war camps. But Conrad Adenauer and John Foster Dulles seem to have accepted him as their oracle on Soviet politics. Because of his inadequate qualification as a student of Soviet politics, the ideological nature of his writings, and the dire consequences of his advice, I am tempted to place Walt Whitman Rostow in his company.

But, frankly, the old Russian hands from the State Department and the German Foreign Ministry who also were prominent among presidential advisors for a long time were not all that more enlightened. The predominance of unprofessional and unscholarly advisors, of course, is not necessarily the fault of political science or area scholarship. Instead, one must assume that political leaders generally receive whatever counsel they desire, and that they avoided the formal theories of the political scientists and the erudition of the area specialists because they preferred to listen to ideologists of various kinds—to the Billy Grahams of Sovietology, or, to stay with an analogy I drew earlier in this essay, the Norman Rockwells, Edgar Guests, and Mickey Spillanes of Sovietology. The analogy I made was between area studies and art; and the disarray of Soviet and East European studies, as well as that of the discipline—the competition between orthodoxies, academics, fads, styles, and topics—these and other developments are quite analogous to the development of the arts in our century. In the following section of this essay I should like to explore this analogy, knowing full well that the comparisons I plan to make will have to be sketchy and unsystematic, and that they must be offered with considerable reservations; comparing two things does not mean they are identical. Yet I do find the similarities suggestive enough to share them with my readers.

III

Pictorial art depicts. Verbal art describes. Like political science, art in some fashion "refers" to reality even if it does not very obviously represent it. The reality which serves as referent for art as well as political science is human experience, human action, and human interaction. It is generally assumed, though not without some sharp dissent, that art and political science originate in *disturbing* experience: awe in the face of nature and the fear of death; disasters, disorder, and violence; tyranny and anarchy. The impulses behind art and political science can be summarized, perhaps, as the experience of overwhelming power and overwhelming disorder. If art, as many scholars seem to take for granted, arises out of alienation, then surely political science arises out of political disorder and discomfort, from a feeling that the world of human relations has gone out of joint. The greatest political scientists and the greatest artists seem to have flourished in the most troubled periods.

While there is considerable controversy over the functions and purposes of political science and art, surely one of their aims or justifications is to comprehend this threatening or disturbing reality, to help us come to terms with it by fixing it in the mind, by portraying it, and by imposing some semblance of order onto it. In doing so, the artists and the political scientists not only justify their activities, but they may also justify this reality by bringing out the beauty, the rationality, the legitimacy inherent in it. The urge to do so has usually been strong, and these professions therefore have had a persistent tendency to omit the ugliest details from their portrayals of reality, either by placing an outright taboo on them or by describing them through circumlocution. A high level of abstraction is one of these circumlocutory devices. Placing ugly features into a totally foreign culture is another of many ways by which the taboo can be obviated. In short, both art and political science have usually been guided by a sense of propriety and decency and have designated some things as too obscene to depict.

Whatever portions of their subject matter they share, art and politics are obviously quite different genres. Treated as a genre, political science is definable as the art of depicting human relations with the help of certain concepts and words. Since every genre changes its styles continually, the key concepts are not always the same. Yet we would recognize many words as clearly belonging to the genre of political science: state, government, sovereignty, power, right, duty, crime, sanctions, laws, leadership, authority, legitimacy, compliance, executive, administration, to name but a few.

All science is to some extent an art, feeding on emotions and inspiration, and utilizing both imagination and intuition. It has its own aesthetics, though that is not discussed much, being considered extraneous by most practitioners. Some scientists seem to assume that the scientific validity of a work is inversely proportional to its aesthetic qualities.[17] Similarly, art partakes of science in that it has often been based on careful observation of reality and on scientific principles, to say nothing of materials and techniques. The discovery of perspective and its use in painting and the use which Impressionists made of the color spectrum are nice examples. Cubism may have been a conscious application of principles inherent in contemporary scientific method and philosophy. Art, like science, has often aimed at a rational comprehension of reality; and I would count many artists among the contributors to our knowledge of politics. This can be argued best by reference to dramatists and novelists, but is also true of many pictorial artists. Goya, Daumier, Hans Holbein the Elder, as well as many Gothic illustrators and sculptors tell us much about the politics of their time and do it well. So do Hogarth, Grosz, Munch, and Steinberg, not to mention Herblock. Among great political scientists whose work we ought to assign to our students I suggest we include Shakespeare and Swift, Stendhal, Balzac and Zola, Grimmelshausen, Grass, Gogol and Tolstoi, Gheorghiu as well as Kafka. The *Divina Commedia*, written in the language of the people, is a beautiful panoramic picture of the *purgatorio* and the *inferno* of Florentine and Italian politics around the year 1300. Nobody ever since has described politics in quite the same manner. In contrast,

De Monarchia, which Dante wrote in the jargon of scholars, is an abstract model which suffers in comparison. There is one well-known American political scientist—no Dante, perhaps—to whom I have said in all seriousness that the very nice novel he wrote about Latin American politics is better political science than the quantitative matrices with which he has been playing in more recent years.[18] But perhaps they are better art. After all, many sociologists of art would argue that much seemingly abstract or nonrepresentational work in various genres of art also, in its way, makes statements about contemporary politics.

Art, like political science, uses the device of comparison. It does not "imitate nature" any more than computer simulation imitates a political process. Instead, it renders reality with the help of imagery, simile, metaphor, and allegory, i.e., by comparisons with other realities. To be worthy of our attention, the comparisons must be bold as well as apt. Startling comparisons are useful cognitive and didactic devices. They estrange us from what is familiar and familiarize us with what seems strange, thus placing the objects of our investigation into new perspectives. To see African political systems compared with old-fashioned American political machines, as Henry Bienen has suggested,[19] the Soviet Union with General Motors, or the Komsomol with Greek-letter fraternities,[20] may give us insight not only into Ghana, the U.S.S.R., and the Communist youth organization, but also into the Daley machine, American corporations, and Sigma Chi. But, in addition to being bold as well as apt, comparisons must continually be fresh and new. Old imagery gets stale. We get tired of it. Worn-out comparisons, like worn-out theoretical models, become clichés. They also become false because reality is in constant flux, and our devices for rendering it must change in turn with this continual shift. When we cling to worn-out models, images, concepts, etc., they become delusions. There is a persistent belief, which has come to us from the era of magic, that we acquire control over things by naming them; power was once identified either with the right to give names (e.g., the right conferred on Adam to give names to all the animals[21]) or with knowing the names of things (as in the Rumpelstiltskin tale). A good deal of social science seems to revolve around this search for magic power. Many of our theoretical models and our esoteric vocabulary constitute elaborate classification schemes, i.e., devices for identifying, pigeonholing, or naming whatever we observe. Having given names, we are often satisfied that we have acquired knowledge. Much of our professional ingenuity is spent on the invention of neologisms or new names. The great political scientists are those whose words we all use.

But, as contemporary philosophy has shown, words, models, comparisons, and concepts turn into intellectual traps. The quest for magic power induces complacency and self-deception precisely when the magic word has been accepted as common coinage. Therefore whoever teaches some tried-and-true method in this never-ending quest for the right word or the most adequate model to render the elusive reality in which we live is sure to mislead his students. *Instead, the creative intellectual's and artist's task is to call things by their wrong names.* Art and political science must forever shock us out of the complacent use of symbols, and there is therefore nothing sick, degenerate, or neurotic about continual rapid changes in the styles of these genres. Indeed, given the knowledge explosion, the rapid changes in the real universe, the possibilities for rapid communication to mass audiences, and other technological advances, the pace of stylistic change must be dizzyingly rapid in our day.

The so-called exact sciences, too, are deeply affected by technological change. Each advance in scientific knowledge and technological capability widens our scientific window into the universe and sharpens the lenses of our viewing glasses. But the sciences do not share in the search for ever new symbols and modes of expression; the social scientist's preoccupation with *words* is foreign to them. Their reality is changing, too. The galaxies expand. Biological species have their histories. Yet in comparison with the realities art and political science seek to comprehend, the universe of the natural scientist is a universe of constants. Our knowledge of these constants and their interrelations becomes more and more refined. But the universe remains the same. Hence natural science, instead of searching for ever new modes of expressing a maddeningly elusive reality, is capable of employing the old modes of expression and very ancient categories; and instead of rejecting old wisdoms for new ones, it carefully builds on the old knowledge. Laws formulated by Pythagoras, Euclid,

Archimedes, Galileo, Leibnitz, and others who have been dead for many centuries remain essential stepping stones to more advanced scientific knowledge. In political science there is no such systematic progression. Indeed there is no such thing as a steady advance, only new modes, new models, new terms, new styles. In that sense it is much closer to art than to science.

Political science as a discrete genre can, as I have suggested, be characterized by the devices it uses, its concepts and paradigms. Like the artistic devices of other genres, the symbols of politics have a tendency to become stale after a given period. Styles inevitably exhaust themselves. Innovators among the practitioners of the genre are perpetually searching for novel ways of expressing their ideas and of representing reality. The novel ways often turn out to be devices that are quite old but have not been used for a while. One could write a history of political science from, say, the Sophists to our day in terms of the ebb and flow of stylistic devices, though that might be a narrowly formalistic exercise. Styles, after all, are related to broader matters such as prevailing life styles, the spirit of the age, the preoccupations, problems, and social relations within which the artist and political scientist operate and which they seek to comprehend. All these parts of the universe change. At the same time, the reality with which all genres seek to deal is basically the same for all of them at one and the same "point in time" and "moment in space." We may therefore find that the styles of political science and art run, roughly, parallel to each other or that, in some fashion, they are mirror images of each other.

Hence the history of political science might be fitted into a history of art or into a history of styles or of culture. I see no reason why one should not explore the possibilities of speaking about the politics of the Gothic, the Cinquecento, or the Baroque, in the manner suggested by Friedrich Burckhardt or, more recently, Max Dvorak.[22] In all cases, the contemporary genres, broadly speaking, deal with similar subject matter, have similar notions of what is and what is not considered proper. Thus burghers and peasants were not considered worthy of portraying in the high art and the high political science of the Baroque. Art and political science at any one period share the basic assumptions made about the nature of the universe and are aware of the same scientific laws. Erwin Panowsky has sought to show that some French architects in the thirteenth century thought, acted, and built in "scholastic" terms.[23] Similarly, without having specialized knowledge of the matter, I would guess that the mathematical knowledge which led to the discovery of perspective also left its traces in the political philosophy of Occam and other late scholastic political scientists, just as, centuries later, Newton's revolutionary discoveries had their impact not only on Hobbes but also on his contemporaries in the fields of art.

Again, the conflict between Classicism and Romanticism may be reflected also in the differences between the political writings of Hume and Burke, or Kant and Fichte. Géricault, Delacroix, and Berlioz are not only contemporary with Fourier, Blanqui, and Bakunin, but are similar to them also in what interests them, the style of their treatment, and the spirit or ideology they express in their work. The list of suggestive parallels could be extended at will.

At any one period, each genre usually has its academy, which consists of the profession as a whole or of its established, recognized senior members. The academy, collectively, determines the style and content of art and political science; it sets the professional standards. This is usually done in an informal process revolving around the screening-out of all works and persons not measuring up to that standard. In the art academies, much of this is done by so-called juries. Political science today has its juries, too. They consist of doctoral committees, departmental curriculum committees, editorial committees of professional journals, association program committees, and special awards committees. Each department by its faculty recruitment policy fulfills similar functions.

Every academy comes under attack from the younger practitioners, the avant-gardists, the rebels, as well as from their followers among the public. Sooner or later every academy is denounced for perpetuating a stuffy, outdated style, for catering to the establishment or the ruling classes, and for being out of touch with the people. The academy, in turn, is quite honestly concerned only with one thing: craftsmanship and "academic" excellence. But inevitably the time approaches when the academic style has become superannuated. By that time the important works of art and political science will be done by people outside the profession. In introducing the panelists in this discussion, Lucian Pye asked, "where does the area student fit?" The answer, of course, is that the creative intellectual never fits. Still, in time, yesterday's rebels will constitute today's academy, even though there will always be some nostalgic people asserting that genuine art or genuine political science has not been produced since the Greeks, or the Middle Ages, or the eighteenth century. Overheard on a college campus was this conversation: "I hear you visited Bruges this summer. How did you like it?" "Bah! The Renaissance spoiled it."

Academy-like processes go on today in art and political science. There are committees, juries, foundations, journals, and galleries, setting standards by selection and screening-out. But in fact the academy is in disarray in all the genres. It has been dissolved into a congeries of mini-academies, each claiming that it is promoting true art or true political science. A proliferation of schools, all of them rivals of the others in a competition that may be healthy and beneficial. They fight each other bitterly over scarce resources, such as professorships, foundation grants, critical acclaim, and commercial success. Winning and losing seem dependent on rapid shifts in fashions and fads. The profession as a whole, however, has lost its bearing and its confidence. It no longer has hard-and-fast criteria of excellence or even of technical competence. It no longer knows how to define good workmanship. It no longer knows what ancillary skills are prerequisite for admission to the study of the profession. Hence our interminable debates over standards of admission to graduate study in political science, debates which are inconceivable, at least in this form, in the natural sciences.

Stretching the labels, perhaps cruelly, one might be able to say that contemporary political science includes Romantics and Realists, Primitives, Fauves, Naturalists and Impressionists, Symbolists, Futurists, Nonobjectivists, as well as Socialist Realists. In all the welter of styles, techniques, ideologies, and orientations vying with each other, however, some predominant trends stand out. One of them is formalism and abstractness. Formalism and abstraction are rampant in modern art as much as in modern political science. Another predominant trait is a fascination with technique at the expense of content and the urge to make use of the most up-to-date hardware. There is a fascination with science and mathematics, but the symbols which in science are essential to communicate scientific information often have become ends in themselves—beautiful objects or empty forms. Realism, mere description, and indeed the old-fashioned skills of observing carefully and sketching meticulously—these are viewed with contempt as methods from the horse-and-buggy age. Hence painters no longer need to know how to draw, and the student of politics no longer needs to know anything about the cultures from which he seeks to draw his "data." Indeed, knowing too much about them might bias him. Similarly, it is possible today to obtain a doctorate in linguistics from a highly respected university without knowing a single foreign language; and geographers, I am told, no longer travel a lot. In all fields, preoccupation with the subject has given way to preoccupation with methods. In line with this, each special field, each subfield indeed, develops its own technical language, and as this happens, the need to write a good English style disappears also, if we can judge from a great deal of work published in our journals. However, just as there are "primitives" in art whose freshness overcomes the limitations of their techniques, so there are successful political scientists who have got by without a knowledge of statistics or computer modeling.

Further, one might note a narrowing of the focus of inquiry. Since the Gothic period, when artists and political scientists sought to represent the entire universe, complete with the Trinity, heaven, earth, angels, humans, plants, and animals, and the denizens of hell underneath, through the vast panoramic canvases of more recent centuries, the problems which artists and political scientists have posed themselves have tended to become smaller and smaller all the time. Both now seem to prefer dealing with mini-problems and micro-problems. Hence much of political science work somehow resembles the giant doodles hanging in our galleries today, in which a minimal number of lines, shapes, and colors are correlated in a fashion which the artist hopes is novel and arresting.

Thus formalism, abstract models, the preoccupation with techniques, and the resultant emphasis on micro-problems dominated the profession. The result, which I have called the loss of content, indicates a loss of touch with reality, that reality which art and political science supposedly seek to comprehend, each in its own fashion. The routinized avant-gardism of contemporary art and contemporary political science is an indication of their functioning in a void. That may be very liberated, and a great deal of fun. But whatever functions in a void has lost its function, at least its original one.

What the function of art is, or what it may have been in previous cultures, is a matter of heated controversy I must leave undiscussed in this essay. Pictorial and verbal representations have obviously fulfilled magic, sacramental, and ritual functions. They have served as cognitive modes and as didactic means. They have glorified and legitimized the established powers and the established systems and served as repositories of the community's myths, history, and self-understanding. In societies divided by conflict between estates, classes, nationalities, or other groups, each contending subsociety may have developed its own art; and in the age of individualism art has often been said to serve as a highly recognized and exalted mode of self-expression and self-orientation. Today, it seems, art functions primarily as a spectacle. It is to be looked at, perhaps for entertainment or edification, perhaps to show off its owner's wealth, sophistication, or eccentricity. Of course, it also provides incomes to artists and their families, dealers, agents, curators, and critics. Anything can serve these functions. Hence anything becomes art by being treated as if it were art. An old crankshaft mounted on a block of wood when displayed in a penthouse apartment is art.

Political science, too, has served magic, ritual, and sacramental functions. It has been a means of legitimation and a weapon for challenging the legitimacy of incumbent elites, a means of individual self-orientation and socialization, and a guidance for policymakers. Today it still serves all or most of these functions on rare occasions, but its chief purpose seems to be to pad the curricula vitae of the practitioners, to the greater glory of departments, schools, and foundations. The fact that political scientists communicate almost exclusively with each other indicates that they too are operating in a void, that political science has lost its function very much like modern art. This loss of function, this *dispensability* of political science, from the point of view of the community, accounts for the neurotic self-consciousness and the sense of bewilderment gripping the profession. Of course, the products of artists and political scientists still find sponsors and markets, and lucrative ones, indeed. But I have often wondered whether the

foundation executives who commission much of our work understand our articles and books any better than they understand the
mod canvases and mobiles they hang up in their fancy offices.

In art as well as in political science there are many professionals who regard this "loss of function" as a good thing. They
describe the purposes served by art and political science in
previous eras and other cultures as extraneous and tyrannical
influences skewing these professions in their true pursuits and
transforming them into handmaidens of contending social forces.
Sacramental art, hidden away in some sanctuary, and restricted in
theme and style, was fettered art. Art had to liberate itself from
these and many other determining forces to become free self-expression in the creation of beautiful objects. Political science at the
service of kings or revolutionaries, or worried about social problems and human values, was ideology rather than the scientific
penetration of politics and the perfection of our tools of inquiry.
Yet in both genres formalism, abstractionism, and the preoccupation with technique and with micro-topics have recurrently come
under attack by those who assert that political science as well as art
must have a social conscience, that they must have content, and
that this content must be the most serious human concerns of the
time. Many of these same people would add that art and political
science must communicate with the people, especially with the
victims of exploitation, domination, and other inequities. Other
critics insist on the need for an awareness of values. The artist
should not merely experiment with novel techniques but should
have aesthetic standards: his work should be beautiful. The
political scientist should not choose his topics merely because they
are nicely researchable with current techniques, but should pick
them on the basis of their relevance. But we no longer know what is
beautiful or what is relevant.

In the beginning of this essay I criticized Sovietology for the
biased evaluation it has been prone to make of Soviet and East
European politics. I also described some of the more recent work
done in the area as reacting to this bias, without being any less
evaluative. It ought to be possible to transcend this provincialism
and ask questions that reflect concerns other than stability,
economic growth, pluralism, private property, or freedom to
criticize. It ought to be possible to inquire about the quality of

political life in other cultures in a fashion reflecting their values as much as ours, their conceptions of citizenship and authority as much as those we tend to take for granted. Doing this, we might even come to the conclusion that the malaise afflicting art and political science is related to an analogous malaise of contemporary American politics and culture, and that the absence of these symptoms from art and political science in other areas reflects a better integrated, a better functioning, a happier style of politics. I know of some promising research being done in this vein, among it Hough's comparative study of responsive political systems and Apel's survey work on citizens' happiness in Greece and Bulgaria. One of the keys to a method of evaluation which takes into account the assumptions and feelings about politics of people in the areas we study is the concept of legitimacy, which is sorely in need of careful redefinition. In attempting this, the provocative definition of exploitation recently offered by Kenneth Boulding deserves careful attention.[24]

Once we focus on legitimacy, we must abandon abstract models of political systems because conceptions of what is and what is not legitimate are culture-bound. In order to understand notions of legitimacy we must be aware of the sum total of historic developments and influences that have helped shape the political self-consciousness of different nations, classes, and groups. Legitimacy can be understood only within that panoramic view of nations and cultures which has been the hallmark of the area studies approach.

But what is culture? Culture is the totality of attitudes, beliefs, behavior patterns, and institutions which any generation of human beings inherits, as it were, from its predecessors in the same nation or group. It is the totality of human relations and institutions viewed as a specific national (or group) *style*. Style, however, is an aesthetic category, which defies the rigorous methods of contemporary political science; so that the comprehension of culture demands an aesthetic rather than "scientific" approach to the study of politics. While doubtless the area specialist may wish to learn from the political scientist how to quantify, determine correlations, and construct abstract models, political science in its turn must apply the area studies approach; i.e., it must view different cultures in their own terms, it must incorporate an awareness of different national styles and national values into its comparative work. Where it has been abstract it must become concrete.

Finally, one result of the analogy between art and political science I have suggested might be fresh insights into the causes of our professional bewilderment. If seemingly unrelated pursuits manifest similar malaises, perhaps the causes are the same. In examining ourselves and our activities—and that is what we are supposed to be doing here—we might attain some self-understanding by applying to our own discipline that technique which is known as the sociology of art. If the sociology of art has singled out a wide variety of factors that have made modern art what it is, perhaps our profession ought to contemplate itself in similar sociological, cultural, historical, psychological, and other mirrors. We might, of course, come to the conclusion that the broader processes within which political science and its development can be fitted are nonreversible and that therefore we are stuck in our state of disarray. Other problems of the genre may be perpetually insoluble: for instance, the need we may feel to communicate with the people, to disseminate our knowledge among the mass of the nonprofessionals. In a highly specialized society that may be too difficult. While the predicaments when closely examined may drive some of us out of the profession in despair, others may learn to laugh at them, go on doing their several things, though with eyes a bit more open. Some of us may even enjoy political science more.

NOTES

1. See, for instance, Sir John Maynard, *Russia in Flux* (New York, 1963, Collier Books); and James H. Billington, *The Icon and the Axe: An Interpretive History of Russian Culture* (New York, 1966, Knopf).

2. The best known work of this kind is Geoffrey Gorer and John Rickman, *The People of Great Russia* (New York, 1950, Chanticleer Press). See also Margaret Mead, *Soviet Attitudes toward Authority* (New York, 1951) and Nathan Leites, *A Study of Bolshevism* (Glencoe, 1953, Free Press). Some echoes of this approach can be discerned also in Leopold H. Haimson, *The Russian Marxists and the Origins of Bolshevism* (Cambridge, 1955, Harvard University Press).

3. Merle Fainsod, *How Russia Is Ruled* (Cambridge, 1963, Harvard University Press).

4. The approach is exemplified most clearly in Waldemar Gurian, *Bolshevism* (Notre Dame, 1952, University of Notre Dame Press). It also pervades Hannah Arendt's work on the origins of totalitarianism.

5. The standard model is presented in Carl J. Friedrich and Zbigniew K. Brzezinski, *Totalitarian Dictatorship and Autocracy* (Cambridge, 1956, Harvard University Press).

6. See Herbert Spiro's article on "Totalitarianism" in the *International Encyclopedia of the Social Sciences*, vol. 16.

7. To annotate this statement, one would have to cite representative samples from the entire vast literature in the field that has been produced in the last ten years.

8. Harold J. Berman, *Justice in the USSR* (New York, 1963, Vintage).

9. John N. Hazard, *The Soviet System of Government* (Chicago, 1957, University of Chicago Press).

10. Alfred G. Meyer, "Legitimacy of Power in East Central Europe," in Sinania, Deak, and Ludz (eds.), *Eastern Europe in the 1970's* (New York, 1972, Praeger). Also Alfred G. Meyer, "Authority in Communist Political Systems," in Lewis J. Edinger, *Political Leadership in Industrialized Societies* (New York, 1967, John Wiley).

11. Jerry F. Hough, *The Soviet Prefects: The Local Party Organs in Industrial Decision-Making* (Cambridge, 1969, Harvard University Press).

12. Joseph S. Berliner, *Factory and Management in the USSR* (Cambridge, 1967, Harvard University Press).

13. Robert V. Daniels, *The Conscience of the Revolution* (Cambridge, 1960, Harvard University Press).

14. M. Lewin, *Russian Peasants and Soviet Power: A Study of Collectivization* (London, 1968, Allen & Unwin).

15. David Joravsky, *The Lysenko Affair* (Cambridge, Mass., 1970); and *Soviet Marxism and National Science* (New York, 1961).

16. Kenneth Jowitt, *Revolutionary Breakthrough and National Development: The Case of Romania, 1944–1965* (Berkeley, 1971, University of California Press).

17. Lawrence B. Mohr, "Social Sciencecraft," Smirking papers, Institute of Public Policy Studies, University of Michigan, 1973.

18. Robert Carver North, *Revolt in San Marcos.*

19. Henry Bienen, "One Party Systems in Africa," in Samuel P. Huntington and Clement H. Moore, *Authoritarian Politics in Modern Society* (New York, 1970, Basic Books).

20. Alfred G. Meyer, *The Soviet Political System* (New York, 1967, Random House).

21. *Genesis* I/26, 26; II/19–20.

22. Friedrich Burckhardt, *The Civilization of the Renaissance in Italy* (New York, 1966), and other works; Max Dvorak, *Kunstgeschichte als Geistesgeschichte* (München, 1924).

23. Erwin Panowsky, *Gothic Architecture and Scholasticism* (Latrobe, Pennsylvania, 1951).

24. See the interview with Kenneth Boulding in *Challenge*, July-August, 1973, p. 35.

Political Science and
South Asian Studies

Myron Weiner

MASSACHUSETTS INSTITUTE OF TECHNOLOGY

EDITOR'S NOTE

Awakened academic interest in the subcontinent of India coincided
with both the coming of age of empirical social science research and
America's discovery of not only the importance of the developing world
but also foreign aid as a new instrument of foreign policy. Instead of
having to break down the barriers of encrusted academic traditions, the
emergence of the contemporary generation of South Asia specialists was
engulfed in a spirit of novelty and experimentation. India itself under the
exciting leadership of Nehru, a man who more than most world leaders
seemed to grasp the potentialities of at least economics if not all the social
sciences, represented the boldest and largest experiment with democracy
and planned economic growth.

The scholars recruited to South Asian studies in the 1950s and early
1960s tended to focus on the present and on possible futures. Most felt that
India's past could take care of itself while they joined in studying problems
relevant for the present. Except for economists, however, the majority of
social scientists began soon to drift away from the questions which
preoccupied policy makers and often rejoiced in taking counter-popular

perspectives. These South Asia scholars were equally skeptical of Western public views, which vacillated between the extremes of innocently expecting that aid and planning could bring rapid development to gloom over the prospect that India would fall apart from all of its linguistic, ethnic, and caste divisions.

Experience derived from adopting the stance that things in the subcontinent are always more complex than public officials pretend them to be helped lead South Asia scholars into more profound and less reassuring studies. The mood of believing that knowledge, instantly attainable, would facilitate desired changes gave way to increasing awe of the tenacity of an increasingly mysterious India. The first wave of scholars of post-independence India wanted to reject any taint of colonial thinking and to believe that a completely fresh start could be made in the new countries. As the tenacious persistence of tradition could no longer be ignored, the initial reaction was to cling to optimism and design theories of the ways in which traditional modes of behavior were in fact functional to change and modernization. With further experience Western scholars began increasingly to respect the uniqueness of the subcontinent and its blends of cultures. Myron Weiner's chapter reflects this appreciation of the perverse capacity of South Asian societies to defy all the generalized knowledge derived by the social sciences from work in other parts of the world. His analysis evokes a new level of excitement and wonder about South Asia and especially India, but as part of our review of the relationship between the disciplines and area studies we must add the distressing observation that just as Western scholars are becoming more mature in their understanding of India and poised to discover what makes that fascinating society so distinctive the political climate has unfortunately changed so as to complicate access for the further research which is now so patently important.

Social scientists are divided between those who ask of every empirical study, how does it contribute to general theory, and those who ask of every purported theoretical contribution, how does it contribute to our understanding of specific empirical situations. Nowhere has this dichotomy been sharper than in the divergent ways in which scholars have approached the study of South Asia. One scholarly tradition has viewed South Asia as a place in which to test and develop theories of political and social change, while the other tradition has sought to understand the region for its own sake. For many years this latter tradition did not hold an honorable place among social scientists, for while studies of political behavior in the United States and Europe seemed intrinsically valuable, the study of South Asia and of other developing countries had to be justified by some higher intellectual calling. The tension between these two perspectives proved to be intellectually invigorating as the area specialists, seeking legitimacy within their own disciplines, sought first to apply general concepts and theories, not to test them but to use them to understand specific features of South Asian society and politics, but in the course of doing so amended or rejected many of the paradigms of their discipline.

I

The application and testing of theories of political and social change to the Indian subcontinent has a distinguished intellectual heritage. Indeed, some of the most influential concepts in political and social theory have been inspired by attempts to explain why one or another phenomenon in South Asia differed from that of the West. Karl Marx, for example, was acutely aware of the inapplicability of his own dialectical theory of development to either India or China, since neither country had experienced the ancient, feudal, and bourgeois modes of production that were so central to his development theory. He offered as an alternative the concept of an "Asiatic mode of production," as much a geographic as an analytic concept, to explain these deviant cases; in retrospect, we can find in Marx's efforts the precursor of contemporary efforts to find an all-embracing model for so-called "non-Western" and "transitional" political systems.

Max Weber, whose approach was chosen by subsequent generations of social scientists as the foremost alternative to Marxism, saw India and China not as exceptions to his general theory, but as supporting cases. If Protestantism was the exceptional case, the unique instance of a religious doctrine and social structure providing an incentive for capitalist entrepreneurial behavior, then Weber needed to demonstrate that other religious traditions played a completely different role with respect to the economic order; in this respect, Hinduism provided him with his most extreme case.

An entire generation of English social theorists viewed India as a place in which social theory could be applied if not tested by public interventions; underlying the policies of each of the great imperial figures of English authority in India stood, often quite explicitly, a social theory; Whig, evangelical, utilitarian, and liberal doctrines underlay decisions affecting land policy, the establishment of a legal code, interventions in social policy, the creation of landed classes in some regions and peasant proprietor classes in others, tax policies, and educational policies. In contemporary terms one could describe the writings of Mill and Bentham, as applied to India, as early examples of interventionist theories of political development.[1]

Finally, India provided a testing ground for the classical theory of imperialism, a theory that simultaneously attempted to explain the expansion of capitalist societies and the persistent backwardness of the economic systems in Asia and Africa dominated by the imperial powers. Just as Whig, evangelical, utilitarian, and liberal doctrines became, in effect, elite guides to public policy, so the theory of imperialism became the ideological foundation of mass nationalist movements.

India, as a testing site for development theories, continues to find a central place among contemporary American social scientists. Four examples come to mind: David McClelland tested his need achievement theory, which attempts to specify the motivational basis of entrepreneurship, in a controlled experiment in a South Indian town; Karl Deutsch applied his theory of the relationship of communications to the growth of nationalism to the study of Indian language development; Reinhard Bendix compared Western Europe's political structures with that of India in his analysis of the relationship between local and national authority in the process of development; and, finally, Barrington Moore turned to an analysis of the Indian agrarian system to test his concepts of the way in which landlord-peasant relationships affect the social costs of modernization.[2]

From Marx to Moore, Weber to McClelland stands a tradition of scholarship more concerned with developing social theories, and using India to test those theories, than with understanding India as such. Each viewed India not simply as another statistical case to add to their "N," but rather as a place where their theory had to work if they were to make any claim for having created a general theory of development or social change.

Almost all general theories of political behavior and political change cry out for testing in one or more countries of South Asia: how "general," for example, is a theory of agrarian revolution that fails to explain why not one of the countries of South Asia has experienced large-scale peasant revolts; or a theory of radical politics that does not explain why radical parties have done badly in most of South Asia; or a theory of national integration that cannot explain why India has remained intact while Pakistan has not; or a theory of party institutionalization and political stability that does not throw light on why India's Congress party continues to thrive and govern twenty-seven years after independence, while nationalist parties elsewhere have disintegrated; or a theory of the role of the military in the less developed countries that does not explain why the military has dominated the politics of Pakistan but not of India; or a theory on the role of the monarchy which does not explain why the authority of the monarchy in Nepal has grown rather than diminished; or a theory concerned with the political effects of distribution policies that does not explain why Sri Lanka (Ceylon), the South Asian country with the most far-reaching program of income distribution, has come closest to a social revolution; or finally, a theory which relates economic growth to governmental performance that does not explain why some states within India have miracle economic growth rates, while others are stagnant though they coexist within the same national political system? No single exception necessarily destroys a theory—unless the theory claims universal validity under specified conditions, as opposed to a probabilistic theory—but most social change theorists have understandably assumed that any development theory they propose must attempt to come to grips with the five countries of South Asia and the seven to eight hundred million people who live in them.

II

Area experts have approached the South Asia region with a different perspective. Their primary concern has been with understanding South Asia, not with generating universal theories. For the past twenty years a small number of American political scientists, an even smaller number of British, Canadian, Australian, and German political scientists, and a growing number of Indian political scientists, all much influenced by contemporary American political science concepts, methods, and theories, have sought to analyze various aspects of Indian political behavior and institutions. The initial influences came more from the contemporary behavioral science revolution than from social theories, though clearly the former were themselves influenced by the latter. The earliest studies in India were of parties and party systems, much influenced by Duverger, V. O. Key, Leiserson, and Eldersveld; studies of electoral behavior drew from scholarship on American elections and later from the work of Butler and Stokes on Britain; as urban studies in India developed, these were influenced by contemporary American controversies, both conceptual and methodological, over the question of who governs; and studies of political participation were much influenced by American scholarship on political socialization.

Typically, a graduate student studying South Asia initially borrowed concepts and methods from the disciplinary field in which he was working—urban politics, political parties and interest groups, electoral behavior, political socialization, and so on. The student had to demonstrate to his doctoral thesis committee that he was not "merely" studying South Asia, but that his research had some larger, more universal theoretical significance. As Lucian Pye points out in his paper in this volume, many thesis committees imposed a higher theoretical requirement for students working on South Asia or other non-American, non-European subjects, on the assumption that there was no intrinsic intellectual value in studying these regions for their own sake.

In practice, the fields often proved constricting, for in political science departments these were actually subfields of American politics, and hence provided little guidance for relating political change to the larger processes of modernization taking place in South Asia or other developing countries. Moreover, as Samuel Huntington has pointed out elsewhere in this volume, the paradigms of American politics were hardly relevant to the study of modernization. "Born free," Americans—with the obvious exceptions of Blacks and Indians, and, as Huntington notes, the South generally—have not experienced the problems of converting from traditional to modern values and institutions.

With the emergence of a separate field of political development concerned with relating modernization to political change and with studying systemic change, one would have expected Marxism to provide some of the central paradigms for research on South Asia. There were some attempts to study class conflict and the emergence of class consciousness in the Indian countryside, and some efforts to show how the distribution of economic wealth has shaped the distribution of political power, but in the main Marx's theories have either not been applied, or when applied, not proven relevant. Indeed, since Marx himself asserted that his dialectical theories were not appropriate for the analysis of India, Marxist analyses have often been misapplied, as Sholomo Avineri has pointed out in his brilliant essay on Marx on colonialism and modernization.[3] Thus, Marxists speak of feudalism in India, when Marx asserted that feudalism did not exist in the Asiatic mode of production; Marxists condemn imperialism, while Marx himself was concerned with the "regenerating" as well as "destructive" elements of the British role in India; and while Marxists seek to show how the distribution of economic wealth determines the distribution of political power, Marx himself emphasized the autonomous character of state power and the ways in which political power affected culture, social structure, and economic relations—a position much closer to contemporary political analysis.

Moreover, neither Marx nor his disciples knew what to do with ethnic cleavages within political systems. Alternatively explained away as "false consciousness," a mask for class cleavages, or a diversionary tactic by the ruling elites (like religion, an "opiate" of the people), ethnicity was to wither away under the impact of a more modern social structure imbedded in a capitalist industrial order. For the sociologist and political scientist studying South Asia, the Marxist dismissal of "ethnicity" (in its many forms) in preference for a class analysis was to neglect a central feature of the social reality of South Asia.

Max Weber's influence on contemporary theories of development as applied to South Asia has been more substantial and enduring than that of Marx, though he too has suffered from gross distortion. While Weber saw Protestantism as a significant *incentive* to entrepreneurial behavior, others have focused on the role of religion generally as an *impediment* to modernization. While Weber analyzed some of the special features of modern industrial societies, especially the patterns of behavior that characterize modern bureaucracies and modern social relations, others have mistakenly proclaimed these characteristics as preconditions to development. There were those who argued that the abolition of the caste system, the joint family, beliefs in fate, rebirth, and duty, ritual observances and the major institutions, practices, and doctrines of Hinduism are a prerequisite for economic development. Some political scientists further argued that urbanization, literacy, and the expansion of the mass media are prerequisites to political participation and the establishment of a modern democratic state. More recently, it has become fashionable to add still another list of prerequisites to development: the "structural" transformation of agrarian systems as a prerequisite to agricultural growth, greater income equality as a precondition to a stable political order, and even a "revolutionary" transformation of the political system as a precondition to economic development, all of which add up to what Milton Singer has pointedly called an "off-with-their-heads" prescription.

Scholars of South Asia have been in the forefront of the attack against this particular approach to modernization. In place of a rigid conception of prerequisites, they have emphasized a model of adaptation of tradition and the principle of substitutability. Milton Singer, in his study of entrepreneurship in India,[4] suggests that a class of entrepreneurs has developed in India with its own industrial cultural tradition, though caste has not been replaced by class, the joint family has not been replaced by the nuclear family, and ritual and religious beliefs have not given way totally to science and secular ideologies. In a similar vein, Lloyd Rudolph[5] has persuasively shown how caste associations can serve as substitutes for the economic and professional interest groups found in modern societies, but serve the same functions of articulating groups' interests in a democratic framework. The complex overlapping of ethnic groups in India, the heritage of a national movement, the Indian devotion to legal processes, the peculiar pattern of central authority and local autonomy, the persistent though at times waning belief in British liberal institutions and values on the part of

India's governing elites, have all helped to preserve India's democratic system, even though literacy remains low—hardly one of five Indians lives in an urban area—the proportion of newspaper readers has not increased (and may have even declined), while exposure to any mass media, including radio, is still small.

Other general development theories have fared no better in the hands of political science-area specialists working on South Asia. One of the major theoretical concerns of students of political development has been the question of which social class or institution would provide the cutting edge for the modernization process. Would it be the one-party state? A revolutionary party committed to transforming the social order? A modernizing oligarchy centered around the bureaucratic and entrepreneurial classes? A modernizing monarchy? A democratically elected party leadership with its roots in the urban middle classes? An important candidate has been the military as an institution that purportedly has the capacity to stimulate both modernization and integration. The argument, put in oversimplified terms, is that armies, affected by the requirements of the technologies they employ, the orderliness that characterizes a chain of command, and their identification with the national structure, can provide the rational, instrumental, pragmatic, and orderly framework for nation-building and modernization in a way that neither party politicians nor bureaucracies are able to do. For some time, this theory seemed particularly applicable to Pakistan, a country dominated by a military-bureaucratic elite, maintaining a high rate of economic growth and, until recently, with little internal disorder. But the recent civil war in Pakistan demonstrated that an army could be imbued with a martial spirit so racial in character that it becomes unable, both by virtue of its composition and temperament, to cope with the issues of ethnic and regional conflict in the society at large. The Pakistan army, with all its American equipment and British spit and polish, proved to be more Moghul than modern, in spirit more akin to the Imperial Japanese army of the 1930s than to the armies of the contemporary West. Rounaq Jahan's study of the Ayub Khan era[6] provides an excellent account of the way in which the transfer of power from party politicians who governed the country badly, but who nevertheless came from both parts of the country, to a narrowly recruited military-bureaucratic regime from the West made the task of reconciling East and West Pakistan increasingly difficult. Her main thesis—that the composition and orientation of the governing elite is a critical factor in whether a multi-ethnic state is able to remain intact—is an important correction to many of the deterministic models of integration in which the variables are so exclusively nonpolitical.

Looking ahead at the tensions which still persist within what now remains of Pakistan, can we say that existing theories of national integration provide us with the tools to explain and predict the forces at work? What theory adequately alerts us to the two factors that may prove most crucial to the survival of Pakistan as a single state—the policies of the government toward the dissident Pathans and Baluchis, particularly the extent to which the government chooses to emphasize coercion as against the accommodating options implied by the newly created federal structure; and secondly, the role played by outside powers, especially Afghanistan, India, Iraq, and Iran, each of whom has the capacity through the provision or denial of arms and policy support to affect either the behavior of the minorities or the response of the government.

The relationship of authority and participation, a core issue in the study of political development, has also been the subject of much research on India, particularly through the study of electoral behavior. As one of the few countries in the developing world with a history of periodic local, state, and national elections based upon universal adult suffrage, India provides political scientists with a rare opportunity to look at the impact of social and economic changes (such as urbanization and the expansion of the mass media) upon political participation, and to look in turn at the impact of changing patterns of political participation on the functioning of parties and government. The political science literature in this area is quite rich—studies by Morris-Jones and Das Gupta[7] isolating some of the social and economic correlates of party preferences, Donald Zagoria's study[8] of the ecological basis of peasant support for radical parties, Francine Frankel's examination of the electoral consequences of the Green Revolution, Mary Katzenstein on the electoral consequences of different patterns of migration to urban areas, and a study by John Field and myself[9] on the way in which voting in urban constituencies is related to the rural areas in which cities and towns are located. One electoral study warranting special attention is Paul Brass's examination[10] of the relationship between political participation, institutionalization, and stability in India. In his analysis of election data for each of the Indian states, he finds no significant association between variations in electoral participation and variations in the vote for the dominant Congress party, and no relationship between levels of electoral participation and stability or instability of state governments; to the contrary, he finds a close relationship between rapid increases in electoral participation and the institutionalization of the party system. In the Indian case, rapid increases in political participation have not been accompanied by destabilization of the party system or of governmental authority.[11]

I have singled out two theories by political scientists that have not withstood the test of empirical scholarship in South Asia; I could as easily single out theories in the other social sciences that have also been substantially amended or rejected by South Asian area experts. The social science literature on South Asia is replete with studies whose starting point is a widely accepted theory that proves to be unsupported or refuted by empirical study. In this connection I would cite Richard Lambert's book[12] on the persistence and adaptation of caste relations in factories of Poona, Morris Davis Morris's study of the way in which British trade and investment actually stimulated rather than undermined traditional craft industries,[13] and the previously cited work by Singer[14] on Hindu entrepreneurship.

Ever since Lord Hastings was tried for impeachment by the House of Lords it has been said that India is a graveyard for men's reputations; as much can be said for many nonempirical theories applied to India. India has always been a difficult country for Westerners to understand. Indians seem to be perversely passive on matters that would lead men elsewhere to revolt, but are politically provoked at what many Americans would dismiss as mere symbolism without substance. They govern themselves more or less democratically under conditions that are suppposedly conducive to authoritarianism. They appear to govern themselves best under situations of greatest adversity—managing famines, refugees, and wars—but remain extraordinarily inept when it comes to the routines of government. Their leaders appear to be skillful at the management of political conflict even when it involves the resolution of intensely felt ethnic sentiments, but they show far less skill in making policy decisions to maximize economic objectives. And Indians find it easier to hate others who belong to another religion, speak another language, or identify with another caste or tribe than to hate others because they are wealthy or powerful but belong to the same linguistic, religious, caste, or tribal community. Nor do Indians see any contradiction between hating one another and loving their country!

No wonder then that South Asian area scholars invariably become their own theorists, resting their theories on the solid empirical research that is now the most important contribution of area studies to the social sciences. Let me now call attention to several problem areas which increasingly occupy the attention of political scientists working on South Asia[15] that are in need of that combination of theory and empirical research that the area expert often provides. Each of these is an important issue in development, and each reflects the concerns not only of area experts but of thoughtful people within South Asia.

III

There is an increasing awareness of the pervasive effects of population growth on social and political change and the extent to which its study has been neglected. One important consequence of this neglect is that we have underestimated the magnitude of many social changes in India, because these changes have been obscured by the rapid increase in population, especially changes in urban growth and migration, agricultural development and education.

Percentagewise, India's urbanization rate is low. The country was only 17.3 per cent urban in 1951, 18 per cent in 1961, and slightly under 20 per cent in 1971. But while the urbanization rate, that is the increase in the proportion of the population living in urban areas, continues to be low, the urban growth rate remains high. India's urban population increased from 79 to 109 million from 1961 to 1971, a 38 per cent population increase. India's urban areas gained thirty million people, slightly under twenty million through natural population increase and more than ten million through migration. India's high rate of natural population growth (24.7 per cent in the decade) disguises the magnitude of her

cityward migration. Had India's rate of natural population increase
been smaller, then the urban growth rate would be lower but,
paradoxically, the urbanization rate would have been higher. If
India's population had increased at half its present rate during the
past decade, then the proportion of her population living in the
cities would have leaped from 18 per cent to 25 per cent while the
cities themselves would now have 99 million rather than 108
million persons.

Migration has accelerated the growth rates of some cities well
beyond the average urban growth. In the past decade Delhi has
grown by 54 per cent, Bombay 44 per cent, the port city of Vizak 71
per cent, the new capital of the Punjab, Chandigarh, 134 per cent,
and the steel town of Durgapur by a staggering 397 per cent.
India's cities now have forty-three million migrants, or one out of
every thirteen Indians. But India's high population growth rate
tends to obscure substantial increases in cityward migration, with
the result that we have tended to pay little attention to migration
processes, their determinants and consequences, both for the city
and the countryside.

Similarly, India's food production per capita has increased at
around 1 per cent per year since independence, an unimpressive
rate which reflects favorably neither on the bureaucracy nor on the
peasantry; even the effects of the Green Revolution appear modest
when translated into per capita terms and averaged for the country
as a whole. Actually, grain production has increased at about 3.5
per cent per year from 1950 to 1970, a doubling of production in
two decades. But again, the high rate of population increase has
meant only small increases in per capita food production, a
doubling rate in seventy years. Still, it is important to note that
Indian agriculture has made impressive strides, and that the growth
in food production has probably been the single most important
factor in the declining death rate,[16] in itself a significant achievement but one which paradoxically tends to hide accomplishments
in other areas.

Finally, we should note the way in which population growth
has also obscured increases in literacy. Twenty-nine per cent of
India is literate as of 1971, only a modest increase over the 24 per
cent in 1961. How inadequate this change has been is shown by the
growth in the number of illiterates from 333 to 383 million, a fifty

million increase. Yet the number of literates has also risen impressively from 106 million in 1961 to 165 million in 1971, a 55 per cent growth.[17] Again, had the rate of population increase been half as great, the literacy rate would have been higher in 1971—up to one out of every three Indians—and in absolute terms the number of illiterates would have declined.

In food production, urban growth, cityward migration, and literacy one can point with equal persuasiveness to the extraordinary pace of change in absolute terms or to the slow pace of change in relation to population growth. Clearly, what has obscured all these rapid changes is that in the past decade India has added a mind-boggling 109 million persons. Under such conditions of rapid population growth, all indices of development appear low when translated into per capita changes.

Though we have many *a priori* assertions concerning the political, economic, and social effects of rapid population growth, we have little in the way of empirical research. We know little about the effects of a changing age structure, the impact of population growth on political demands and on the capacity of government agencies to meet demands, the effects of population growth on social mobility, on income distribution, on the size and functioning of the joint family, on the fragmentation of land, and on the use of resources. Political scientists have paid little attention to the study of political demography with its concern for the political determinants and consequences of changes in the size, composition, growth, and distribution of populations, particularly as these changes relate to other aspects of development.[18]

Attention needs to be given not to the "crises" that purportedly result from population growth, but to the innumerable ways in which a society and its political system cope with and adapt to population changes. Who would have quarreled with Sir Henry Maine when he wrote over a century ago, "How can 180 million souls govern themselves? Responsible and representative government are terms without meaning when they are applied to such a multitude. Societies of that magnitude have seldom held together at all under the same political institutions, but when they have, the institutions have been sternly despotic." [19] If in retrospect Maine was wrong in his conception of the relationship between population size and representative government—for India with a population now three times larger is held together by a single nondespotic political system—it suggests that we need to understand the kind of adaptive mechanisms at work that make it possible for institutions to cope with growing populations.

A second problem area concerns the growing income disparities within South Asia. It is widely asserted and well documented that income disparities are large and that they have grown since independence; it is not clear, however, to what extent these disparities reflect regional differences as opposed to class and occupational disparities within each region. According to a study by Irma Adelman and Cynthia Taft Morris, the lowest 40 per cent of India's population earns 20 per cent of the country's income, those between 40 and 80 per cent of the population earn 38 per cent, and the top 20 per cent earn 42 per cent of the income.[20] Given the substantial differences in regional development in India as between states (e.g., Punjab versus Orissa) and within states (e.g., western versus eastern Uttar Pradesh), there is reason to believe that the lowest 40 per cent of the population are unevenly dispersed. Nor do income distribution data tell us what proportion of the lowest income groups belong to India's scheduled castes and tribes, who constitute 21 per cent of the population.

These various income disparities are related to variations in investment as between one region and another, to either unequal access or unequal performance in schools and colleges, to the differential effects of the Green Revolution on those who have land and those who do not, to who finds jobs in the modern industrial sector as against those who remain in the low skilled, low wage, low technology occupations that characterize the dual economics of developing countries, and to who does or does not find employment in government service, India's largest employer.

Some of these disparities are more easily explainable than others. The technology of the Green Revolution, for example, is available to peasants with an adequate water supply, but that currently excludes some four-fifths of the land. Disparities in industrial investment are often related to earlier investment decisions in transportation and electric power. Other disparities are more complicated. According to studies conducted by the Indian Council of Social Science Research, tribals and harijans have a low school attendance and a high dropout rate even when educational facilities are provided, fees are paid to schools and stipends to students and, in some instances, jobs are virtually assured. The complexities of the role of ethnicity in income distribution are further demonstrated by the fact that in some regions the establishment of new industries has provided employment opportunities for migrants from other regions, rather than for native populations who for one reason or another are unable to compete effectively. There is often an ethnic component to the question of who finds employment in the relatively privileged modern industrial sector.

Nor are the social and political consequences of these disparities well understood. What new political demands and cleavages will arise as a consequence of increased disparities? Will backward regions within states press for statehood in the hope that they would thereby command more attention from the central government, a phenomenon already at work in some states? Will there be even more pressure for laws and ordinances to protect certain social groups against competition—through, for example, restricting interstate migration, and systems of employment preferences? Very little is known concerning the actual effects of public policies on reducing disparities through reservations for harijans and tribals in schools, colleges, and in employment—India's version of a quota system for the underprivileged; nor do we have studies evaluating the efforts to develop backward areas through programs of regional development as against programs to increase the skills of people who live within backward regions.

Simply to pose these questions is to point to the obvious convergence between the concerns of South Asia area experts and of informed people in India, and some of the current concerns of social scientists studying social change in the United States. Some of the efforts to develop social indicators, to develop quality of life measures that are more comprehensive than income measures, to isolate the factors which affect school performance, employment, and social and spatial mobility, and to develop improved methods for measuring the effects on individuals of social policies could all prove useful to area experts and to South Asian social scientists. These efforts may be more significant than the studies by economists of income distribution in India and other developing countries which pay no attention to either the spatial or the ethnic dimension, both of which may prove, especially in South Asia, politically more salient than class and occupational disparities.

A third problem area of concern to South Asian area specialists continues to be the study of changing cultural identities. On the one hand there have emerged in South Asia distinctive *regional* cultures, attachments to historic empires, distinctive heroes and events, and regional cultural practices and literary traditions; and on the other hand we are witnessing the spread through India of Hindu puranic and epic mythology, the conversion of cultural events into national events, and the use of the modern mass media to reinforce traditional beliefs and symbols and to elevate them to a *national* Indian culture. These two tendencies exist side by side, sometimes in conflict but often interrelated in complex ways. Moreover, the regional and national cultures each in their own way reflect the extent to which modernization has created a popular culture out of the roots of ancient beliefs and practices and contributed to the shaping of new political as well as cultural identities. The relationship between these regional and national identities, the role of the region as a bridge between local and national politics, the disparities between regions with respect to levels of economic development and the effect of these disparities on national loyalties and national conflict all continue to remain important areas for research.

The issue of identities is closely linked to our need to understand the spatial dimensions of life in South Asia. What are the spatial regions with which Indians identify and how are these changing? What is the relationship between these spatial conceptions and linguistic and other cultural identities? And how do these spatial concepts affect people's decisions with respect to where they choose to move, where they invest, and whom they accept as a local person as against whom they view as a stranger?

As India's regions become more multi-ethnic under the pressures of interregional migration and the resistance on the part of linguistic and tribal minorities to cultural assimilation, we may begin to see the emergence of territorial as distinct from ethnic identifications. Can someone born and raised in Maharashtra be a Maharashtrian though his native language is Gujarati? Can a tribal living in Bihar ever be a Bihari, or a Bengali living in Assam be Assamese? The terms themselves make territorial identities difficult. To be Maharashtrian, Bihari, or Assamese is to be a member of a linguistic group, not a life-time resident of a state or region. In a few instances we can see Indians assert their attachments to particular cities (Bombaywallahs, Delhiwallahs), subregions of states, or to their states, while most continue to assert their cultural identities, a difference which could have important consequences for political behavior and institutions. In this connection it should be noted that not all the movements for smaller states in India are based upon ethnic claims: the call for a Telengana state to be carved out of Andhra, a Chota Nagpur state to be carved out of Bihar, and a Vidarbha to be carved out of Maharashtra.

IV

This review of theories applied to South Asia and new problems posed by political scientists working on South Asia points to a number of observations concerning the relationship between the area expert and his discipline:

Firstly, the area expert is a contextualist; he is sensitized to look at a wider range of relationships than the political scientist who is not an area expert. If he has difficulty applying some general theory to the area in which he works, it is not because he is perversely committed to the uniqueness of his region, but because he often finds the general theories do not work or are at a level of generalization that makes them trivial. It is because of this contextual orientation that area specialists have often been attracted to the systems approach, not necessarily in its current quantitative incarnation, but as a way of thinking which emphasizes the special—yes, perhaps even the unique—configurations that characterize a society and its political system.

Secondly, area specialists recognize that late development has a dynamic all its own. Those who do research in the developing areas are witnesses to change processes and problems that have often never occurred before. The demographic dimension, for example, is new, for historically none of the countries of the West has experienced natural population increases of the magnitudes now taking place in the developing countries. No existing theory based upon historical experience is likely to be adequate for predicting the consequences for, say, the performance of governmental agencies, the kinds of demands likely to be generated, the tensions and violence that might result from crowding, and so on. As Hirschman has pointed out, paradigms and models can be a hindrance to understanding by excluding relevant factors from our vision, and by their tendency to exclude the unexpected. Area specialists are thus properly cautious in the face of general theories and models and at aggregate cross-national analyses. This is not to say that the models or paradigms do not have utility. For as Hirschman has written, "they are useful for the apprehending of many elements of the complex, and often are stimuli to action before the event and indispensable devices for achieving a beginning of understanding after the event has happened. That is much, but that is all." [21]

Third, and finally, let us note that political scientists working on South Asia will increasingly turn even more than before to the work of political and social scientists studying political behavior and development in other developing areas, for it is in the expertise of the area scholars, their capacity to combine theory with empirical scholarship, their ability to observe and analyze change with regard to the context in which it occurs that we have the building blocks for comparative analysis.

NOTES

1. The best accounts of the application of nineteenth-century political theory to governance in India are Eric Stokes, *The English Utilitarians and India* (Oxford University Press, Oxford, 1959), and Francis G. Hutchins, *The Illusion of Permanence: British Imperialism in India* (Princeton University Press, Princeton, 1967).

2. Since the works of the theorists discussed here are all well known, I shall not provide the usual list of citations except to note that the McClelland experiment is described in David C. McClelland and David G. Winter, *Motivating Economic Achievement* (Free Press, New York, 1969).

3. Sholomo Avineri, ed., *Karl Marx on Colonialism and Modernization* (Doubleday and Company, Anchor Books, New York, 1969), pp. 1–31.

4. Milton Singer, *When a Great Tradition Modernizes* (Praeger, New York, 1972). Singer has been the principal opponent of the view that the modernization of India necessitates the rejection, politically and intellectually, of the core elements in Indian culture. His critique of Weber is further pursued in *Entrepreneurship and Modernization of Occupational Cultures in South Asia*, Milton Singer, ed. (Duke University Program in Comparative Studies on South Asia, Monograph Number Twelve, 1973). The theme of the papers in this volume is that there exists within Hinduism (and according to Hanna Papanek in her paper on Pakistan's new industrialists, in Islam as well) "functionally equivalent belief and value systems" to the "Protestant ethic" and the "spirit of capitalism" (p. 14).

5. Lloyd Rudolph, "The Modernity of Tradition: The Democratic Incarnation of Caste in India," *American Political Science Review* (December, 1965). The argument is further developed in Lloyd and Susanne Rudolph, *The Modernity of Tradition: Political Development in India* (University of Chicago Press, Chicago, 1967).

6. Rounaq Jahan, *Pakistan: Failure in National Integration* (Columbia University Press, New York, 1973).

7. W. H. Morris-Jones and B. Das Gupta, "India's Political Areas: Interim Report on an Ecological Investigation," *Asian Survey* (June, 1969).

8. Donald S. Zagoria, "The Ecology of Peasant Communism in India," *American Political Science Review* (March, 1971).

9. The papers by Francine Frankel, Mary Katzenstein, John O. Field, and myself appear in a volume John Field and I have edited, *Electoral Politics in the Indian States: The Impact of Modernization* (Vol. III) (Manohar Book Service, Delhi, forthcoming).

10. Paul R. Brass, "Political Participation, Institutionalization and Stability in India," *Government and Opposition* (Winter, 1969).

11. The concept of institutionalization is, of course, associated with the work of Samuel P. Huntington, "Political Development and Political Decay," *World Politics* (April, 1965), 386–430, and *Political Order in Changing Societies* (Yale University Press, New Haven, 1968).

12. Richard Lambert, *Workers, Factories and Social Change in India* (Princeton University Press, Princeton, 1963).

13. Morris D. Morris, *The Emergence of an Industrial Labor Force in India* (University of California Press, Berkeley, 1965). See also his "Towards a Re-interpretation of Nineteenth Century Indian Economic History," *The Journal of Economic History* (December, 1963).

14. Singer, cited.

15. For a comprehensive examination of political science research on South Asia, its quantitative dimensions, a review of approaches, and a survey of data, research and educational needs, see "South Asia in American Political Science," a report submitted to the South Asia Committee of the Association of Asian Studies by Henry C. Hart, David

H. Bayley, Samuel J. Eldersveld, George H. Gadbois, Jr., and Khalid B. Sayeed, 1967.

16. The death rate declined from 27.4 per thousand in 1951 to 17.5 in 1969. During this same period, the infant mortality rate dropped from 183 to 136 (per thousand live births).

17. Between 1950 and 1970, the number of children below 14 in school increased fourfold, while the number of literates more than doubled.

18. For a review of approaches and hyptheses see Myron Weiner, "Political Demography: An Inquiry into the Political Consequences of Population Change," in *Rapid Population Growth*, published for the National Academy of Sciences by the Johns Hopkins Press, Baltimore, 1971. A significant contribution to the understanding of the social and political demography of South Asia is W. Howard Wriggins and James F. Guyot, eds., *Population, Politics and the Future of Southern Asia* (Columbia University Press, New York, 1973).

19. Quoted by Anil Seal, *The Emergence of Indian Nationalism* (Cambridge University Press, Cambridge, 1968), p. 185.

20. Irma Adelman and Cynthia Taft Morris, *Economic Growth and Social Equity in Developing Countries* (Stanford University Press, Stanford, 1973), p. 152. India's income distribution problem is no worse and is often better than that of most developing countries. According to Adelman and Morris, the lowest 40 per cent in India earns a larger proportion of income than the lowest 40 per cent in Mexico, Brazil, Nigeria, Tanzania, Pakistan, and Argentina and, surprisingly, Japan and Israel. In each instance the top 20 per cent in these countries earns the same or an even larger percentage of the national income than the top 20 per cent in India. India's middle population group earns a larger share of income than that of most other low income countries. However, from a social justice point of view what has been disturbing is that the share of the lowest income group in India, as in other developing countries, has declined in spite of the growth in GNP, and that the absolute income levels for the lowest groups in India remain below any reasonable standard of human decency.

21. Albert Hirschman, "The Search for Paradigms as a Hindrance to Understanding," *World Politics* (April, 1970), p. 343.

Politics and the Study
of Latin America

Kalman H. Silvert

NEW YORK UNIVERSITY AND FORD FOUNDATION

EDITOR'S NOTE

For some time the serious study of Latin America has been concentrated in a few North American universities while many otherwise very strong faculties offer nothing on the neighboring continent. There is thus a strikingly uneven quality about Latin American studies: in some respects it is a mature field with established authorities in several disciplines, while in other respects the field is underdeveloped.

Latin American studies have two distinctive features in comparison with other area studies. First, the Latin American political and social systems do not readily conform to standard categories: Latin American states are not underdeveloped countries in the Afro-Asian sense of newly independent, emerging nations; nor are they readily comparable to European societies in spite of their heritages. As a consequence of their distinctive characteristics the issue of whether the concepts and theories basic to most social science disciplines that were formulated out of study of American and European systems are appropriate when applied in such a different setting becomes peculiarly acute in Latin American studies. Kalman Silvert's chapter which follows is a strong reminder of the dangers of allowing ethnocentric concepts to be treated as universal categories and the need for modesty among outside researchers in the face of different traditions.

The second distinction of Latin American studies, which Silvert also notes, is that the region has produced its own scholarly interpreters who do not share all the views of Western social sciences but who are also highly autonomous scholars and not advocates of official ideologies. In the early postwar period there was considerable foundation support for building greater empirical social science capabilities in Latin American universities in which the humanistic traditions of an earlier European period were particularly strong. By the 1960s, however, the emphasis shifted toward trying to foster greater cooperation and interaction between indigenous and outside researchers. For various reasons, relating mainly to political perceptions, it has not been easy to build a community of scholars involving both North and South Americans. The inherent problems of cross-cultural cooperation were further exaggerated by the suspicions of North American intentions after the incident of the Camelot Project. Precisely because of these problems of distrust greater efforts have been made by various foundations to seek more institutionalized forms of research collaboration in Latin America than in any other areas. For example, the Foreign Area Fellowship Program, under the skillful guidance of Bryce Wood, arranged for all North American fellowship recipients to be affiliated with appropriate Latin American institutions.

As both the intellectual and the human relations problems of research in Latin America are more effectively tackled the way will be opened, let us hope, for exciting research developments. The combination of both North and South American traditions for understanding social and political phenomena should provide a strong stimulus for new advances in the social sciences.

Probing the relationships between the disciplines and area studies is a theme with a long and drab history. I have no intention of weaving my way through the extensive literature on the subject. Anybody curious about such matters may begin by consulting the omnibus note whose number is given at the end of this sentence.[1] Furthermore, I have an equal disinclination to defend myself or my fellow political scientists who write on Latin America from chronic charges that we are somehow not up to the task, or at least relatively not as "good" as our disciplinary colleagues who labor in other geographical vineyards. Herewith, I present you with another note number to satisfy any prurient curiosity you may have about such gossip.[2] It has some redeeming social value, but very little academic worth. Instead of treating area studies and political science as essentially different enterprises, I wish to suggest that the latter had best ingest the former if it is to prosper, and not continue to languish in its present state—a discipline which has creditably managed to discredit most of its recently popular theories, but has not summoned itself to the general and scientifically transient acceptance of more useful constructions of reality.

The reasoning I will pursue has little documentary backing, for the historical separateness of area studies and the social science disciplines is the stereotypical strain throughout the available literature. The commonly accepted view is summed up in the following résumé by a leading student and impresario of area studies:[3]

> It is suggested that there have been four stages in the development of relationships between area studies and the social sciences; that is to say—naming the extremes—between the gathering of data and their ordering by theoretical constructs. In the first stage, data about foreign areas were collected through field research by area specialists. A second stage saw the comparison of similar problems in different areas through the broadening of training of area specialists. In the third stage, data from several areas were used by social scientists to develop new theories and to overcome the parochial basis of much existing theory in the social sciences. In the present, fourth stage, the development of theory begins to influence the types of problems area specialists investigate and the kinds of questions they begin to ask as they undertake field research, in part because, more than ever before, the training of area specialists is becoming assimilated to the training of social scientists. This is bound to have effects on both. . . .

On the surface of it, the process as described appears ideal: an inductive gathering of data by area specialists leads to theoretical, disciplinary interpretations which permit the deductive approach to begin.[4] Area studies are "prescientific," while the discipline provides the science which then impregnates the continuance of area analysis, which in its turn moves ever closer to the disciplines.

Would that life so ordered itself. This view of "natural" process is highly reminiscent of the trickle theory in economics, the belief that a well primed pump will be made to continue to shower some water on everybody, for reasonable and rational men will see the personal advantage to keeping consumers alive. The trickle theory breaks down, among many other reasons, because unequal power distributions all too often prevent the flow from permeating the entire society, even most inequitably. Analogously, the flow of data from "areas" to the disciplinary mills and out to the "areas" dries up because the mill is unable to process the raw material; it cannot convert "information" into "data" without changing its own nature, without grappling with the fact that area studies came into existence because of the very ethnocentric limitations of the disciplines. Political science is a weak sister. Area studies are her crutch.

Although this standing on its head of the discipline-area relationship is unusual, comments on the debilities of political science are not. Once again, I do not propose to summarize arguments about neo-positivism, quantification and "qualification," the meaning of "institutional approaches" in political science as distinct from sociology and economics, or the different significance of "structuralism" in our discipline from anthropology. Whatever one's persuasion, *it is a matter of fact* that the discipline has not dealt *conceptually* and hence *scientifically* with some of the more astounding political developments of the past two decades. The failure is beyond debate. Joseph LaPalombara wrote in the inaugural issue of *Comparative Politics*:[5]

> A less generous reaction to much of the recent whole-systems theoretical output of the discipline is the observation that we have returned to the ancient art of scholasticism, armed to be sure with new terminology, but not any more successful than were the ancients in narrowing the gap between abstract formulations and theoretical realities. It strikes me as enormously telling that at precisely that moment in the profession's development when methodological tools will permit the rigorous comparative testing of hypotheses the distance between hypotheses and general theory should be widening and that the linkage between hypotheses and macrotheory is either terribly obscure or of such problematical logical construction that theory itself cannot be falsified.

The literature in all social science disciplines, both in the United States and abroad, is now rich in such observations, and in yearnings after a new "paradigm." [6] The area specialist has long known that he has had trouble with organizing concepts, but understanding precisely the nature of his trouble does not come easily. For example, in the article from which the above citation comes, LaPalombara condemns—rightly, to my mind—the search for "systems theory," "holistic theory," "general theory," or "grand theory." But perhaps the "systems" idea is in itself a major impediment to understanding how to generate hypotheses which will order our understanding. That is, maybe we should seek to know something about total *situations,* but not beg the question by searching for the order, rationalization, self-contained "sense," and bias toward "system-maintenance" that is involved with the very word "system." Certainly, any student of Latin American politics would be hard pressed to describe national phenomena in the region in terms of a single coherent "system" or of a master "system" with its "subsystems." After all, the core of Latin American politics has to do with ambiguities, the interactions of at least different and often opposed views of desired social "systems," the asymmetry of rapid change, and sometimes grotesque adjustments among seemingly contradictory forms, ideas, and practices.

Behind systems theory, however, lie other North American cultural biases which, by influencing the mainstream political scientist[7] in his choice of theoretical views, have also made it difficult for him to "see" Latin American politics and, perhaps, even his own. The rejection of "institutionalism" in comparative politics is an appropriate case in point. Turning away from legalistic descriptions of formal political structures was certainly justified. Not defensible, however, was simultaneously withdrawing from a concern with institutions as historically developed clusters of routinized behavior patterns, with their appropriate sets of sanctions. To abandon the study of institutions in that sense, implying as it does historical and cultural specificity, inhibits our ability to develop causal analyses and to create true syntheses, as distinct from merely adding up analytical statements and labeling the sum "holism." The result has been that we have developed great strength in deciding upon what is "necessary" to an occurrence (the individual elements comprised in a situation), but have been woefully laggard in arriving at "sufficiency" (the configurations of the "necessary"—their *melding* into a social event or a social latency, an integrating task vastly different from a simple addition). What is more interesting, however, than the rejection of the richness of institutional, historically bound research and thought is what was adopted in its place.

The commonplace explanation for the abandonment of historically tied research is that the social sciences hared after the rising star of the physical sciences, determined to find universals, an equally defensible set of "laws" to cover the entire human experience. Consequently, one must not place primary emphasis on clusters of historical uniqueness—institutional situations, ideological sets, social classes, families of social organization—but rather on whatever can be found everywhere, such as stratification, biological "determinants," functions, and allegedly common psychological motivations. That approach is antithetical to area studies, whose prime task is to establish the cultural parameters of social activity. Thus, political science and area studies could not converge; data from foreign fields could not be absorbed by a discipline so fixed on a search for the common that it had no idea-frame for holding the different. Naturally, area studies specialists and mainstream political scientists also diverged theoretically —for it was never true that the area man was without theory, or that the disciplinary person was somehow especially gifted in theorizing. In brief, most American political scientists became modern-day utilitarians,[8] with one or another variation. Contrariwise, most political scientists concerned with the Third World, and particularly with Latin America, have been on a long search through the writings of Locke, Rousseau, Kant, Hegel, Marx, Weber, Mannheim, Durkheim, Lukacs, Gramsci, and the like to find understanding of the partially Mediterranean, partially industrial, partially patrimonial, partially modern, partially traditional, and highly changeful and varied sets of occurrences with whose understanding we have been charged. Our colleagues in the United States, when they knew what they were doing, were adapting Bentham and Marshall and Parsons, while remaining more than slightly contemptuous of anyone who thought that social class, and race, and ideology were "variables" worth worrying about. But the Latin Americanist had little choice in the matter, not least because the Latin American intelligentsia is tied to the European scene and the latter's interest in precisely what we were discarding. Thus, all of Weber was available in Spanish by the late 1940s, long before that was the case in the United States. Generations before the M.I.T. Press bestowed Lukacs on American readers, he was the subject of wide discussion in Latin America, his works available in translation through the good offices of Spanish publishing houses, which have published the writings of even esoteric Marxists and distributed them at relatively low cost.

Concern with such thinking is justified by much more than keeping up with the Sánchezes, however. What is happening in Latin America cannot be understood in light of the common ideas produced by positivistic neo-utilitarianism—such ideas as that stability is *ipso facto* "good," that "ideologies" are important only when "things" are in crisis, that a mean is "happy," and that politics or anything else can be pursued in the absence of ethical and moral values. Neither political scientists nor political men can afford such luxuries in Latin America. Equilibrium theory looks strange to persons trying to change their political orders—whether for right-wing or left-wing "developmentalism," or revolution, or whatever. Amoral politics is a double-edged sword when losing can sometimes mean dying. And ideologies are the essential stuff of party politics when consensus is lacking concerning the definition of the good society. But Latin American social scientists and North American "Latinists" also generally are either of the conviction or trending toward it that neo-utilitarianism is not only of little use for understanding Latin America, but also neither appropriate for the United States nor very good "science." Some of the reasoning is as follows:

1. Utilitarian equilibrium theory and its contemporary derivative, the various forms of functionalism, presume that change occurs because of one or another reaction to "tension" created by deviation from harmony, balance, or the "functional" working of a "system." Even with the introduction of ideas of "tension-management," the theory deals essentially in psychological reductionism. The exercise of reason is epiphenomenal, or at least of less theoretical importance than an inherent striving for evenness. The major implications are two. First, such ideas depart from antecedent liberal views linking social action to a moral basis, expressed by

Locke and Smith, for example, in a "natural" *structure* the search for whose achievement *should,* ethically, motivate behavior. Thus utilitarianism discards a social ethic in favor of an inherent and essentially individual psychological calculus. Second, the downgrading of reason opens the door to technocratic thought, to the assumption that all social problems have essentially to do with manipulating tensions into their resolution. Hence the appearance of "crisis managers" to replace political men, and the confusion among social scientists between "pure" and "applied" research, which leads to our blurring the difference between a scientist and an engineer. Rationalization becomes the principal function of the utilitarian social scientist, even when what he is putting in order is an irrational or anti-rational structure. This class of "social scientist" in Latin America is known as a *técnico,* a word connoting something more than a technician and something less than a freely inquiring scientific spirit.

2. The accent on the universality of motivation slights effectiveness of action as well as the possibility of a rational component in arriving at decisions. Consequently, social muscle as well as intelligence and its exercise are relegated to secondary positions and, indeed, given no comfortable place at all in utilitarian thought or its derivatives. Class as a measure of potential access to manifest power, and culture as the reservoir of justifications for the use of power are concepts critical to an understanding of historical continuities, of the ways in which societies get where they are and move themselves into where they are going. But theories derived from utilitarianism have little to say about these matters. They are as inhospitable to the basic questions of political science as they are to an appreciation of the ethical bases which sustain the relativistic and rationalistic enterprise that characterizes science itself as an institutional social undertaking.

The utilitarian structure of thought is "pure" in the sense that it is unsullied by data; rather, its design establishes data as being "out there," not an integral part of the theoretical structure itself. Hence, the complaint of LaPalombara and many others that "theory" and hypotheses are moving apart. Since hypotheses *must* refer directly to data, and *should* be an application of a theoretical construct, a separation of theory and hypotheses makes of "systems theory" and its cousins mere ideology—or "normative theory," the subject matter of what we usually call the history of political thought. Certainly such constructs are not empirical theory, an intellectual guide to research and the particular methods appropriate to given research problems.

Latin American politics forces us to remember what we have been professionally taught to forget. To put it another way, the exercise of standard American professionalism is incompetence in explaining Latin American politics. Let me make this point by asking you to join me in a vicarious tour of Latin America. Become innocent—naively listen to what is being said, observe what is around you, and make a layman's decision on what is important, what is amusing, and what is ephemeral and casual. Here, in no particular order, are the most commonplace "variables" of Latin American politics:

—Class, power, and color. Words in common use are aristocracy, bourgeoisie, proletariat, upper class, middle class, lower class, decent people, modest people, the *"jailaif"* (high society), accommodated people, marginal populations, professionals, industrialists, workers, white collar employees, elites, and so forth. Similarly fine gradations are used to denote ethnic origins, and neighborhoods are carefully defined as to their status.

—Foreign companies. Dependence. The CIA. Imperialism and colonialism and feudalism and patrimonialism. Sharks and their sardines, and the powerless ones.

—Torture, force, the police and military plots, *guerrilleros*, military equipment, rumors and gossip of who is in jail and who is out, corruption, bribery, theft, and favoritism.

—At appropriate electoral moments, parties and candidates, and at all times ideologies, the persuasions of left, right, and center; Marxism, Communism, Falangism, corporatism, democracy, liberalism, conservatism, and the men who in partisan and ideological pleading incarnate views and parties.

—Nationalism, laws, patriotism, taxes, regulations, bureaucracy.

—Inflation, jobs, industrialization, economic policy, social security, strikes, health care.

—Salacious personal gossip—who is doing what to whom when, how, and how often, and with how much relish.

Now, let us translate these quotidian matters into more formally expressed concepts. To wit:

—Social class, social structure, stratification.

—The nature of community (national community, the relation between nation and the international political order, local-national tensions, the role of a secular state as opposed to or in conjunction with church, economy, and others of the major institutional spheres).

—The rule of law—its extent, the "ins" and the "outs" as a real-type measured against the ideal-type expressed in the formal body of rules.

—Overt values (ideology), the predication of approved behavior, and actual behavior.

—The illegality of the governors, the illegality of the governed, and legitimacy and consensus.

—The place of individual idiosyncrasy in grand and petit politics. The place of accident, taste, personality, and intelligence in political life.

Nothing is new about these lists. They contain the subject matter of all standard political discourse from that of the ancient Greeks to this morning's newspapers. But are such subjects studied in much of the comparative politics literature? Let us discuss this question next, and then turn to a more difficult matter concerning the nature of the idea-sets required to discipline our thinking about the use of such information. It is not intellectually enough to point out that common subjects of discussion about Latin American politics are omitted, or little mentioned, in many scholarly books. We must also attempt to demonstrate that they *should* be mentioned in given ways for the purposes of more efficient diagnosis and, perhaps, prediction.

I will make no pretense to an exhaustive search of the literature. Instead, I have put my hand around four books sitting together on my shelves, all expressions of the functionalist school of comparative politics. They are the very well-known following: Almond and Verba, *The Civic Culture* (1963), Pye and Verba, eds., *Political Culture and Political Development* (1965), Fagen, *Politics and Communication* (1966), and LaPalombara, ed., *Bureaucracy and Political Development* (1963).[9] I mean nothing personal by selecting these volumes, and I am fully aware that all the listed authors have since changed their ideas, some of them profoundly, as earlier mentions in the text indicate. Still, the several indexes to those books should tell us what was not being discussed in this sampling of some of the leading books of the 1960s—which our students, perforce, continue to be assigned to read in the 1970s.

> Class, stratification, etc. Fagen: one mention, "elites, separated from masses." Almond and Verba, one mention, "elites" and perhaps one could stretch items concerning "political competence," "citizenship," and "participation"; Pye and Verba, "class structure, in Mexico" (appropriately), "elite political culture" in India, Mexico, and Turkey, and "mass political culture" in India; La Palombara, "political elites," with twelve page references. Note no references at all to outcasts and others of the least privileged.
>
> Fascism, Nazism, corporatism, authoritarianism, dictatorship. LaPalombara, no mentions; Fagen, three mentions of authoritarianism "as a communications system," "stabilizations, communication changes," and "groups" in "authoritarian systems"; Pye and Verba provide three page references to "fascists," another to "authoritarian personality" in Italy, and five references to Nazism; Almond and Verba, no mentions!
>
> Ideology as an explicitly mentioned concept. Almond and Verba, no listing; Pye and Verba, one reference under "ideologies"; Fagen, no listing; and LaPalombara, no listing.
>
> Nationalism. Almond and Verba, "national character" and "national pride" comes as close to the idea as the volume offers; Pye and Verba provide six page references on "national identity" and four on "nationalism, Japanese"; Fagen has five page references on "national integration, and political development"; and LaPalombara has no mentions.
>
> Corruption, torture, terrorism, lying, etc. (strange index items, to be sure, but commonplace political practices). LaPalombara, no mentions; Fagen, no mentions; Pye and Verba, no mentions; Almond and Verba, no mentions.
>
> Power. Almond and Verba, no listing in the index; LaPalombara, no listing; Pye and Verba, no listing; and Fagen, one page reference ("power, as communication").

A summary glance through the indexes of two books on Latin America will show us how different is the tone to be inferred from the subjects mentioned. Both books are the product of persons sharing mainstream North American social science ideas. One volume is an edited work prepared by two scholars, one deeply involved in North American political sociology, the other in Latin American political sociology. It is *Elites in Latin America* (1967), edited by S. M. Lipset and Aldo Solari, and contains articles written by scholars from both Americas.[10] The other is a so-called "country book" which attempts to study Colombia by applying some of the then reigning notions in comparative politics. Written by Robert H. Dix, *Colombia: The Political Dimensions of Change* was published in 1967. I will not break down the index mentions as above, for there are too many. Instead, I will take each book and, alphabetically, rapidly run through some of the pertinent entries.

Lipset and Solari. The relevant items begin with "Alienation. *See* Class consciousness." Then: Apathy. Authoritarianism (two page references). Bandits (five page references covering nine pages). Bourgeoisie (six page references with cross-listings). Business executives. Capitalism. Class consciousness (six references). Social classes (fourteen page references and an extended discussion). Corruption (five pages listed). Dictatorship (one reference). Elites and elitism (major entry, of course, given the title of the book). Equalitarianism (11 page references, many to multiple page discussions). Falangists (one entry). Ideology (two and a half inches of typically small index type). Integration (national and social) has seven entries. Labor (seven entries referring to 22 pages of text). Left-wing ideology (nine references, many to multiple pages). Masses, materialism, middle classes (28 entries, most to multiple page discussions). Nationalism (close to two inches). Occupations (approximately an inch). Terrorism (four entries). Value-orientation (an inch and a half). Value-system (six entries referring to five pages of text. Working classes (30 page references, including one covering pp. 256 to 296).

The Dix volume is not as richly indexed as is the Lipset-Solari work, but the index reflects the same factual concerns. It starts off immediately with *Abolengo*, the Colombian landed aristocracy (four page references). There are over two inches of entries for *campesinos* (peasants, poor farmers), references to workers' confederations and unions, corporatism (two page citations), corruption (two more), crises of integration and participation, dictatorship (as modernizing regime, one reference), education and social status, about two inches on elites, electoral fraud and intimidation, falangism (four references), fascism (two references), guerrillas (eight page references, including two referring to extended discussions), intellectuals (and their social status, political role, and Communist Party affiliation), extended discussions of the lower classes, about two inches on the "middle sectors," and about a half column on various entries having to do with the military. Modernizing elites earn a separate heading, nationalism has 18 page references, national integration another 12, and so forth.

The narrowest reasonable inference from this somewhat juvenile exercise is that Latin American politics is discussed in factual terms different from those applied in some of the best known comparative politics literature. There is more to the matter, however, for the choice of subjects for study in Latin America implies a way of looking at politics that, until very recently, has been alien to most North American political scientists. The past decade, however, has raised many Latin American questions for the United States. Assassinations, urban *guerrillismo,* racial disturbances, favoritism and corruption and official illegality, debates on the subjects of meritocracy and technocracy, the obviousness and persistence of differences among major groups that can be called class divisions, ideological confrontations, student disorders, the growing political involvement of police and military groups, the down-grading of Congress in favor of a strong and personalistic executive—what a different index Ogg and Ray would have prepared for their text on American government had they (or any other writers of such standard texts) considered the full theoretical possibilities that became reality in this "slum of a decade" just past.

Now that we must explain instability, disjunction, asymmetry, intersystemic change, the creation and uses of power, ideologies and behavior, violence, and so many other manifestations of a total situation in rapid and wrenching change, most political scientists find themselves stranded with values, theories, and methods dedicated to finding and measuring opposite phenomena. That is, our bents, ideas, and techniques are designed to search out stability, conjunction, symmetry, intrasystemic extrapolations, manipulations of existing influence, the separation of ideas and action, and the tameness of a citizenry led by an "elite." Almost our entire statistical enterprise illustrates this point. We search diligently for scalar relations, for we must have evenness, predictability along a single line. If two macrophenomena do not correlate, then they are obviously not "related." One will not "control" or "explain" the other. It may very well be, however, that lineal relations across the major manifestations of any society are rare, and that when found they indicate either a static "organic" society, or one which is in such crisis that its individuals and groups are forced to reconcile their values and their many different sets of institutional behavior patterns. It also may be that only some individuals hold political and social values in a scalar relation, and that others do not wish to do so, or cannot. That is, the very fact of value coherence may be a critical indicator of the *kind* of value posture being held. The f-scale provides a good case in point. As is very well known, one of the most cogent criticisms leveled against this measure of Fascist attitudes was that similar scales could not be constructed for non-Fascists, libertarians, democrats, or whatever one may wish to call such persons. Adorno and his associates long ago pointed out, however, that it is entirely possible that a basic distinguishing characteristic of the Fascist is his inability to tolerate ambiguity, while his opposite number demands it. That is, the non-Fascist cannot maintain full attitudinal consistency and consonant desires for behavioral conformity, because the world is not a consistent one for the person willing to see its dissonance, disharmony, disjunction or, to use less negative words, its variety, cultural richness, and the special overarching synthetic stamps of particular peoples. Methodologically, then, in macrosocial studies the Fascist can respond to a scale, the non-Fascist only to a typology. Significantly, scales are usually constructed inductively, while typologies are almost always built deductively.

But let us not lose ourselves in examples. The point I wish to make, to repeat, is that the factual material pressing in on us from Latin America and, indeed, from almost everywhere, demands theoretical, methodological, and technical change from us. Following are some generalizations out of the Latin American experience which contain implicit within them what I consider imperatives for the evaluation of current theories and their possible amendment in contemporary situations of profound and rapid change:

—A lack of "fit" among elements within social situations is the usual case, and "harmony" is rare. Legal systems only loosely describe behavior, morality, and the power relations within societies. Members of social classes do not share relatively similar ideologies or even more basic values. Industries do not produce uniformly industrial men, and cities are not inhabited only by the urbane. We need a word other than the negatively weighted "disjunction" to describe our normal inconsistency.

—Institutional differentiation does not occur evenly or uniformly as societies "develop"—or industrialize, urbanize, become literate, media-participant, empathic, or whatever other configuration of indicators one may wish to select. Specialization of function may occur within institutions, but overwhelming evidence indicates that certain interinstitutional attachments tend to become strengthened as modernization proceeds. It is notorious that economic and political interests become ever more tangled in many "modern" states. Also, as religious institutions are in many lands pushed out of politics, their attachment to family and education becomes stronger. When one institution is employed to perform some of the functions of another, and when the autonomous interest of one is sacrificed to the interest of another, then one is safe in saying that institutional differentiation is not increasing.

—Latin American political events strongly suggest that the major interinstitutional differentiation is not among individual institutions, but between those serving an affective, immediately satisfying purpose (the family and religion, most importantly) and those seen as serving instrumental purposes (education and the economy). Affective attachments tend to be held unquestioningly, hence ritualistically, unchangingly, or "traditionally." Instrumentalism tends to be viewed as adjustable, changeful, hence in "modern" fashion.

—A prime issue everywhere in Latin America, in varying ways and degrees, is not alone how each institution will relate to the others, but the overall configuration of such relations. That is, the question refers to the total social order, not only to the partialities of "free" or "collective" economies, or the separation of church and state. To reintroduce an earlier concept, a major problem has to do with the nature of social synthesis, with the ways in which a seeming lack of "fit" among major social elements is given sense within a synthetic ordering of the entire situation.

—The role of the state and the polity is everywhere being seen as increasingly a key element in the establishment of total configurations; in some countries, it is seen as *the* key. I am not being so obvious as to say merely that states have much to do with economic development, population policy, health and welfare, and the like—which they certainly do. Much more profoundly, I am suggesting that critically different politics attend the conviction that a polity should be only instrumental in nature, or the opposing view that it should be both instrumental and affective—that politics is something worth doing for itself alone, that influencing the course of one's communities of membership at all levels is an essential element in the reduction of personal and group alienation. Politics as instrumentalism is fatally authoritarian, while politics as an activity worth doing *per se* (as well as for the accomplishment of other goals) sets the foundation for meaningfully participatory systems.

—The part played by the polity in establishing and sanctioning the overarching system of interinstitutional relations defines the secular or sacred nature of any society. Purely instrumental politics are exercised to further sacred purposes and, more often than not, the private purposes of family and individual within rigid status and class systems. Affective politics create the conditions for secularism. Such activities and beliefs make possible some ultimate, mundane commitments to fellow citizens and the communities we inhabit. Secularism allows room for religious belief and the pursuit of some entirely private interests. Sacred society does not allow room for secular relativism. Again to evoke an earlier argument, the sacred view demands coherence, the secular one not merely tolerates but promotes ambiguity.

—These pretheoretical observations drawn from Latin American societies suggest that an appropriately total theoretical construction will dissolve the differences between micro- and macrotheory that now hobble our intellectual freedom. That is, they suggest that individual idiosyncrasy, institutional settings, social structure, and ethos can be reconciled within one intellectual frame.

A study of Latin America pushed me to such observations as those above. The development of comparative politics in the United States since the early 1950s also gave me something to hone myself against, provided me with a useful antagonist inside my own head that sometimes confused me but more often than not sharpened me. I advance these ideas because they have been useful to me in explaining Latin America and, obviously, Watergate and its antecedent occurrences in the United States. What more can one ask of the social sciences? I did not say "political science," or "area studies," or a combination of the two. Obviously, we are all "area specialists." (Indeed, a major problem with most American comparativists is that they are area-bound.) And most persons hearing this paper or reading it will be "political scientists." However, not enough of us are social scientists with a primary interest in politics. It is in that construction of our role that we will arrive at a reconciliation of interdisciplinary, multidisciplinary, policy-oriented, disciplinary, and area studies endeavors.

NOTES

1. See Fred W. Riggs, ed., *International Studies: Present Status and Future Prospects* (Philadelphia: American Academy of Political and Social Science, 1971); Allan A. Michie, *Higher Education and World Affairs* (New York: Education and World Affairs, 1968); Robert F. Byrnes, "The Future of Area Studies," *ACLS Newsletter*, vol. 19, no. 7 (Nov. 1968); Hugh Borton et al., *Report of the Committee on the College and World Affairs* (New Haven: The Hazen Foundation, 1964); the numerous issues of *Far Horizons*; many issues of the SSRC's *Items*, and so on and on.

2. Charles Wagley, ed., *Social Science Research on Latin America* (New York: Columbia University Press, 1964); Manuel Diégues Jr. and Bryce Wood, eds., *Social Science in Latin America* (New York: Columbia University Press, 1967); Howard F. Cline, ed., *Latin American History: Essays on Its Study and Teaching, 1898–1965* (Austin: University of Texas Press, 1967, 2 vols.); Richard M. Morse, "The Strange Career of 'Latin American Studies,'" *Annals of the American Academy of Political and Social Science*, no. 356, Nov. 1964; many issues of the *Latin American Research Review*, and particularly Peter Ranis, "Trends in Research on Latin American Politics: 1961–1967," no. 3, Summer, 1968; and so on.

3. Bryce Wood, "Area Studies," *International Encyclopedia of the Social Sciences* (New York: Macmillan and Free Press, 1968), vol. I, p. 405.

4. I am using "induction" and "deduction" vulgarly. We all know that data cannot be "gathered" in the absence of previously extant notions of order and significance. Thus the "induction" of initial area data-gatherers in truth describes searching around without explicit recognition of the guideposts actually being employed.

5. Joseph LaPalombara, "Macrotheories and Microapplications in Comparative Politics: A Widening Chasm," *Comparative Politics*, vol. I, no. 1 (1968), p. 54.

6. I am using the word "paradigm" in the sense of Thomas S. Kuhn, *The Structure of Scientific Revolutions* (Chicago: University of Chicago Press, 1962).

7. I am specifically not addressing myself to the many competing schools of thought in the discipline, but rather to the principal figures and tendencies in the field of comparative politics. The principal omissions have to do with those political scientists working within Marxist ideas, or those others who, implicitly or otherwise, assume the "inevitability" of governments of force.

8. See, of course, John Rawls, *A Theory of Justice* (Cambridge: Harvard University Press, 1971). The great impact of Rawls' book, primarily because of its discrimination between Utilitarian and Liberal thought, is again somewhat surprising to a Latin Americanist, for in that part of the world the distinction has always been clearly recognized. Still, it is a pleasure to read such a painstaking attempt to disaggregate what has become an undifferentiated mass in so many heads.

9. The Fagen volume was published by Little, Brown in Boston, the other three by the Princeton University Press.

10. The Lipset and Solari book was published by Oxford Press, the Dix volume by Yale University Press.

The Middle East

Dankwart A. Rustow

CITY UNIVERSITY OF NEW YORK

EDITOR'S NOTE

Of all the regions of the world, historically scholarship on the Middle East has been possibly the most remote from the mainstream of political science. The work of Egyptologists did not contribute to political science theories about dynastic court or imperial bureaucratic policies as much as the work of Sinologists and their findings about Imperial China. Westerners who became fascinated with the life of the desert Arabs did not make systematic contributions to political science and thus the Middle Eastern systems of tribal life and nomadic organization have not become a recognized category in the usual typologies of communities analyzed in political science.

Unquestionably, political science has been the poorer for this neglect in the past of the Middle East. The discipline, for example, would have certainly developed far more sophisticated views about the ways in which religion can relate to politics had it earlier sought to incorporate the unique bonds between Islam and Arab styles of authority and rule. Running through the social sciences has been an assumption that generally a sharp divide exists between the sacred and secular, and while the one may impinge (usually improperly) upon the other, the two can never be truly blended—especially in the domain of politics. To the extent that there have been studies of the relationship of religion to politics the almost universal presumption has been that the problems involve essentially secular governments having to respond to pressures from Christian churches, Buddhist leaders, or the interests of other religious bodies or communities. Also, of course, the relationship of religious identification to party affiliation and public opinion attitudes has been routinely studied. Generally, however, political science has been devoid of understanding of the complex ways in which religion and politics can mix as they do where Islam permeates politics in the Middle East.

As Dankwart Rustow shows in the following chapter, recent advances in research have occurred in the study of Middle East politics but much still remains to be done. His analysis is based on a close review of the literature which helps to dramatize the extent to which impressive studies have been done by outstanding scholars, but it also reveals how relatively underdeveloped this field is.

Given the pull of Israel, the importance of oil, the strategic significance of Suez and of the northern tier of Turkey and Iran, it is puzzling why more scholars have not been attracted to Middle East studies. It seems that the region lost out in the early years of enthusiasm for foreign area studies because of the more dramatic popularity of such developing countries as those in South Asia and Africa. Most Middle East states were at the time more engaged in ideological politics than in the pragmatic approaches toward development which then attracted American scholars interested in nation-building. Later Latin America and Southeast Asia occupied most of the limelight when more critical views of "development" theories emerged. By the mid-1970s the Middle East could no longer be ignored as a center of world tensions, but at the same time there has been a decline in interest among aspiring scholars for foreign area studies.

It is possible that when the revival of interest in foreign studies comes one of the areas of focus will be the Middle East. In any case, Dankwart Rustow has provided us with a guide to the research which awaits doing.

The study of Middle Eastern politics as a subfield of American political science is little more than twenty years old. Two decades ago, there were no universities that offered regular courses on the politics of the Middle East. There was at most one book, Lenczowski's *The Middle East in World Affairs*,[1] that might have been suitable to serve as the text in such a course. There were no more than a handful of specialized monographs relating to Middle Eastern politics and international relations, and some of these were byproducts of an interest in naval strategy stemming from the Second World War. Among members of the American Political Science Association around 1950, there can have been no more than half a dozen with a working command of either Arabic, or Persian, or Turkish.

Wherever there was already a demand for expert knowledge of the politics of the contemporary Middle East—for example in the Office of Strategic Services and the Office of War Information during the Second World War and in the State Department or at the Library of Congress immediately after the war—the deficiency was not uncommonly supplied by persons trained in law, history, philology, biblical studies, anthropology, or even archaeology. Graduate and undergraduate courses in Middle Eastern politics were being developed at a number of universities in the mid-1950s; but a look at some of the early reading lists indicates that they were composed mostly of books and articles relating to ethnography, comparative religion, current history, jurisprudence, diplomatic history—almost anything, in fact, except politics.

All in all, it is fair to say that the study of the contemporary Middle East and its politics by North Americans had made little substantial progress since the spring of 1919, when Woodrow Wilson dispatched a commission of inquiry to the Middle East to ascertain the political aspirations of its peoples and, on that basis, to advise on United States policy with regard to the distribution of Mandates over former Ottoman territories among the victorious Allied Powers. Wilson's commission, it will be recalled, was composed of Dr. Henry C. King, president of Oberlin College, with a fine reputation as a biblical scholar; and Charles R. Crane, Chicago plumbing manufacturer, generous financial contributor to presidential campaigns, and an enthusiastic world traveler. And the commission was assisted by an Ottoman historian, a teacher at an American missionary college, and an army intelligence officer who had once served for the Standard Oil Company.[2]

By the 1970s the picture had dramatically changed. The field of Middle Eastern politics today claims well over 100 established practitioners who form a recognizable subgroup in the political science profession. Similarly, within the field of Middle Eastern area studies, political scientists not only are a recognizable subgroup; their influence far overshadows that of archaeologists, Old Testament scholars, and even specialists in language and literature, and indeed is rivaled only by that of the historians. Perhaps the situation in the Middle East Studies Association of North America (founded in 1967) can be taken as representative. It has about 600 fellows (this implies, beyond dues-paying membership, election by the Board on the basis of recognized scholarly attainment). Of these over one-third teach in area studies programs of one kind or another. Among those affiliated with disciplinary departments, historians, language and literature people, and political scientists are about equally numerous (about one-sixth of the total roster of fellows each). Nearly all the Association's offices are honorific, and (since honor is as always in scarce supply) they rotate periodically. But two offices are of real significance and have, in effect, been permanent since the Association's founding; of these the editorship of the *International Journal of Middle Eastern Studies* has been held by an historian and the office of Executive Secretary by a political scientist.

But this quantitative and organizational growth in the subdiscipline of Middle Eastern politics in the last two decades has had a solid qualitative foundation. It has been possible since the mid-1950s for political scientists to get language training in Arabic, Persian, and Turkish at any one of the leading centers of Middle Eastern area studies, such as U.C.L.A., Chicago, Princeton, Columbia, or Harvard; and through intensive summer sessions staffed by teachers from several universities, these language training facilities have also been available to graduate students or younger faculty from other institutions. There also has been a recognition of the needs of the social scientist for a type of language training distinct from that traditionally given to the historian or the philologist. Students of Turkish therefore no longer are forced to master the Arabic script (which for written Turkish was abolished in 1928) or the richly Arabic and Persian vocabulary of Ottoman Turkish (which fell into disuse just a little later). Students of Arabic can concentrate on contemporary newspaper

Arabic in preference to the classical Arabic of the Qur'an—the two being about as distinct as the English of the *Canterbury Tales* or the *Faerie Queene* is from that of *The New York Times.*

To such possibilities of language training correspond a vastly expanded set of library holdings that make possible original research from published sources such as newspapers, government documents, and political pamphlets without taking a trip to the area. And in the 1950s and 1960s opportunities for research travel also were relatively ample. The revamping of language training and the expansion of library holdings were the work primarily of forward-looking linguists and devoted librarians. Yet political scientists, with their customary grip on the secretariat and representing, as it were, a fast-expanding consumer group, have also been able to play a helpful role at crucial points.

None of these language-training, library, and travel grant facilities could have been developed without the generosity of the Ford Foundation in the 1950s, the massive infusion of funds under PL 480 and the National Defense Education Act, or the coordinating mission of the S.S.R.C. Committee on the Near and Middle East (later sponsored jointly with the A.C.L.S.). Yet despite the severe curtailment of these original sources of funds, it would seem that the major centers of Middle Eastern area studies—notably U.C.L.A., Princeton, Chicago, and Harvard—are well enough established to survive on the basis of the usual other sources of financing.

It is worth noting at this point that a very sizable contingent of specialists in Middle Eastern politics consists of native Middle Easterners—Nadav Safran, Hisham Sharabi, Ibrahim Abu-Lughod, Kemal Karpat, to mention a few at random—or others who spent some of their formative years in the region, such as Malcolm Kerr or myself. Yet I have been emphasizing the broader and more purposeful organization of language training. For the viability of Middle Eastern politics as an academic specialty in the United States it is more significant that Frederick Frey has become fluent in Turkish and Leonard Binder in Arabic than that Kemal Karpat retains the command of his mother tongue, or that Kerr or Rustow continue to use one of the languages of their adolescence.

The vast improvement of language, library, and research facilities coincided with a revolution in method throughout our discipline. As a result, political scientists 45 years of age or younger working in the Middle Eastern field generally know their theory of stratified or random sampling and their two-tailed tests of significance as well as they do their quadrilateral nouns or their doubly-weak verbs.

The most impressive test of development of the field, of course, is the enormous expansion of available literature. There are at least half a dozen textbooks on Middle Eastern politics (Harari, Rustow, Lenczowski, among others)[3] or related books of readings. There are competent studies of the recent domestic politics of many individual countries, notably Israel (B. Halpern, Fein, Safran),[4] Iran (Binder, Cottam, Bill),[5] Turkey (Karpat, Weiker),[6] Lebanon (Binder et al.; Hudson, Suleiman),[7] Jordan (Vatikiotis),[8] Syria (Torrey, Seale),[9] Iraq (Khadduri),[10] Egypt (Dekmejian, Vatikiotis),[11] Tunisia (Cl. H. Moore),[12] Algeria (Quandt),[13] and Morocco (Ashford, Waterbury).[14] Nor are most of these just narrative descriptions: the theme of social composition of the political elite runs through the studies by Bill on Iran, Dekmejian on Egypt, Quandt on Algeria, and Waterbury on Morocco; it also forms the subject of detailed monographs by Frey on Turkey[15] and Seligman on Israel.[16] Indeed, the recruitment of political elites would seem to be the topic on which we have at this point by far the richest store of information. Other topics that have received attention in a number of studies include ideology and political thought (Safran, Binder, Khadduri);[17] and the political role of the military (Fisher et al., Hurewitz, Be'eri).[18] The pioneering work by Lerner et al. remains the major study based on an attitude survey—in this case a comparative study of radio audiences in several Middle Eastern countries.[19] A truly pathbreaking survey by Frederick Frey of the political and social attitudes of the peasantry of Turkey—unique for the richness of its data and sophistication of its treatment—still remains available only in multilith.[20]

In the subfield of international relations the literature, understandably, shades off quickly into the journalistic. But there are notably competent studies of inter-Arab relations (e.g. Kerr, McDonald, Khadduri),[21] an impressive array of works of meticulous scholarship on the Palestine question of the Mandate period and the subsequent Arab-Israeli conflict (Hurewitz, Khouri, Safran), and the excellent general study by Campbell.[22]

Finally, there have been a number of attempts at overall interpretation of Middle Eastern politics—ranging from a cursory sketch of mine on *Politics and Westernization*[23] to the full-size account by Manfred Halpern of political change as crucially affected by newly emerging social strata,[24] and J. C. Hurewitz's well-documented and comparative *Middle Eastern Politics: The Military Dimension.*[25]

But any recital of accomplishments in the field of Middle Eastern politics would be grossly misleading unless accompanied by a listing of the enormous gaps that still remain. There are some topics for which we can rely, to a greater or lesser extent, on the work of scholars in neighboring disciplines. For example, the best biography of a Middle Eastern political leader is probably that on *Sayyid Jamal al-Din "al-Afghani"* by Nikki R. Keddie, and the fullest account of a particular Middle Eastern political party is that of Turkish Communism by George S. Harris.[26] The origins of Arab nationalism in the early twentieth century have been illuminated by the scholarship of Haim, Kedourie, and Dawn[27]; and for the transformation of Turkey since the Ottoman period we have the imposing work of Bernard Lewis.[28] All these authors are professional historians (even Kedourie, who holds a chair in political philosophy at the London School of Economics, is probably more justly classified, for most of his work, as a historian), and if political scientists are as serious about their scientific method as they often claim, they would do well to learn something from these historians about meticulous documentary and archival research, about use of primary and secondary materials in all relevant languages (these, for Keddie's work on Afghani, included Persian, Arabic, Turkish, and Urdu as well as English, French, Russian, and German), about a sense of responsibility in formulating broad conclusions, and about clarity of style in expressing them. And on that basis, aspiring political scientists might proceed to political biographies of figures such as Atatürk, Inönü, Zaghlul, Nahhas, Musaddiq, Nuri Said, Bourguiba, and many others; to accounts of Arab nationalism in its post-1945 and post-1967 phases; and to studies of political parties such as the Ba'th, the Wafd, the Republican People's Party, and the Neo-Destour.

Economists, much like historians, have a good deal to teach us, but in this case we must go beyond the themes that we can adopt and the methods that we can learn from them. For example, in view of the dominant role that agriculture still plays in much of the Middle East, it is remarkable that patterns of land tenure have received as good as no attention from political scientists. The work of economists such as Doreen Warriner[29] and Eva Hirsch[30] is a good starting point—and Hirsch's work, in particular, shows what a rich field of application for quantitative method there is. But agricultural economists tend to be concerned with such factors as return on investment, potential for irrigation or mechanization, or changing commodity prices. What is badly needed is a study that would attempt in some detail for one or more Middle Eastern countries what Barrington Moore has done in his broad comparative synthesis for major countries outside the region: the economic politics of lord and peasant relations.[31] The relevance of such studies to elite analysis should be readily apparent. We know much about the career patterns of members of the elite who wind up in politics. We know little or nothing about the basis of ownership and exploitation that makes them members of the elite to start with.

Other crucial topics of economic policy that have been almost totally neglected by political scientists include the structure and incidence of taxation; the centrally planned use of foreign funds (U.J.A., German reparations, etc.) by public or semipublic authorities in Israel; the use of labor unions as instruments of oppositional expression or governmental repression; and, above all, the current revolution in the Middle Eastern petroleum industry. Here we need studies that go beyond the digests of concessions and administrative regulations provided long ago by Shwadran, Lenczowski, and Longrigg[32]; that have firmer political anchoring than the abstract economic analyses of Adelman or Penrose[33]; and that bring up to date the political and economic analysis provided long ago by perceptive economists such as Issawi and Yeganek, or more recently by Schurr and Homan.[34]

Implicit in my remarks about what we can learn from historians or contribute to border disciplines such as political economy is a plea for new breadth in a particular direction. The young political scientist of the future who wishes to make a solid and lasting contribution in the Middle Eastern field should acquire competence not only in the applicable language and the relevant concepts in comparative politics or international relations, but also in one other technical field—whether psychobiography or petroleum economics, whether agrarian sociology or public finance. Yet he or she ought to acquire that expertise after choosing a major topic, rather than before, for only then can the new methodological skills become what all method ought to be: a means to the acquisition of accurate and meaningful knowledge, and not an end in itself. And only when systematic interest and research skill are happily blended can the study of Middle Eastern politics contribute to the advancement of comparative politics—a task so far attempted only sporadically, as in the study edited by Ward and myself on Japan and Turkey[35] or that by Ashford on political participation.[36]

NOTES

1. Lenczowski, George, *The Middle East in World Affairs* (Ithaca, 1952, 1956).

2. Howard, Harry N., *The King-Crane Commission* (Beirut, 1963).

3. See: Harari, Maurice, *Government and Politics of the Middle East* (Englewood Cliffs, N.J., 1962); Rustow, Dankwart A., *Middle Eastern Political Systems* (Englewood Cliffs, N.J., 1971), and Lenczowski, George, *Oil and State in the Middle East* (Ithaca, 1960), *The Middle East in World Affairs* (Ithaca, 1952, 1956), and *Russia and the West in Iran* (Ithaca, 1949).

4. See: Halpern, Ben, *The Idea of a Jewish State* (Cambridge, Mass., 1961); Fein, Leonard J., *Politics in Israel* (Boston, 1967); and Safran, Nadav, *The United States and Israel* (Cambridge, Mass., 1963), *From War to War: The Arab-Israeli Confrontation* (New York, 1969).

5. See: Binder, Leonard, *Iran: Political Development in a Changing Society* (Berkeley, 1962); Cottam, Richard W., *Nationalism in Iran* (Pittsburgh, 1964); and Bill, James A., *The Politics of Iran* (Columbus, Ohio, 1972).

6. See: Karpat, Kemal H., *Turkey's Politics: The Transition to a Multiparty System* (Princeton, 1959), and Weiker, Walter F., *The Turkish Revolution 1960–1961* (Washington, 1962).

7. See: Binder, Leonard, et al., *Politics in Lebanon* (New York, 1966); Hudson, Michael, *The Precarious Republic: Political Modernization in Lebanon* (New York, 1968); and Suleiman, Michael W., *Political Parties in Lebanon* (Ithaca, 1967).

8. Vatikiotis, P. J., *The Egyptian Army in Politics* (Bloomington, Indiana, 1961).

9. See: Torrey, Gordon, *Syrian Politics and the Military* (Columbus, Ohio, 1964); and Seale, Patrick, *The Struggle for Syria; A Study of Postwar Arab Politics 1945–1958* (London, 1965).

10. Khadduri, Majid, *Independent Iraq* (London, 1951, 1960).

11. See: Dekmejian, Richard H., *Egypt under Nasir* (Albany, 1971); and Vatikiotis, P. J., *The Egyptian Army in Politics* (Bloomington, Indiana, 1961).

12. Moore, Clement Henry, *Tunisia since Independence* (Berkeley, 1965).

13. Quandt, William, *Revolution and Political Leadership: Algeria, 1954–1968* (Cambridge, Mass., 1969).

14. See: Ashford, Douglas E., *Political Change in Morocco* (Princeton, 1961), and *National Development and Local Reform: Political Participation in Morocco, Tunisia, and Pakistan* (Princeton, 1967); and Waterbury, John, *The Commander of the Faithful: The Moroccan Political Elite* (New York, 1970).

15. Frey, Frederick W., *The Turkish Political Elite* (Cambridge, Mass., 1965).

16. Seligman, Lester, *Leadership in a New Nation* (New York, 1964).

17. See, Safran, Nadav, *Egypt in Search of Political Community* (Cambridge, Mass., 1961); Binder, Leonard, *The Ideological Revolution in the Middle East* (New York, 1964); and Khadduri, Majid, *Political Trends in the Arab World: The Role of Ideas and Ideals in Politics* (Baltimore, 1970).

18. See: Fisher, Sydney N., ed., *The Military in Middle Eastern Society and Politics* (Columbus, Ohio, 1963); Hurewitz, J. C., *Middle East Politics: The Military Dimension* (New York, 1969); and Be'eri, Eliezer, *Army Officers in Arab Politics and Society* (New York, 1970).

19. Lerner, Daniel, et al., *The Passing of Traditional Society* (New York, 1958).

20. Frey, Frederick W., et al., *Rural Development Research Project*, 10-part multilith, M.I.T. Center for International Studies, 1967.

21. See: Kerr, Malcolm H., *The Arab Cold War* (London, 1965, 1967, 1971); McDonald, Robert W., *The League of Arab States* (Princeton, 1965); and Khadduri, Majid, cited.

22. See: Hurewitz, J. C., *The Struggle for Palestine* (New York, 1950); Khouri, Fred J., *The Arab Israeli Dilemma* (Syracuse, 1968); Safran, Nadav, cited; and Campbell, J. C., *Defense of the Middle East* (New York, 1958).

23. Rustow, Dankwart A., *Politics and Westernization in the Near East* (Princeton, 1956).

24. Halpern, Manfred, *The Politics of Social Change in the Middle East and North Africa* (Princeton, 1963).

25. Hurewitz, J. C., cited.

26. Harris, George S., *The Origins of Communism in Turkey* (Stanford, 1967).

27. See: Haim, Sylvia, ed., *Arab Nationalism* (Berkeley, 1962); Kedourie, Elie, *England and the Middle East: The Destruction of the Ottoman Empire* (London, 1956); and Dawn, C. Ernest, *From Ottomanism to Arabism* (Urbana, Ill., 1973).

28. Lewis, Bernard, *The Emergence of Modern Turkey* (London, 1961, 1965).

29. Warriner, Doreen, *Land Reform and Development in the Middle East* (London, 1957).

30. Hirsch, Eva, *Poverty and Plenty on the Turkish Farm* (New York, 1970).

31. Moore, Barrington, *Social Origins of Dictatorship and Democracy: Lord and Peasant in the Modern World* (Boston, 1966).

32. See: Shwadran, Benjamin, *The Middle East, Oil, and the Great Powers* (New York, 1955); Lenczowski, George, cited; and Longrigg, Stephen Helmsley, *Iraq 1900–1950* (London, 1953) and *Oil in the Middle East* (London, 1954).

33. See: Adelman, M. A., *The World Petroleum Market* (Baltimore, 1972); and Penrose, Edith, *The Large International Firm in Developing Countries: The International Petroleum Industry* (Cambridge, Mass., 1969).

34. Schurr, Sam, and Paul Homan, *Middle Eastern Oil and the World* (New York, 1971).

35. Ward, Robert E., and Dankwart A. Rustow, eds., *Political Modernization in Japan and Turkey* (Princeton, 1964).

36. Ashford, Douglas, E., cited.

African Studies, Afro-American Studies, and Political Analysis

Martin Kilson

HARVARD UNIVERSITY

EDITOR'S NOTE

The two newest, and complexly related, fields in American universities are African and Afro-American studies. During the era of European colonialism a few adventuresome, and indeed distinguished, American scholars explored in relative isolation African developments. But then with the drama of African nationalism and the excitement of the birth of new nations across that continent, the idiosyncratic pursuits of the few were overwhelmed by a flood of interest which soon compelled foundations and universities to inaugurate full-blown curricula of African studies.

It is hard to find an explosion of interest in the history of American higher education comparable to the burgeoning of African studies in the 1960s. Even the onset of the Cold War and the emergence of the Soviet Union as a world force did not produce such numbers of academically curious. The wave of interest swept quickly from fashion-prone undergraduates to serious graduate programs, and in a few years America was turning out more certified specialists on this newest of academically recognized continents than experts on the more established regions of the Middle East, South Asia, China, and Japan.

The fact that African programs generally required no new foreign language might explain why so many decided to take up African studies, especially given the proverbial American repugnance for learning foreign tongues, but any theory of popularity based on preferences for soft options collapses in the face of the numbers of young social scientists who committed themselves to the rigors of African field work. Beyond geographical novelty, African research offered genuine intellectual challenges. Nation-building in Africa brought to the surface vivid issues basic to all political theory.

African specialists were quickly confronted with questions about whether Africa might have novel responses to age-old dilemmas in political thought. Can the balance between the imperatives of authority and the aspirations for democratic variety be reconciled in a one-party system? How far should the principle of self-determination be carried in societies composed of many tribes? What is the relationship between demagogues and democracy; between army technocrats and civilian proponents of democratic rhetoric? The realities of African politics in the postcolonial era have brought to life in stark form these and other basic questions which lie at the core of all peoples' experiences in trying to build civic communities.

Unfortunately, in American universities the excitement of understanding Africa was engulfed in the larger tides of passion and confrontation which swept the campus scene in the late sixties. In the atmosphere of tension at that time, the African Studies Association was dramatically divided, as black and white, radical and liberal academics confronted each other over the issue of how the American scholar should relate personally and politically to African developments. Some argued that the ultimate value for African specialists should be support of African causes, defense of African practices, and refusal to hide behind pretensions of objectivity. On the other side were those who felt that the relationship between students of Africa and the countries of their study should be no different from that of scholars to any other political class.

To some degree tensions about African studies were fueled by the emergence of the new phenomenon of Afro-American studies on American campuses. As the civil rights movement raised the political consciousness of black students in American universities, and as that very movement increased the number of blacks on American campuses, there emerged, not surprisingly, a new area study which took as its domain the entire experience of black Americans from their origins in slavery through the trials of plantation suffering, Jim Crowism, and the struggles for equal citizenship. What obviously sets off Afro-American studies from other "area" studies is that its students are generally identified with the phenomenon being studied.

This distinctive character of Afro-American studies has made it a matter of some controversy in intellectual circles. Whereas Martin Kilson has in the past participated in this debate, in the chapter which follows he has sought to place the question of Afro-American and African studies in a larger perspective. More specifically, he has identified two fundamental issues in political philosophy which have been of major importance in both African and Afro-American political life, and through his analysis of these problems in the two "area" settings he has concretely demonstrated how study in these two fields can contribute to the enrichment of theories of comparative politics.

I. Introduction

African Studies and Afro-American Studies do not as such pose a problem for political science. Well before either of these fields of study acquired an organized curriculum within the university, some of the finest minds in political science applied political analysis to them. Harold Foote Gosnell, a leading and innovative political scientist at the University of Chicago in the 1920s–1940s, undertook the first systematic analysis of the position of Negroes in city political machines in the 1930s.[1] Ralph J. Bunche, a former president of the American Political Science Association and the first black to hold the post, was perhaps the major student of the political status of Negroes in the pre-World War II era, commencing these studies in the late 1920s while a graduate student at Harvard University.[2] Bunche, who spent most of his career as an international bureaucrat, was also one of the first political scientists to apply systematic political analysis to the colonial power systems in Africa, producing a doctoral dissertation in this field in the 1930s.[3] Following in the steps of these two pioneers, numerous other American political scientists—seminal students in the field—studied modern political patterns among Africans and Afro-Americans in the post-depression era.[4]

I am indebted to the Ford Foundation, and especially its President, McGeorge Bundy, for financial assistance to my research into ethnicity in American political

For a variety of reasons—notably those related to the foreign policy needs of the U.S. government—African Studies acquired an organized status in American universities before Afro-American Studies. It developed along with other so-called area studies in the immediate post-World War II era and spread rather quickly throughout the 1950s. Afro-American Studies is less than a decade old as an organized area of teaching and scholarship, although a small but first-rate group of black and white social scientists—including political scientists—pursued research and teaching in this field in the years between two world wars and into the postwar era.[5] The stimulus for the inclusion of Afro-American Studies in the academic regime of many universities was the militancy of the new crop of Negro students on white campuses in the middle 1960s. Thus far the main result of this mode of inclusion of Afro-American Studies into the university curriculum has been an excessive politization of this field of study. This politization has been so massive that it spread, willy-nilly, to African Studies. This produced in turn the hybrid field of studies known as Black Studies.[6]

What about African and Afro-American Studies as fruitful areas for comparative political analysis? There is no doubt about their value in this respect. Two facets of modern politics can be used to demonstrate this—namely, institutionalization and cleavages. For many reasons these facets of modern politics have a special salience in the new African polities and the Afro-American subsystem. The primary reason for this is, of course, that African polities and the Afro-American subsystem are developing or modernizing systems. They are, that is, in the process of realizing a greater capacity both to create and to allocate power, as Lucian Pye would say—a process we have come to call modernization.[7]

II. Institutionalization

Institutionalization is, essentially, a question of political order. By *political order* I mean something more than the maintenance of peace: political order is, in its modernization dimension, a matter of creating political relations that are stable and capable of

culture and the political patterns of Negro Americans. The Harvard Center for International Affairs—and especially its former Director, Robert Bowie—has supported my African research in a modest but consistent way for thirteen years.

mediating conflicting interests in a manner that does not impede the modernizing (power-creating) functions of other social relations, especially economic relations.[8] So defined, institutionalization is not a preserve of competitive or democratic polities; authoritarian or totalitarian systems can and have realized it.[9] The study of institutionalization in African polities and the Afro-American subsystem might enable us to uncover dimensions of this process not necessarily found in other modernizing (or already modern) political situations.

Although all emergent political systems find institutionalization hampered by the central problem of delimiting the secular and sacred constituents of political relations, African polities display a special problem in this regard.[10] The definition of both mutual and divergent interests of competing groups and sectors (e.g., center vs. periphery) in African polities is plagued by this issue. Indeed, the crux of political institutionalization in emergent African systems is a "boundary problem." [11]

1. The African Pattern

This may be illustrated briefly by reference to a variant of this problem in Ghanaian politics during its formative emergent period of the 1950s.[12] The major opposition to the dominant Convention People's Party in the 1950s was the Ashanti nationalist subplot, known popularly as the National Liberation Movement (NLM). Although the NLM was in many respects a secular affair, stemming from the key position of the Ashanti tribe and region in Ghana's cocoa industry and endeavoring to give Ashanti greater leverage over the politics of cocoa, the NLM was also a sacred movement. Its operative *raison d'être* was linked in a profoundly normative and symbolic way to the historic role and status of traditional Ashanti. Its *élan*—a crucial variable in the differentiation of the secular and sacred constituents of modernizing political relations[13]—was, moreover, derived more from this link with the glorified Ashanti past than from the secular fact (that is, the *interest-related fact*) of Ashanti's dominant contribution to modern Ghana's economic life.[14] Thus insofar as the typical Ashanti, although a participant in modern social relations to some degree, is still enmeshed in traditional values that shape self- and group-identity, modern Ashanti politicians seeking support could hardly ignore this.

The sacred-secular dimension of political relations in modern Ashanti posed a major dilemma for the central government, controlled by the CPP. A response to the purely secular or interest-related factor in the Ashanti nationalist subplot would be satisfactory only if it dovetailed in some measure with the sacred attributes of the NLM. But such a response carried two politically significant implications: First, it would have entailed major concessions from the central government, bordering on a veritable constitutional reorganization of the largely unitary polity Ghana inherited from colonialism; for the sacred attributes in the Ashanti nationalist subplot were projected in terms of the historic sovereignty of the Ashanti *as a polity,* especially this polity's traditional hegemonic relations with other Ghanaian tribes—those to the south who dominated the governing CPP (e.g., Ga, Fanti, and Ewe).[15] Second, it would have involved some modification too of the mode of national-power legitimation employed by Kwame Nkrumah's CPP government—a mode which was charismatic and thus in part sacred.[16] To some extent this mode of national-power legitimation was due to the personality characteristics of Nkrumah and to the recognition by the CPP government of the appeal of charismatic-type authority to most Ghanaians. But it was also utilized as a substitute for reliance upon a secular political appeal, which necessarily entails material incentives and rewards which in Ghana had a problematic dimension: they were not plentiful and were generated to a significant degree in the 1950s by Ashanti cocoa production. Indeed, nearly 70 per cent of Ghana's foreign earnings were derived from this source.

Thus the political dilemma posed by the character of the "boundary problem"—the pattern of secular-sacred delimitation of political relations—in Ghana in the 1950s was pregnant with serious conflict. *All things equal, a poor differentiation of the secular and sacred constituents of political relations is productive of highly contentious and violence-ridden politics.* The Ghanaian situation in the 1950s exemplified this: violence was rife in the political interactions of the activists on both sides.[17] This in turn limits the options—actual and perceived—available for a solution. As it happened, the central government chose an essentially coercive solution. The investigatory, police, and political-regulatory powers of the CPP government were employed to squash the NLM. The

NLM in turn perceived this solution not merely as a rebuff to the Ashanti secular demands relating to the political-economic power of cocoa, *but more significantly as an attack on sacred Ashanti—on its pride, virtue, and past glory.*

The succeeding decade of Ghanaian politics was plagued by this solution to the Ashanti nationalist subplot. It set in train numerous dysfunctions to institutionalization, both within the Ashanti and in other regions, both at the center and periphery, and between the center and the periphery.

In Ashanti—the prominent producer of Ghana's foreign exchange—the central government was often unwilling to allocate to local councils that supported the NLM the financial and technical resources they required, *not merely because they were dissident (a secular reason) but because the Ashanti might interpret concessions from the center in sacred terms.* When the central government did make concessions they were often dysfunctional: for example, demands from non-Ashanti groups within the Ashanti region that backed the CPP or gave only superficial support to the NLM were often granted without regard to their impact upon institutionalization at the periphery. Thus in 1958 and later in 1963 onward demands from such groups to divide local councils into smaller administrative units, deemed more suitable to parochial perceptions of political influence, were frequently granted.[18]

As a consequence, by the middle 1960s the viability of local councils as agents of local institutionalization was problematic. This was particularly so in Ashanti, but elsewhere as well. The central government's solution to the political dilemma posed by the pattern of secular-sacred delimitation of its relationship with Ashanti spawned a distinctive habit of mind or governmental outlook in regard to center-periphery relationships. The manner of handling the Ashanti situation was applied, willy-nilly, to cognate situations. In short, a serious crisis of institutionalization had ensued.

2. The Afro-American Pattern

Political order in the Afro-American subsystem is not different in kind as a problem from the situation in African polities, although the milieu is different and thus the modalities of the problem differ.

The Afro-American subsystem differs markedly from other ethnic subsystems in the United States like the Irish, Jewish, Italian, etc. Most significantly, what might be called the *ultra-stigmatization* of Negroes in American life—racism if you will—more distinctly demarcates the black subsystem from that of other ethnic groups. Until the middle 1960s this is commonplace for the political status of blacks in the South, but not much less so outside the South.

Why did the *ultra-stigmatization* of blacks in American life truncate the political institutionalization of the Afro-American subsystem? *Ultra-stigmatization* is essentially a sacred behavioral category; it is mystical, mythical, and like all forms of primordial group behavior (e.g., tribalism in Africa) it defies rationalization, or rather is difficult to rationalize.[19] Politically, it cuts several ways: First, efforts by blacks to translate the social and economic indices of modernization into *power equivalents* are not perceived by whites—and thus by the dominant political interests—as secular acts. Instead, *ultra-stigmatization* endows the endeavors to institutionalize the Afro-American subsystem with special qualities, unnatural and demonic. Until the middle 1960s the authoritarian power of the white population in the South simply precluded any reasonable institutionalization of the black subsystem. Outside the South the experience is checkered since the 1930s.

There is another facet that requires mention in this brief characterization of the essential features of the Afro-American pattern of institutionalization. *The ultra-stigmatization of Negroes in American life creates internal as well as external impedimenta to effective institutionalization of the Afro-American subsystem.* That is to say, blacks internalize some of the values and myths associated with their *ultra-stigmatization.*[20]

This situation, only recently attenuating, plays havoc with the limited capacity available for the institutionalization of the Afro-American subsystem. More specifically, dysfunctional cleavages and modes of cleavage perception emerge; they become key—although not the only—agents of the weak institutionalization of the Afro-American subsystem. This unique crisis of institutionalization is in turn complicated by other cleavage patterns that are in some respects basically Negro—emanating, that is, from the *culture indigène* of Afro-Americans. Thus greater understanding of the problems of Afro-American political institutionalization requires a closer analysis of cleavage patterns.

III. Cleavages[21]

The Afro-American subsystem, unlike other American ethnic subsystems, lacks a well-articulated group cohesion. This prevails even among those sectors of blacks who have acquired a significant measure of the social and economic indices of modernization, as well of course as between the advanced sectors and the poorly advanced—the Negro masses. This has several crucial political implications: first, cleavages are convulsive; second, power- or influence-allocation patterns are distorted.

By convulsive cleavages I mean a dynamic of centrifugal conflict. Rather than producing compromise, bargains, trade-offs and thus a network and hierarchy of competing yet overlapping interest clusters, *convulsive cleavages emphasize the characterological specificity of competing interests.*[22] This in turn leaves a distinctive imprint upon the perception of competing interests: the sacred attributes (symbols, paraphernalia, heritage, etc.) are accorded greater salience than their secular features. This perception, moreover, cuts two ways: both the self-perception and other-perception of competing interests move along the sacred axis.

One consequence of this is that political pathology disproportionately characterizes cleavages in the Afro-American subsystem. In particular, violence or threats thereof and dysfunctional corruption are not infrequent, for the restraining force of overlapping secular interests is absent or highly diffuse.[23] Thus in the early twentieth century competing pressure groups within the Afro-American subsystem openly warred at street rallies and meeting halls (e.g., followers of Booker T. Washington vs. backers of Monroe Trotter and W. E. B. DuBois). Archie Epps' work on the nineteenth and early twentieth century development of the elite sector of the Negro church—the African Methodist Episcopal Church—has turned up numerous conventions of bishops which were riotous, with chair slinging and some gun display.[24] A similar pattern of convulsive cleavage appeared in the Chicago branch of the AME Church in the 1930s when the highly secular emergent Negro political machine, controlled by Edward "Bulldog" Wright

—perhaps the first consummate Negro machine politician—attempted to politicize the AME hierarchy.[25] The institutional development of the popular sector of the Negro church—the Baptist organizations—has also experienced convulsive cleavage throughout this century, marked by violence. Numerous other instances, some of recent vintage, could be cited.

Convulsive cleavage is particularly important to the power-allocation patterns of the Afro-American subsystem. *Power resources (money, voters, supporters, strategic position, access, etc.) tend to be deployed in terms of the sacred axis, both within the interest clusters and between them.* Thus leaders of Afro-American social movements throughout this century, and still today, allocate significant political resources to elaborating the personalistic (charismatic) dimensions of leadership. Prototypical in this respect was Marcus Garvey, founder-leader of the Universal Negro Improvement Association—popularly known as the Garvey Movement—in the 1920s.[26] A case study of the Garvey Movement from this vantage point would throw enormous light upon these processes. The competition between the Garvey Movement and the NAACP, in which W. E. B. DuBois played a leading role in this era, also evidenced the distortion of political resources through sacred-oriented allocations.[27] Current instances are numerous—although significantly this pattern is beginning to attenuate, owing to the greater institutionalization of the political status of Afro-Americans through more extensive inclusion into the dominant American power patterns.[28] As a greater capacity to translate the socioeconomic indices of modernization into power equivalents—the crux of Afro-American political development—accrues to blacks, convulsive cleavage and its dysfunctions can be rationalized.[29]

The convulsive cleavages and dysfunctional power-allocation patterns within the Afro-American subsystem are not different in kind from similar situations in African polities. Ethnicity or tribalism in African politics is the functional equivalent of ultra-stigmatization of blacks in the United States. And although it is unlike the latter in that it is not imposed from without but rather is fundamental to African societies, the sacred qualities attached to tribalism produce comparable problems. Convulsive cleavages have, in fact, combined with dysfunctional power-allocation patterns to become the bedrock of mal-institutionalization in African politics.[30]

There is, of course, a point where a comparison of African polities and the Afro-American subsystem breaks down, for the latter is a *subsystem*—a dialectical variant of a dominant system. In the past decade, therefore, the changes in the racial aspects of cleavage patterns in the Afro-American subsystem have been unique in their highly paradoxical quality. A militant black group consciousness—what I call elsewhere black ethnocentric revitalization[31]—has been the main instrument used by blacks to redefine their weak institutionalization in the American system. On the one hand, the thrust for greater institutionalization requires a strident black-white polarization, for the mobilization of Negroes into greater power-mustering capacity is virtually inconceivable otherwise. On the other hand, as black ethnocentric mobilization realizes the benefits or payoffs from a greater power-mustering capacity, continued attachment to such mobilization becomes ambivalent. Thus during the very period of the maturation of black ethnocentric mobilization the proportion of Negroes preferring housing in racially mixed neighborhoods increased from 64 per cent in 1963 to 74 per cent in 1969.[32] A similar pattern prevails for another basic area in black-white interactions—the job milieu. Negro preference for a racially mixed job milieu increased from 76 per cent to 82 per cent between 1963 and 1969, and the middle-class preference (86 per cent) is somewhat stronger than the total black preference—a significant fact in view of the disproportionate role of the Negro middle classes in the movement of black ethnocentric mobilization.[33] Viewed from another set of data, in 1969 some 59 per cent of Negroes disagreed with the statement that "Negroes can get what they want only by banding together as black people against the whites, *because the whites will never help Negroes.*" Yet in the same year only 27 per cent of Negroes felt that whites wished a "better break" for blacks.[34]

Why the ambivalence in the Negro perception of black-white cleavages suggested by these data? The key to this ambivalence is that black ethnocentric mobilization occurs within a framework not of rigid sociopolitical constraints upon Negroes but of steady modification of the historic parameters dividing blacks and whites in American life. For example, the proportion of Negroes who are poor or lower class has declined from 48 per cent in 1959 to about 30 per cent in 1971; and blacks in white-collar and craftsmen-cum-skilled occupations have increased 76 per cent in the past decade, from 2.9 million in 1960 to 5.1 million in 1970, compared to a 24 per cent increase for whites—41.6 per cent to 57 per cent. These occupational changes are associated with significant educational change: median school years completed for Negroes aged 25–29 increased from 7 years in 1940 to 12 years in 1970; for 10 per cent of Negroes aged 18–24 were enrolled in college in 1965 (26 per cent of whites) and 18 per cent in 1971 (27 per cent of whites) and the black-white differential is now only 9 per cent. Negroes are also 9 per cent of the college population.[35]

In short, it seems that despite nearly a decade of intense black-white polarization consequent to the movement of black ethnocentric revitalization, this cleavage is not perfectly continuous at the institutional level, or rather a significant proportion of Negroes do not wish it to be. More recent data covering 1969 through late 1972 support this conclusion: there is a sharp decline in black perception of discrimination in all major spheres of black-white interaction. For example, there is a 17 point decline in Negro perception of housing discrimination—from 83 per cent in 1969 to 66 per cent in late (December) 1972.[36] It seems, then, that as the black ethnocentric mobilization realizes benefits for Negroes the pluralistic political pressures of American society function as a counterweight to long-run cleavage polarization of blacks and whites. This tendency toward equilibrium is found in other historic areas of conflict in American society, as Robert Dahl demonstrates in regard to ethnic and class cleavages in twentieth century New Haven between lower- and working-class Catholics, on the one hand, and patrician WASPS on the other.[37]

IV. Summary and Conclusion

I have attempted to illustrate the relevance of African Studies and Afro-American Studies to the field of comparative politics through an analysis of the nature of political institutionalization and cleavages in new African polities and the Afro-American subsystem. A case study of institutionalization in Ghana in the

1950s is presented. Institutionalization is conceived as a problem of delimiting the "political boundary" between the secular and sacred constituents of political relations. A major region in Ghana—the Ashanti region—spawned a political opposition to the central government, controlled by the Convention People's Party. The political behavior of the Ashanti nationalist subplot displayed a poor differentiation of secular and sacred attributes. Indeed, the *raison d'être* of the Ashanti opposition—known popularly as the National Liberation Movement—was thoroughly sacred, based upon the past political glory of the traditional Ashanti authority groups. Transposed to the context of modernizing Ghanaian politics, the political style of the Ashanti opposition inevitably created a major political dilemma. Why?

The prominence of Ashanti in the production of Ghana's cocoa represented the secular factor—the interest-related factor— in the NLM, but a response to the Ashanti opposition solely in terms of the political economy of cocoa would not be satisfactory. The sacred dimension of the Ashanti opposition required a *distinctive deference* from the central government in accord with Ashanti's historical (precolonial) hegemonic status vis-à-vis the tribes of southern Ghana—a status which political modernization had reversed. The requirement of *distinctive deference*, originating in the poor delimitation of the political boundary in the NLM's political style, implied a major constitutional concession to Ashanti—a devolution of the unitary power the Ghanaian state inherited from colonial rule. As it happened, the CPP government responded negatively to both the secular and the sacred dimension of the Ashanti nationalist subplot, squashing the NLM. This decision, in its turn, combined with, and in fact facilitated, a dysfunctional pattern of power-allocations—erratic and opportun- ist—between the center and periphery to produce a major crisis of institutionalization throughout the 1960s. The military coup of January 1966 capped this process, ostensibly containing but actually complicating the problem of differentiating the secular-sa- cred constituents of political relations in Ghanaian politics.[38]

The *ultra-stigmatization* of Negroes in American society is the key factor in the mal-institutionalization of the Afro-American subsystem in that it ensures that blacks who realize the socioeco- nomic indices of modernization are hindered in their capacity to translate these benefits into power equivalents. This in turn imposes a dysfunctional conflict dynamic upon the subsystem. First, cleavages are convulsive: a hierarchy of competing-but-overlapping interest groups is precluded through emphasis upon the characterological specificity of competing interests. Second, power-allocation patterns in the subsystem are distorted; the absence of overlapping competing interests causes power resources to be deployed disproportionately in the service of the personalistic (sacred) dimensions of leadership.

Only in the past decade have the convulsive cleavages in the Afro-American subsystem begun to alter, owing to the role of black ethnocentric revitalization in the politization of the Negro lower classes and of the elite-mass linkage. This crucial development has been characterized by sharp black-white polarization in American politics. But as the benefits or payoffs of a greater power-mustering capacity by Negroes increase, blacks display ambivalence toward ethnocentric political mobilization and the polarization (separatism) associated with it. This outcome confirms Robert Dahl's observations about the equilibrium role of pluralistic political pressures in American society when politics provides upward mobility.

Thus our analysis gives some indication of the type of comparative political analysis—middle-range in theoretical thrust—available in the fields of Afro-American and African Studies. These fields are as intrinsically fertile for seminal analysts as other interdisciplinary fields. The quality of comparative analysis in African Studies in particular is advancing markedly, owing to the works of theoretical comparativists like Lucian Pye, Samuel Huntington, and Samuel Beer.[39] The situation in Afro-American Studies, however, has been bedeviled by the powerful black separatist movement of recent years.

The black separatists have argued that Afro-American Studies cannot be treated as a field of comparative political analysis because the modernizing experience of blacks in American society has very little in common with other ethnic groups or subsystems.[40] This viewpoint claims that the historical uniqueness of the Afro-Americans' status precludes an adequate understanding of it through comparative analysis. Instead, it is argued that Afro-American modernization is to be understood, as it were, *on its own terms;*

as a field of inquiry the study of Afro-Americans can generate its own methods and concepts of analysis, requiring no assistance from other related fields of inquiry.

A few critical comments on this issue will be sufficient. First, the claim for the historical uniqueness of the Afro-American modernizing experience is little more than a latter-day variant of the outmoded ethnocentric approaches to history and the social sciences that prevailed before World War II.[41] Second, the spokesmen for the historical uniqueness of the Afro-American subsystem are for the most part ignorant of the extensive scholarship undertaken in the first half of this century, which actually treats the subject largely *on its own terms*. This primitive stage in the development of Afro-American Studies is long past; it is now necessary to enter the more sophisticated stage of the comparative analysis of the Afro-American subsystem.[42] The need to understand this subsystem for both theoretical and practical purposes is too important to allow the sacrifice of Afro-American Studies on the altar of black separatist politics.

NOTES

1. Harold F. Gosnell, *Negro Politicians: The Rise of Negro Politics in Chicago* (Chicago, 1935).

2. See Ralph J. Bunche, "The Negro in Chicago Politics," *National Municipal Review* (May 1928), pp. 261–264. See also Ralph J. Bunche, *The Political Status of the Negro in the Age of FDR* (Chicago, 1973).

3. Ralph J. Bunche, "French Administration in Togoland and Dahomey" (unpublished doctoral dissertation, Harvard, 1934). This excellent analysis deserves publication. It was supervised partly by Professor Rupert Emerson, who played a major role in developing African Studies after World War II. Among the postwar students he stimulated and directed in the field of African political analysis are James S. Coleman, Martin Kilson, W. Crawford Young, Joseph S. Nye, Brian Weinstein, G. Andrew McGuire, and Frances Hill.

4. Several political scientists in the Afro-American field worthy of mention include J. T. Salter, actually a pioneer along with Gosnell and Bunche, who studied a Negro district leader in Philadelphia in the 1930s; Edward H. Litchfield, who studied Negro voting in Detroit in the late 1930s; V. O. Key, who studied the national impact of authoritarian

constraints on blacks in the lily-white Southern politics; Hugh D. Price, who studied Negro voting behavior in Florida in the 1950s; Harry Holloway, who studied Negro politics in Texas in the late 1950s and in the South generally in the 1960s; John Morsell, who studied the structure of Negro politics in New York city in the 1940s; Donald R. Matthews and James W. Prothro, who studied Negro politics in the South in the 1960s when authoritarian constraints were attenuating; Edward Banfield, who studied the Chicago Negro machine's role in the politics of urban housing in the 1940s and early 1950s; James Q. Wilson, who studied the political styles of Chicago Negroes in the 1950s; and Charles V. Hamilton, who studied changing patterns of the accommodationist politics of Southern blacks in Alabama in the late 1950s.

5. Among the Negro social scientists worthy of mention are Charles S. Johnson; E. Franklin Frazier, sociologist; Horace Mann Bond, sociologist; Robert Weaver, economist; Abram Harris, economist; Allison Davis, social psychologist; John Aubrey Davis, political scientist; St. Clair Drake, anthropologist; Ira de Augustine Reid, sociologist; and John Hope Franklin, historian. The white social scientists worthy of mention include Thomas Wofter, economist; Sterling Spero, economist; Harry Stack Sullivan, psychologist; Robert Warner, historian; Edward Reuter, sociologist; Melville Herskovitz, anthropologist; John Dollard, social psychologist; and Hortense Powdermaker, anthropologist.

6. See Martin Kilson, "Reflections on the Structure and Content of Black Studies," *Journal of Black Studies* (Spring 1973).

7. Cf. Lucian W. Pye, *Aspects of Political Development* (Boston, 1966).

8. Cf. Samuel P. Huntington, *Political Order in Changing Societies* (New Haven, 1958), pp. 20ff., passim.

9. Cf. Zbigniew Brzezinski and Samuel P. Huntington, *Political Power: USA/USSR* (New York, 1964). This study deserves much more attention than it has received.

10. Cf. Martin Kilson, *Political Change in a West African State* (Cambridge, 1966).

11. My notion of the "boundary problem" is influenced by Gabriel Almond and James S. Coleman, eds., *The Politics of Developing Areas* (Princeton, 1960).

12. For an extended analysis which influences what follows, see Martin Kilson, "The Grassroots in Ghanaian Politics," in Philip Foster and Aristide R. Zolberg, eds., *Ghana and the Ivory Coast: Perspectives on Modernization* (Chicago, 1971), pp. 103–123.

13. The function of *élan* has been curiously neglected by political analysts. *Élan*—a dimension of ideology—can, I suggest, be fashioned in a manner that allows the manipulation of the sacred constituents of modern political relations in behalf of greater differentiation from the secular *but without seemingly surrendering to the secular*. This partly is what *effective* "radical" or "revolutionary" modernizing regimes appear to do, of which

there are many varieties ranging from Kemal's Turkey to Mao's China. But modernizing systems not usually designated "radical" or "revolutionary" also display this use of *élan*—e.g., early twentieth century Japan.

14. See the excellent piece on historical Ashanti by Ivor Wilks, "Ashanti Government," in Daryll Forde and P. M. Kaberry, eds., *West African Kingdoms in the Nineteenth Century* (London, 1967).

15. On the central role of the Ashanti King in the nationalist subplot, see Justice Sarkodee Adoo, *Report of Committee of Enquiry . . . into Affairs of the Kumasi State Council and the Asanteman Council* (Accra, 1958). On the NLM's translation of traditional Ashanti sovereignty into constitutional restructuring of the Ghana state, see Gold Coast Government, *Report of Select Committee on the Federal System of Government and Second Chamber for the Gold Coast* (Accra, 1955).

16. The best study of this issue remains David Apter, *The Gold Coast in Transition* (Princeton, 1955).

17. See Martin Kilson, *Chiefs, Peasants and Politicians: Grassroots Politics in Ghana* (forthcoming).

18. Ibid.

19. Cf. Gordon W. Allport, *The Nature of Prejudice* (Cambridge, 1954).

20. The classic study of this issue remains Kenneth B. Clark's *Prejudice and Your Child* (Boston, 1955). See also Allison Davis and John Dollard, *Children of Bondage: The Personality Development of Negro Youth in the Urban South* (Washington, D.C., 1940); E. Franklin Frazier (with Harry Stack Sullivan), *Negro Youth at the Crossways: Their Personality Development in the Middle States* (Washington, D.C., 1940).

21. I deal here mainly with Afro-American cleavage patterns. For an analysis of African patterns, see Martin Kilson, "Elite Cleavages in African Politics: The Case of Ghana," *Journal of International Affairs*, vol. XXIV (1970), no. 1, pp. 75–83.

22. Lipset's writings are central to a grasp of most forms of modern cleavages. See Seymour Martin Lipset, *The First New Nation* (New York, 1963).

23. On political pathologies, see C. J. Friedrich, *Political Pathology* (New York, 1972).

24. Epps' researches are still unpublished but some will appear in a study I am organizing, *The Professions and Afro-Americans*.

25. See Gosnell, cited.

26. Cf. Edmund Cronon, *Black Moses: The Story of Marcus Garvey* (Madison, 1955).

27. Cf. ibid.

28. Cf. Martin Kilson, "Black Politics: A New Power," in Irving Howe and Michael Harrington, eds., *The Seventies: Problems and Proposals* (New York, 1972), pp. 297–317.

29. Cf. Martin Kilson, "Blacks and Neo-Ethnicity in American Political Life," in Nathan Glazer and Daniel P. Moynihan, eds., *Ethnicity in Modern Society* (Cambridge, Mass., 1975).

30. Cf. Henry Bretton, *Power and Stability in Nigeria* (New York, 1962). Cf. also René Dumont, *L'Afrique noire est mal partie* (Paris, 1962).

31. Kilson, "Blacks and Neo-Ethnicity in American Political Life."

32. Peter Goldman (with Gallup Poll), *Report from Black America* (New York, 1970), p. 179.

33. Ibid., pp. 266–267.

34. Ibid., pp. 260, 250.

35. These data are found in Ben J. Wattenberg and Richard M. Scammon, "Black Progress and Liberal Rhetoric," *Commentary* (April 1973).

36. *The Harris Survey* (December 1972).

37. Robert A. Dahl, *Who Governs? Democracy and Power in an American City* (New Haven, 1961), esp. chapters 5–6.

38. The reason for this in post-coup Ghana, and elsewhere in Africa where armies have seized power, is the failure of military leadership to fashion an *élan* and ideology capable of facilitating the process of functional differentiation of secular and sacred constituents of political relations. The only other possible contribution the military leadership could make to this process is to facilitate viable economic development, for there is some evidence to suggest that the "boundary problem"—essentially a matter of legitimation of political relations—is lessened in modernizing societies where viable economic and social change is a prominent feature. (Cf. Lipset, *The First New Nation*.) Neither the military regimes in Ghana since 1966 nor in most other African states (save Nigeria) have good records in the economic sphere.

39. Huntington's *Political Order in Changing Societies* and Pye's *Aspects of Political Development* are invaluable for political scientists interested in closely-knit and middle-range theoretical analysis of African political modernization. Pye's contributions to *Crises and Sequences in Political Development* (Princeton, 1971), which he conceived and organized, are equally invaluable, as is Samuel Beer's introductory essay to the revised edition of *Patterns of Government* (New York, 1972).

40. See, e.g., chapter by Houston Baker in Nathan Huggins, Martin Kilson, and Daniel Fox, eds., *Key Issues in the Afro-American Experience* (New York, 1971).

41. Cf. Robert K. Merton, "Insiders and Outsiders: A Chapter in the Sociology of Knowledge," *American Journal of Sociology* (July 1972).

42. For an attempt to inaugurate this new stage in comparative analysis of the Afro-American subsystem, see Martin Kilson, *Political Dilemma of Black Mayors: A Study of Carl Stokes' Mayoralty in Cleveland, 1967–1974* (Washington, D.C., 1975).

A Critique of Area Studies from a West European Perspective

Harry Eckstein

PRINCETON UNIVERSITY

EDITOR'S NOTE

Traditionally comparative politics in America meant the study of the great powers of Europe, instruction in international relations focused on Europe, and the learning of a foreign language meant French, German, or Spanish. Therefore there was no need for European area programs since the common basis of all educated people was knowledge about Europe and its traditions. Until recently those who taught European subjects saw no purpose in specialized programs, which were seen as necessary only for less developed fields of study.

By the late 1960s, however, it was apparent to some specialists on Europe that in the competition for bright students and research funds work on Western Europe was losing out to the better organized area fields. During the previous years when the foundations and the government were providing extensive funds for building area studies programs with respect to the more esoteric regions, Western European research was increasingly neglected and therefore some felt a crisis was approaching because inadequate numbers of younger scholars were being trained. In response to this situation eight universities (Berkeley, Columbia, Harvard, Michigan,

M.I.T., Princeton, Wisconsin, and Yale) banded together to form a consortium called the Council for European Studies. The Ford Foundation also recognized the need for stronger support for Western European studies and made appropriate increased allocations for fellowships and research support. Subsequently the Council for European Studies has expanded to include nearly thirty universities.

These developments have not, however, made Western European work comparable to other area studies. No university, for example, has initiated master's degree programs in European studies. There is also some debate as to whether Western European studies should focus on the unique characteristics of a total civilization or whether they should be combined with work on America and Japan as a part of comparative studies of advanced industrial societies. Advocates of this latter approach see in a very general way the world as being divided between developed and developing societies, and therefore they feel that it is appropriate to distinguish between the comparative analysis of policy outputs in complex industrial and postindustrial society, and political development for the whole Third World.

In this chapter Harry Eckstein takes up the question of the appropriateness of area studies and arrives at the paradoxical conclusion that while remaining skeptical about area studies, as contrasted to general disciplinary work, he finds that of all the regions of the world Western Europe is the most homogeneous according to a variety of measurements and thus Western Europe should be the most legitimate candidate for area study.

Among these essays mine represents the skeptical attitude toward area studies. It seems appropriate that doubts about such studies should be expressed by someone whose principal area of empirical expertise is Western Europe, for Western Europe has been the poor relation among area programs. It was late to be admitted to the family of "areas" considered worthy of special research programs, and, once admitted, was treated stingily by the funding agencies. It is appropriate too that the role of skeptic should be played by someone who thinks that the ultimate (perhaps only) task of comparative politics is to find general solutions of general problems that cut across both geographic areas and periods of history—for organizing researches around such problems is the

obvious alternative to organizing them in terms of geographic areas
of expertise.

The term "skeptical" is used here literally, to imply doubting
but not absolutely denying. Disapprobation must not be categori-
cal. Good work has certainly been done by area specialists working
in area programs. Area studies were probably an unavoidable
phase in the development of contemporary comparative politics.
And area programs can no doubt still contribute to the further
development of the field. But doubt predominates. To say that
good work has come out of certain programs is not to say that
better work might not have come out of others; to say that a way of
organizing research can still be serviceable is not to say that other
ways would not be more so. This is precisely what I propose to
argue: the organization of comparative political research in terms
of geographic areas, while explicable and perhaps in its time
inevitable, was misconceived, and ought now to be transcended by
a different, better focus.

The argument will be conducted in four parts. First, I will try
to explain why the admission of Western Europe to the roster of
"areas" came late and in a niggardly way; since Western Europe
certainly is a geographic area this surely calls for explanation—and
can tell us a good deal about the animus and intellectual
credentials of area programs. Secondly, I will argue that Western
Europe's claims to be treated as an area for special research
programs are at least as good as those of any other, indeed
better—anyway to the extent that geographic "areas" make sense
at all as categories for a division of labor in research. Next, I will
try to demonstrate that the area concept has important weaknesses
even in the case of Western Europe. Finally, I will discuss an
alternative to area studies—a better way to attain what area studies
pre-eminently did accomplish: the formation of close-knit "communities" of scholars.

I

To explain why Western Europe played only a late and minor
role in area studies, we consider first the kinds of rationales on
which the organization and funding of area programs might be
based. Four such rationales are conceivable:

i. Area programs might be organized to *fill in conspicuous voids in factual knowledge*—if such gaps happen to occur principally in special geographic regions.

ii. Area programs might be organized as *rubrics for interdisciplinary collaboration*. Academic fields carve up the world by types of subject; hence, geographic regions provide an obvious point of intersection among them: all regions have particular histories, polities, systems of social structure, economies, and so on.

iii. Area programs might be organized because it is felt that *different geographic regions pose distinctive problems*, or (much the same) that different problems arise with particular emphasis and urgency in different regions of the world.

iv. Area programs might be organized because it is considered that *the societies and polities of different regions constitute distinctive types:* cases that have more in common with one another than with cases in other geographic areas.

These rationales, of course, are not mutually exclusive: all might have played a role in the formation of area programs. The third and fourth are especially likely to be related since different types of phenomena always give rise, to some extent, to different problems. It should also be evident that, from the theorist's point of view, the third and fourth considerations provide the weightiest reasons for carving up a subject, or set of related subjects, geographically.

Of all the above rationales, the one that most obviously played a role in the creation of area programs (and also best explains the initial exclusion of, and subsequent minor emphasis on, West European studies) is the first.

In the wake of the second World War, American social scientists could hardly be insensible to the fact that non-Western societies were largely *terra incognita* to them. Political scientists were especially likely to perceive them as areas of ignorance. Anthropologists, of course, had studied non-Western societies all along, even if from perspectives that seemed increasingly inapplicable; so had some historians and a handful of sociologists with special interests (e.g., in extended families). Political scientists, though, had long concentrated almost exclusively on Western polities; for evidence, look at just about any text in comparative politics produced before the war—and most after. They also were most familiar with the study of phenomena of only marginal significance outside the West, such as the analysis of formal constitutional structure or the operation and influence of pressure groups and democratic parties. There had, to be sure, been a brief efflorescence of political anthropology early in the twentieth century, concerned mainly with a problem similar to that of "nation-building": the origin of the State.[1] Work done on this subject, however, was hardly informative about contemporary non-Western polities (and exceedingly flawed as history as well); most of it was done in the twenties, or before; and names like Jenks, MacLeod, and Oppenheimer were hardly common fare on political science syllabi.

We need not dwell long on what made non-Western societies obtrusive during the war, especially in the Middle East and Asia; a nucleus of people competent to study them had in fact been generated by special military training programs and work in the wartime and immediate postwar intelligence services.[2] They became more conspicuous as a result of decolonization and the accelerating growth of new nations. And the intrinsic appeals of studying exotic peoples and social structures and being *au courant* with rather dramatic current events were hardly lessened by the fact that the market for expertise in non-Western societies was bullish, especially, of course, in Washington. It need only be added that the most obtrusive and most marketable aspects of non-Western social life were political, or highly tinged with politics. There was a manifest need to diagnose and adapt to likely political trends in the Third World; and most of what was "new" in the new nations was either directly political (the appearance of nation-states or of parties of national "mobilization") or engineered by political structures (e.g., attempted industrialization, land redistribution, and so on).

Nothing like the same considerations operated in favor of Western European studies. The blanks of knowledge to be filled in were certainly much smaller to begin with. Americans aside, local scholars were busily at work, and reporting in accessible languages. Nor was there much of a sense of new political drama, or of practical problems requiring specialized scholarly assistance. If anything, it seemed necessary to de-emphasize Western studies precisely in order to right a balance, and to keep scholarship in equilibrium with changed forces in the world's politically significant affairs.

Of course, large voids existed in our knowledge of Western societies and polities. We knew little, for instance, about the smaller European countries—and still do not know a lot about them. New things were going on in the old nations as well: not just that much-studied process, transnational integration, but the development of advanced welfare states, changes in party systems, the greater significance of pressure groups. Old things, still very imperfectly understood, and anything but undramatic, had gone on too, such as the malfunctioning and collapse of democratic orders and appearance of totalitarian regimes. Still, there was every reason to accord priority to non-Western studies, simply as a response to imbalance, as a corrective to forces of academic inertia that still steered many scholars toward Europe (*sans* area programs), and on the ineluctable postulate of scarce research resources. (In the case of East European and Soviet studies, the case for emphasis could be made from a slightly different perspective: the inherent difficulty, and fatefulness, of having accurate knowledge of the polities, and the extreme improbability of accurate studies being done by local scholars.)[3] The late, attenuated appearance of West European programs thus can be explained as itself a response to imbalance, resulting from the too lopsided earlier use of research resources.

But this argument is insufficient. It only explains special emphasis on non-Western studies. It does not explain why these studies were organized in terms of *areas*. Other ways of organizing them surely existed. Consequently we need to look at the other rationales on which area programs might be based for further illumination.

There is certainly a link between area studies and interdisciplinary research. A distinctive trait of the area programs has been that they combine the work of scholars in fields as diverse as languages, history, literature, and the various social sciences. They are the only programs that have consistently linked just about all of the social sciences, and the social sciences with the humanities. In doing so, they have created extraordinary communities of scholars —people who share common knowledge, are able to communicate across lines of specialization, meet often, interact much, read one another's works, discuss one another's concerns, constitute "societies" of a sort. One may question, however, that the area programs were created for that purpose. I see the matter less as one of deliberate design than as a contingent outcome produced by factors that have little to do with the "proper" organization of research.

Any program of study must have a nucleus of personnel who possess certain indispensable skills and knowledge. In studies of alien societies the most obviously indispensable requisites are language and some modicum of factual, not least historical, knowledge. Social scientists interested in (to them) esoteric societies thus had perforce to go to school with linguists and historians. Languages and history, moreover, were precisely those fields that could best muster critical masses of personnel for programs of non-Western studies (anthropology aside). From the outset, therefore, programs in non-Western studies, even if principally intended for social-scientific research, had to take on the internal contours of the humanistic fields, or tended naturally to do so. It happens that the internal divisions in these fields are principally geographic, simply because languages, cultures, and histories differ along geographic lines. In the sciences the more "natural" division of labor is by general types of phenomena or problems, since their aim is "extensive" knowledge (nomothetic generalization); in the humanities divisions by cultural and historical entities are more apropos, since their object is "intensive" knowledge (particular "understanding"). The division of non-Western studies by geographic areas can thus be seen, in the first instance, as an outcome of the central role that linguists and historians had to play in them.

Linguists and historians had, in fact, already been the core personnel of the wartime training programs in foreign societies, which served as models for the postwar programs—and out of which had come many of the social scientists already competent to deal with non-Western societies. Furthermore, resistance to dividing social-scientific studies along geographic lines was no doubt inhibited by the fact that the general theoretical problems to be investigated in non-Western contexts initially were ill defined (they have since become much more clearly defined) and since the filling of factual voids had clear precedence over attempts at theoretical generalization. Resistance was probably also inhibited by a general sense that studying non-Western societies intrinsically required the sort of broad interdisciplinary collaboration that a division by areas could accommodate. Partly, such collaboration seemed required because the tasks undertaken in the new nations (e.g., the achievement of social-economic-political "development") manifestly had aspects that involved all of the social sciences. Partly it seemed required because social structures in non-Western societies were themselves much less concretely differentiated along lines paralleling those of the social sciences than those of Western societies. And the surest way to de-emphasize Western studies was, of course, to draw geographic boundaries around the studies to be promoted.

The third and fourth rationales for area programs (different regions present different problems, or constitute distinctive types) thus provided little or none of the impetus for their organization. In view of the initially secondary role of social scientists in the programs it seems inevitable that the rationales most weighty from their point of view should have been secondary, or negligible, also.

This is explanation, not criticism. It might in fact initially have made most sense to conduct non-Western studies on an area basis, because of the factors mentioned. And it is not inconceivable that area programs might now be justified by factors that did not initially provide impetus to them. Major problems for theoretical inquiry might in fact largely cluster along geographic lines, and general types of societies and polities might do so as well. It is also conceivable that, while problems and types cluster in areas like Africa, East Asia, or the Middle East, they do not do so in the West—that there is greater social and political heterogeneity in Western Europe than in other geographic areas. If so, we would, of course, have an alternative, or supplementary, explanation for the exclusion (and subsequent downgrading) of West European studies from the roster of area programs. Are these suppositions really tenable?

II

I now propose to argue two related points. (1) If *problems* differ by geographic regions, then it is the West European area that is most distinctive—provided only that one does not make too much of the fact that countries like the predominantly white British Dominions, or other countries chiefly populated by "Western" European immigrants, are not actually located in Western Europe. And (2) if any area of the world consists of nations that have distinctive, rather homogeneous traits, and thus might qualify as a distinctive *type,* then again—with the same proviso—it is Western Europe that best fills the bill. In effect, the geographic region that has figured least in area programs has the strongest claims to be treated as an "area."

We start with traits, for the argument that Western Europe poses distinctive problems depends on West European countries having distinctive characteristics. Since these essays are chiefly aimed at political scientists it is, of course, political traits that need particularly to be stressed; parallel findings, however, would almost certainly turn up if economic and social traits were emphasized.

Some findings highly pertinent to my purpose are reported in a recent study by Gurr.[4] This study covers 82 nations in all areas of the world and in a time period that runs from 1800 to 1971. During that period 337 distinct "polities" existed in the nations covered, including 69 that still operate. Gurr's chief purpose is to account for persistence and change in "political authority structures." To do so he must, of course, identify basic variable traits of political authority. Five such traits are used[5]: openness of executive recruitment, constraints on executive autonomy, extent and institutionalization of political competition and opposition, scope of governmental direction of society, and complexity of governmental structure.[6] These variables are made "dimensional" so that minor and major political changes—changes "in" and changes "of" polities, adaptive changes and disruptive changes—can be distinguished. The five variable traits are used further to identify three general types of polities, which allows making very broad as well as very fine distinctions among them (and the identification of undeniable "major" changes). These types are democracy (in which there is a relatively high level of subordinate participation and low level of superordinate control), autocracy (where the opposite is the case), and "anocracy" (a neologism denoting polities that govern little and are highly decentralized, but are ruled by caesaristic figures and not characterized by regularized competition—in short, polities in which both elites and masses are weak). Finally, as well as measuring the persistence of polities, Gurr identifies such dynamic traits as their adaptability: the tendency of changes "in" them, not changes "of" them, to occur in response to changing pressures and circumstances; thus he presents information about both structural traits of polities and aspects of their performance.

In short, the study paints on a broad geographic and historical canvas, identifies both rather small and very large differences among polities, and looks at polities both in rest and in motion. The conjunction of a large, geographically scattered sample of cases and a long historic time span makes it particularly suitable for the argument I want to make here—and later, as will be apparent in the next section. The work is also notable for using particularly systematic, apparently highly reliable, techniques for coming to grips with traits of authority.

Some of Gurr's pertinent findings are summarized below[7]:

i. In the most general terms, there seem to be three rather distinctive geographic clusters of polities: the European, the Afro-Asian, and the Latin American. One of these clusters, the Afro-Asian, it should be noted, combines most of the areas *distinguished* in area programs—particularly those that have generated the most long-lived, best-funded, *separate* communities of scholars. The finding does not, of course, allow one to divide the world into "European" nations and all others, because of the distinctiveness of the Latin cluster. But while that cluster does have some peculiar traits, it is distinctive also in that it resembles the European cluster in some respects and the Afro-Asian in others (a finding perhaps not unrelated to the fact that Latin-American countries intermix people of European and non-European stock more than any others). Thus, the European area still is the most distinctive of those that have been used as foci of area programs, with Latin America a close second.[8]

ii. European polities are particularly distinctive on three of the authority variables: complexity of governmental structure (high), constraints on executive autonomy (also high), and governmental directiveness (low). On these dimensions, Latin and Afro-Asian polities closely resemble one another. A marked difference between Europe and other areas, by the way, turns up despite the facts that Europe includes a large proportion of the older polities and that there has been a general temporal increase on all three dimensions. The inference is that if only modern Europe were considered the differences would loom still larger.

   iii. In the case of participation, the Latin cluster is distinctively high, but chiefly because of the very high incidence of "factional/restricted" competition, as against the "institutionalized/electoral" competition more characteristic of the European cluster. Overall level of competition does not distinguish the latter from other clusters, but qualitative modes of competition do. Lack of institutionalized competition and the proscription of competition probably also account, respectively, for the facts that openness of executive recruitment is distinctively high in the Latin cluster and distinctively low in the Afro-Asian.

   iv. The European cluster is characterized by the typical occurrence of democracies; the Afro-Asian by that of autocracies; the Latin by that of anocracies. Here again, lumping most geographic areas together would not appear to be unwarranted—provided that the European (and Latin) area is still distinguished.

   v. European polities are distinctively adaptable, no less than peculiar in their static traits. They tend, on the whole, to undergo minor changes "in" their structures rather than major changes "of" them over time. In that regard, however, Latin polities do resemble them, at least superficially. In them, too, changes tend to be minor—but less because of peaceful adaptation than because violent change rarely produces major transformations.[9] In the rest of the world change seems generally to imply upheaval.

   vi. Perhaps most significant of all, durable European polities turn out to have authority traits quite different from all others. This is particularly significant because it implies more than that descriptive differences between Europe and other conventionally defined "areas" are greater than among the other areas themselves. It implies that Europe is distinctive also in the ways dependent and independent variables are there related, compared to the rest of the world; surely the strongest argument for treating a geographic area as a special universe for inquiry is that it calls for special theories that relate variables. To be more specific, only in Europe are highly open political recruitment, high constraints on executive autonomy, high participation, low governmental directiveness, and high complexity positively related to the ability of polities to endure. In the Afro-Asian cluster just the opposite is the case; in Latin nations only constraints on executives have a clear relation to durability.

Surely then Europe is a distinctive political area, but the different Afro-Asian "areas," the cores of area programs, are not.

Many other findings could be adduced to the same effect. Consider as just one example the Feierabends' study of the world-wide incidence of "instability-events" in the period 1955–61[10]—the period during which most area programs were founded. The study shows that Europe (Western and Eastern) furnishes virtually all the cases of high stability: all but four of the twenty-one countries in the highest quartile of cases. Only France and Italy fell below the quartile. The cases in the lowest quartile, on the other hand, are a geographic hodge-podge. Similarly, on the Feierabends' "coercive-permissive" scale all but three cases in the highest quartile of permissiveness were West European[11]; none in the lowest quartile were; and the latter again was a strange geographic mixture of cases.

The essential peculiarity of Western Europe then is this: (1) From the standpoint of static descriptive traits, it is the distinctive area of complex government, controls on executives, relatively autonomous citizens, and "institutionalized/electoral" competition and opposition. (2) From the standpoint of dynamic traits, it is the pre-eminent area of adaptive change and the relatively low incidence of instability events. (3) From the standpoint of theoretical relationships, it is the one area in which "democratic" traits promote rather than hinder the persistence of polities.

Do other areas have anything like that set of distinctive characteristics? Culturally and from the standpoint of social structure, maybe; but politically not. If then we must continue to divide the world geographically for purposes of political inquiry, a distinction between Western Europe (broadly conceived) and all the rest seems tenable—although a distinction into four clusters (Western Europe, Eastern Europe, Latin, and the rest) may be still more tenable.

As for distinctive "problems," Gurr also provides the essential clue—which should in any case be apparent from the argument thus far and from common sense. The differences between the European cluster Gurr identifies and other areas closely parallel, according to his findings, differences between contemporary polities in general and those that appeared earlier in history. They can thus be considered epiphenomena of historical development, a point to which we return in the next section. The term "development," as we all know, is beset with definitional ambiguities—varied and loose usage. But for the present purpose these ambiguities can be ignored. The simple point is that Western Europe (again in the broad sense of the term) is distinctive as a source of problems because it alone poses problems, practical and theoretical, of high development. (The area also, of course, pre-eminently raises problems about "democratic" politics in general, government through highly complex structures, government under considerable executive constraint, and competition through institutionalized/ electoral devices.) No one should still need convincing nowadays that problems of high development are, from the standpoint of "praxis," fateful and dramatic—whatever may have been thought when area programs were first organized—and, from the standpoint of theory, interesting and peculiar. Other areas of the world, to be sure, pose similarly fateful, interesting, and peculiar problems about underdevelopment or processes (especially earlier processes) of development; but the point is that the areas do not greatly differ in the political problems they pose.[12]

I do not, of course, imply that non-Western countries are all alike. Obviously they are not; neither are Western ones. The differences between particular countries might well suffice to justify case studies—but that is not the matter under consideration. The issue here is what geographic areas, as clusters of countries, make sense—if any do. On that score, the argument that Western Europe does so *more* than other areas seems to me compelling. Whatever differences might exist among non-European cases seem to cluster much less along clear-cut regional lines.

III

But how compelling is the case for treating even Western Europe as a rubric for organizing political studies? Although stronger than the case for so treating other "areas," it is, in some important respects, far from sufficiently persuasive. I base this position on three principal arguments.

First, the notion of "Western Europe" as a typological category entails some conspicuous anomalies of its own. For one thing we have seen already that countries like Australia, Canada, New Zealand, Israel, and the United States clearly belong to the category on any grounds other than actual geographic location;

but since these countries can be considered "European" without obvious procrustean stretching that objection should perhaps not be taken too seriously. More important, Western Europe itself is hardly all that homogeneous an entity, even if average measures on dimensional variables make it appear to be. Again and again, for example, major contrasts turn up between what might be called Latin Europe (Spain, Portugal, Italy, and France) and the rest. The "Latin European" countries, for instance, are hardly notable for democracy, for adaptive change, or for a low level of instability events: in the Feierabends' study of instability they are located— along with another Mediterranean country, Greece, but unlike all other European nations (except Belgium)—in the fourth column (which denotes rather high instability), in company with a large assortment of Latin American and Asian nations. Not least, when countries are ranked on the basis of such variables as incidence of civil strife or type of elite recruitment, certain non-Western nations nearly always creep in with the European ones: above all Japan, the Philippines, Costa Rica, and sometimes Saudi Arabia or India. The "European" syndrome thus is far from uniform, and not really restricted to Europe, or even countries whose populations mainly originated in Europe.

Secondly, if we take a decently long historical view—sometimes not very long—differences between Western Europe and other areas also tend to dissolve, or to grow fuzzy at the edges. Certainly the complexity of European polities was not always markedly greater than that of others. Executives in Europe were not always highly constrained (e.g., in Nazi or Imperial Germany). Competition was not always "institutionalized/electoral." It seems a vast oversimplification to associate Europe, even in the broadest sense, with democracy, or low governmental directiveness, considering that it has also been the aboriginal home of totalitarian rule. Not all European polities have been notably "adaptive" over the period covered by Gurr; in many cases (Germany, Italy, Austria, for instance) explosive change obviously did occur, and Gurr finds that the average "life-span" of European polities during his period was 12.8 years as compared to 12.2 years in all other cases—hardly a difference on which to base an academic division of labor. Differences between Europe and other areas are more pronounced if only the more recent postwar period is considered, but that is a temporal rather than geographic distinction, or a combination of the two.

That leads directly to the third, and most important, argument. Whatever differences might exist between Europe and other areas, much more pronounced differences exist between contemporary (twentieth-century and/or presently existing) polities taken as a whole and older polities, also undifferentiated (those of the nineteenth century). Distinctions by historical periods thus seem to work much better than distinctions by geography. The implications surely are that the variable of "development" is critical; that Europe is now distinctive precisely because distinctively developed; that the Afro-Asian cluster of nations is not readily divisible into geographic subsets precisely because of similarities in the development of the Afro-Asian nations; and that the distinctiveness of Europe tends to disappear if earlier European polities are compared with contemporary non-European ones for the same reason. (Again, it is possible here to circumnavigate the thorny issue of just what "development" means, and whether more appropriate, more informative terminology might be available for the same phenomena; what matters is that the historical factor does seem to matter critically.)

From this argument there follows another, concerned with general problems. To the extent that we want to solve theoretical problems distinctively raised now by non-Western nations—e.g., the conditions that promote or hinder nation-building, or those that impede or facilitate democratization, or institutionalization in political competition, or the achievement or civil order—it would be obvious folly to deprive ourselves of the experience European countries furnish. Problems do seem now to arise in European contexts on which experience in other areas can shed no light, but surely the reverse is much less the case. The European experience certainly is supremely relevant to all problems raised in the contemporary study of "development" in other contexts: e.g., the effects of conditions prior to development on the developmental process; the significance of the process beginning in one or another sector of society (economic, political, or intellectual, for instance); the significance of the process originating in violent upheaval or more moderate change; and such problems as the effects of more or less rapid rates of development, or the effects of the coincidence, or separation in time, of "critical" problems that typically arise in the developmental process.[13]

This is quite apart from the fact that many theoretical problems that arise in political study (probably all the most important) are universal and susceptible to general solutions that transcend both geography and history. One thinks here of such problems as the conditions of legitimate rule, of civil order and disorder, of forces that make for political power or weakness, of forces of cleavage and cohesion, of factors that govern the scope of public direction and of private autonomy, of the impact of economic structure or class structure on politics, of the interplay between levels of political demands and governmental outputs, of the preconditions and effects of revolutionary violence, and many more. The solution of some of these problems may, to some extent, take different forms in different contexts (we mentioned a noteworthy example earlier), but even these may ultimately be subsumed under general statements of regularity that ignore context. And it seems probable that if different solutions do pertain to different areas, they do so only because nongeographic forces happen to work differently in geographic clusters, at particular moments in history and for contingent reasons.

IV

Having criticized the area-concept as a basis for organizing political researches, I am anxious that my argument should not be misconstrued. As stated at the outset the area programs did generate much good work, and also useful work. Most of all, they in fact filled in gaping voids in our common stock of knowledge, and counteracted the parochialism that had afflicted earlier political studies. In so doing they not only broadened our range of factual knowledge but also fertilized theoretical imaginations, as wide comparative knowledge usually does. They generated novel and basic theoretical problems—all the more important to have on the agenda for applying to Western no less than non-Western nations; they did much, in short, to sensitize political scientists to what is problematic in political experience, including that of their own societies. They also generated novel approaches to political study (the political culture approach and functional analysis, for example)—the more important also for their utility in studying polities that were played down in the area programs. They produced political scientists with skills, like language skills, previously almost nonexistent. Not least, they helped overcome disciplinary parochialism and scholarly isolation by creating scholarly "communities" worthy of the name. Perhaps nothing else could have done all this as well—at the time area programs were widely organized.

My argument, then, is not that area programs were useless. But I do contend that they have by now largely outlived their usefulness. Originally created chiefly to correct imbalances in factual knowledge, they have by now contributed to an imbalance of another kind: between factual knowledge of alien countries, chiefly of the "humanistic" kind, and our ability to make theoretical sense of that knowledge—to solve general theoretical problems in macropolitics (many of which were initially generated in area studies). Granted that we do not entirely lack that ability. Still, our ranks surely remain far better stacked in area specialists than in general theorists. There would seem now to be a primary need to counteract the manifest parochialism of the area programs themselves (and they *are* parochial, in their own ways) and to create, in political and other social sciences, communities of the sort that have always been common in the physical sciences: "problem-communities," united by common interests in coming to grips with general theoretical issues not unique to peoples and places.

There is no reason why such problem-communities should be any less exciting than area-communities. There is, in fact, every reason why they should be more lively. What, after all, is more inherently exciting to scholarly investigators than the process of dispelling the common mysteries that diverse experience presents to them? There is also every reason to expect such communities to be more close-knit, for the area programs certainly created, along with cohesive groups, their own frictions and discords, originating in fundamentally different ways of scholarly life: divergent conceptions of the nature and aims of scholarship. Nor would a problem-focus necessarily discourage cross-disciplinary work, although the collaborating disciplines might be different. And a focus on general problems certainly need not prevent intensive specialization in particular cases, or sets of them (types of polities, or even areas).

The essential point is that the area programs have by now largely succeeded in, and thus transcended, their original purpose. There is, of course, more to learn about the societies and polities they emphasize, but still more to learn about other matters. By now area programs have also uncovered most of the general problems for research they are likely to uncover. We are, in fact, now overrun by general problems still awaiting general solutions.

If further argument is needed, readers might ask themselves two questions. (1) What is the nature of the most influential work to come out of the area programs? (Most of it, in my view, seems in fact to be study conducted along the lines of some general theoretical approach or study in which a very general theoretical problem is raised; and empirical materials used in the studies, more often than not, are individual cases, not geographic clusters of them.[14] In these studies something more general than an area—a general problem or general research approach—is at the heart of research; and usually illumination is sought in a pertinent case, not a geographic cluster of cases.) And (2) who has profited more from whom: area specialists from general theorists or vice versa?

NOTES

1. I have in mind works like Edward Jenks, *A Short History of Politics* (J. M. Dent: London, 1900) and *The State and the Nation* (J. M. Dent: London, 1919); W. C. MacLeod, *The Origin of the State* (Philadelphia: University of Pennsylvania Press, 1924) and *The Origin and History of Politics* (New York: Wiley, 1921); Franz Oppenheimer, *The State* (New York: Vanguard, 1927); and E. M. Sait, *Political Institutions* (New York: Appleton-Century-Crofts, 1938).

2. It would be interesting to do an analysis of the early staffs of the area programs from this point of view. Their nuclei, I would suppose, came chiefly out of the military ASTP programs and organizations like OSS (and later the CIA).

3. The main factors that actually account for the flourishing of Communist studies no doubt were the easy availability of research funds and the existence of certain "old boy" networks between universities and government departments.

4. Ted Robert Gurr, "Persistence and Change in Political Authority Structures," *American Political Science Review* (forthcoming).

5. These traits were selected from a dimensional analysis of authority patterns done by Gurr and myself, with help from a number of graduate students at Princeton. The full analysis will appear in our work, *Patterns of Authority: A Structural Basis for the Study of Politics* (New York: Wiley, forthcoming). The traits selected by Gurr are those on which reliable data are widely available.

6. The first four variables are probably sufficiently self-explanatory. The fifth, complexity, includes such matters as decision-making by collectivities rather than individuals, the presence of several overlapping decision-structures at the same level, and the vertical differentiation of polities.

7. Readers are referred to Gurr's article for full discussions and numerical expressions of his findings.

8. If Gurr had distinguished Western and Eastern Europe a case for treating the latter as an area with distinctive traits of its own would probably have emerged.

9. See the evidence in Ivo K. and Rosalind L. Feierabend, "Systemic Conditions of Political Aggression: An Application of Frustration-Aggression Theory," *Journal of Conflict Resolution*, X (3), (Sept., 1966), Table 1; and Ted Robert Gurr, "A Causal Model of Civil Strife: A Comparative Analysis Using New Indices," *American Political Science Review*, LXII (Dec., 1968), Table A-1.

10. Feierabend and Feierabend, ibid.

11. Here I count New Zealand, Israel, and the United States as "European" nations.

12. Latin America is, in this case again, something of an exception—perhaps because of early, but also early arrested, "development."

13. See Leonard Binder et al., *Crises and Sequences in Political Development* (Princeton: Princeton University Press, 1972).

14. Examples are legion. A few are: David E. Apter, *Ghana in Transition* (New York: Atheneum, 1963); Daniel Lerner, *The Passing of Traditional Society* (New York: Free Press, 1958); Lucian W. Pye, *Politics, Personality, and Nation Building* (New Haven: Yale University Press, 1962); L. I. and S. H. Rudolph, *The Modernity of Tradition* (Chicago: University of Chicago Press, 1967); and Aristide Zolberg, *Creating Political Order* (Chicago: Rand McNally, 1966). These works use contemporary African, Middle Eastern, and Asian materials, but could just as well have been done in reference to other geographic areas and/or time-periods.

Western Europe as a Laboratory for Studying Social Change and Policy Response

Leon N. Lindberg

UNIVERSITY OF WISCONSIN, MADISON

EDITOR'S NOTE

Harry Eckstein has just reminded us that, despite Europe's partition into a multiplicity of states, the continent retains a sense of commonality, rooted in its deep cultural traditions. Furthermore, he has shown that "Western Europe" as an "area" of study should properly encompass political systems of the same traditions which happen to be geographically outside of the continent. There is another argument which also says that the "area" study of "Western Europe" should not be limited to that continent because intellectually there is more to be gained from the comparative analysis of the European systems in the broader context of the problems of the highly advanced industrial societies.

This argument holds that just as South Asian or African studies were greatly strengthened when they were reinforced by the general theoretical concepts of political and social development, so "Western European"

This article appeared in the *European Studies Newsletter*, vol. IV, no. 1, October, 1974, pp. 10–19.

studies can be revitalized by theories of advanced developed, or, as some would say, "overdeveloped" societies. This interest in combining European studies with development theories was stimulated in part by European specialists deciding to partake of the excitement in recent years about theories of political development which had been the monopoly of specialists of the non-Western world. It was, however, also stimulated by the students of non-Western development who were anxious to gain better historical perspectives on the state-building process and thus felt a need to examine the experiences of the "older" states in terms of development theories. This process of "coming home" to Western Europe in search of better understanding of the dynamics of development encouraged not only new approaches to European history but also new ways of seeing contemporary development processes. The stage was thus set for a new subfield of the social sciences, the comparative study of the problems of advanced societies.

The shift of forces in the study of development from the less developed to the most developed nations has produced significant changes in theoretical concerns and methodology. Development, as long as it was associated with the non-Western areas, dealt mainly with the larger social and economic processes which were seen as significant in helping to shape the growth of states and nations. Concern was thus with process and the "inputs" to political life. In the developed countries state structures already exist and therefore the problems of "development" call for the study of how governments can and should cope with the public policy issues common to advanced industrial societies. Concern thus tends to focus on the "outputs" of political systems and the management of all the new types of problems inherent in highly industrial and "postindustrial" societies.

In the chapter which follows Leon N. Lindberg outlines numerous ways in which Western European studies can provide a laboratory for the study of public policies. It is appropriate that we should end our review of the relationship of area studies to the disciplines on this subject since it points to the future with respect to both research needs and the evolution of political society.

We have begun to see in recent years a revival of interest on the part of political science (and to a lesser extent sociology and economics) in Western Europe. On an institutional and program level this is evinced by the establishment of a number of active Western European programs during the late 1960s, by the creation of the Council for European Studies as an inter-University forum of communication and research innovation in European studies, by the major expansion of fellowship resources available through the Foreign Area Fellowship Programs of the SSRC-ACLS, and by the creation by the West German government of a foundation explicitly devoted to advancing European studies, the German Marshall Foundation of the United States. All of these have paid off in a slow but steady increased flow of research reports and monographs.[1]

This major expansion of programs, studies, and available resources has a number of different roots.

1. Within the discipline itself, the behavioral revolution and the strides made in the study of modernization and development in Asia, Africa, and the Middle East have led to an interest in refining our understanding of past developmental sequences, for which Western Europe is the logical and ideal setting. We have also seen a new interest in political structures, and in public policy and policy impacts, and in both cases Europe is attractive as a "most similar system model" basis of comparison.[2] Furthermore, the availability of long-term longitudinal public records and an unparalleled richness of social scientific and historical research, plus a rapidly expanding and increasingly sophisticated European social science community, make Western Europe an especially attractive research site.

2. Recent political events have also contributed. The re-emergence of Western Europe as a major economic power, the functional and geographic growth of the European Community, structural transformations in the international monetary and trade systems, and East-West détente, all recall the economic, political, and strategic importance of Western Europe and make increasingly evident the relative dearth of intellectual, institutional, and financial resources in the field. This was similarly the case with the gradual realization that Western Europe shared with the United States certain common problems such as pollution, urban blight, transportation, and the like, and that much benefit would flow from increasing our pool of knowledge and skills about how such problems have been dealt with.

3. Each of the above also partakes of a third element which may well be the most primordial, namely, a growing preoccupation with our own fate, with the "future of the West," with "postindustrial society," with the prospects for capitalism and socialism. This is to some extent a function of a certain millennial mood of the times, a sense of malaise and pessimism. It is reflected in the passionate, almost theological debates set off by *The Limits to Growth* and other "doomsday" books.[3] But it also reflects the emergence of a serious body of literature that calls into question the ability of advanced industrial societies to continue their past policy practices, and that raises troubling doubts about their capacity to manage the problems that the coming changes seem likely to introduce.[4] And we have begun to realize that, in spite of the strides we thought we had made in the study of political change and development, this work told us very little about the nature or the prospects of modernity.[5]

It will be the argument of this paper that Western Europe offers an especially apt comparative framework for investigations into the present and future implications of contemporary change processes in advanced industrial societies. In the first place, studies and theories of contemporary change, conceptualizations of change processes or of alternative future societies, such as Bell's notion of a "postindustrial society"[6] or Gross's imagery of "friendly Fascism,"[7] are rooted essentially in perceptions of American experience and suffer from ethnocentrism and parochialism. The same is true of studies of capitalism, as Heilbronner has recently pointed out.

[W]e cannot analyze the adaptive properties of capitalism or socialism by confining our attention to the merits or shortcomings of any single example of either system. The range of social structures, traditions, institutions of government, and variations of economic forms is sufficiently great for both socio-economic orders that generalizations must be made at a very high level of abstraction—so high, in fact, that we may seriously question whether an analysis along these lines can shed much light on the adaptive capabilities of, say, "capitalist" Sweden or Japan. . . .[8]

In the second place, Western European countries share with each other and with North America and Japan a number of important similarities that seem to be closely associated with their common "problematique" and that also make them a feasible and fruitful arena for comparison. These include basically capitalist economic systems, comparable levels of economic development and industrialization, roughly similar welfare state policies and institutions, liberal-democratic politics, and involvement in a common set of intensive international and transnational systems, such as the internationalized market system—its commodity, service, and institutional manifestations—and, in the European case most distinctively, membership in that most "involving" of international systems, the European Community.[9] Finally, the countries of Western Europe display relative to each other and to other advanced capitalist systems an interesting range of theoretically relevant variations: in level, type, and timing of industrialization, in the persistence of traditional culture, in political attitudes and values, governmental and political institutions, elite characteristics, party systems, dominant ideologies, and past patterns of policy.

There is a Chinese curse that says, "May you live in interesting times!" Curse or not, the next decades for Western Europe, as for other highly industrialized capitalist societies, seem likely to offer a fascinating laboratory of political and social change. We should take advantage of the opportunity and move quickly toward what Campbell[10] has called "quasi-experimental designs," using disciplined cross-national and longitudinal comparisons of change, problem-solving, and policy-making sequences as "quasi-experiments." A major focus of such research would be upon dynamic and comparative analysis of policy, as Heclo[11] puts it, on "moving events, routines, strategies and adaptations," of "courses of action through time and outcomes which no one may intend or decide upon," of "what sort of learning mechanism governments in fact are." In the pages that follow I will suggest some of the lines upon which such research might be organized.

The Future Development of Industrial Society

Within the broad frame of a concern for the future of advanced industrial societies are a variety of political science questions at different levels of analysis. In delineating these I want to distinguish them and myself from an activity and an intellectual movement commonly called "futurology." Although there are vast differences of emphasis among futurists or futurologists, it is probably fair to say that their dominant concern is with making valid or useful assertions about the future, be these conditional (a prediction based on some model or scientific law), unconditional (a forecast based on projection or extrapolation of trends), or conjectural (an "intellectual construction of a likely future").[12] This is not the place to discuss the epistemological, methodological, and normative problems associated with such activities or my own objections to them. Suffice it to say that the intellectual activity I am proposing falls within an empirical-analytical mode. What is entailed are over-time comparative studies of contemporary processes of change (or development), and their political aspects and political consequences. Perhaps we could speak of *emergent* futures. As I see it, such analyses fall solidly within the tradition of the theory of political development, modernization, or change.

I shall propose below several sets of questions as central foci for comparative political research over the decades to come. Each can be best investigated empirically in the quasi-experimental spatial and temporal analytical frame provided by contemporary Western Europe. They are all premised on the observation that these societies—along with other advanced capitalist societies— seem to have entered upon a period of unanticipated and little understood change. Perhaps, as many believe, the decades of the 1970s and 1980s will be seen in retrospect as having constituted a transitional period or turning-point in the overall history of modernization, in which qualitatively new issues arose, the choices taken to deal with them and the way in which they were taken fundamentally transformed the performance and very character of these societies. Or perhaps it will be seen as a period of retrogression, of incipient ecological and societal collapse as problems pile up that are too complex and demanding for existing institutions and policy imaginations to cope with. At the very least, the next decades promise to be a period of important structural, institutional, and policy change. Sir Geoffrey Vickers asks in *Freedom in a Rocking Boat,*

> Can the political process, as any Western country knows it today, manage the increased volume and complexity of political choices

which the next thirty years will bring to it? If so, by what growth, in what directions? If not, what breakdown will lead to what alternative? [13]

Vickers suggests that however advanced industrial societies come to terms with their present problems they are likely to be radically changed in the process.

The changes that will flow from all of these impacts are unpredictable and perhaps unimaginable, but we can prepare to recognize and understand them more quickly as they emerge, by finding some common frame within which to comprehend them. [14]

It is such a frame that is to be briefly sketched out below. My approach is rooted in what Huntington has called the *"transitional process approach"* to political change and development. [15] Researchers in this tradition have argued that variations in the historical performance of polities are to be explained or accounted for in terms of the nature and circumstances of the transitional process or of historical turning-points.

Was it prolonged or rapid, early or late? Was it peaceful or violent? What was the sequence of change? Differences in these aspects of the transition lead to more or less political stability and more or less democracy. [16]

An attention to historical turning-points would then bring us to focus on the issues of public choice that emerged at particular points in time, on the policy options that were considered and chosen by governing and influential elites, on the way in which the crucial resources of contending actors were affected, etc. Development theorists have argued in a variety of different ways and from a variety of normative standpoints that elites, in the process of reacting to changes or transformations that impinge upon them and their societies, not only determine the specific policy actions that are or are not taken in particular cases, but that they also play a central role in shaping the future political cleavage patterns of the society, which in turn may result in changes in—or perpetuation of—the relative power of different elites. Different patterns of elite response and of interelite coalition formation may also help determine for decades to come the effective political structures, decision rules, kinds of policy outcomes, and hence the stability/instability patterns that will characterize a given society.[17] It seems to me especially important that research into contemporary transitional phenomena be systematically comparative, for industrial societies seem to me as or more likely to develop in different or even divergent ways as in convergent ones, depending upon the particular patterning of change processes and the modes of response. Wiles has criticized Bell on this point specifically, accusing him of being "too Marxist." Wiles stresses

> the basic unpredictability of almost everything. That society is becoming post-industrial as defined is true, the change is very important *per se*. But we do not know what it portends for other aspects of human affairs. . . . [A]bove all it is difficult to infer much from post-industrialism about the form of government.[18]

One of the most interesting questions to ask about the future is whether there will emerge a range of different types of "post-industrial" societies in response to different historical cultural heritages, different structures, different timing and patterning of change, and different public and elite responses.

What are the key characteristics of the contemporary transition? This is, of course, as Huntington remarks in an understatement, "rather hard to pin down." [19] Nevertheless, my own investigations in the literature and preliminary research findings have persuaded me that there are certain interrelated "heavy tendencies" that are sufficiently basic to hold the potential for bringing about fundamental change in economic policy, and in social and political structures.[20] They seem likely to me to trigger the kinds of problems or demands that would qualify as a crisis in Verba's terms, namely those that will require "governmental innovations and institutionalization if elites are not seriously to risk a loss of their position or if the society is to survive." [21] These are:

(1) *The increasing primacy and density of politics*—the trend toward centralization of political power, planning, and control and the decline of the market as regulator and allocator. Vickers' anticipation of a having "to live in a much denser political medium." [22]

(2) *A trend toward resource scarcities*—of environmental amenities, biological species, wilderness, energy, mineral resources, space, land, clean air and water. Boulding[23] speaks evocatively of how "the shadow of the stationary state falls upon our time," of the "imminent closure of the human environment," of "the transition from the infinite plane to the closed, limited round ball of spaceship earth."

(3) *Mounting centrality of a concern for issues of equality, equity, and fairness*—to some extent a secular trend in industrialized societies, but likely to be much intensified by the increase in the scope of overt and discretionary political power and by the renewed importance of scarcity.[24]

(4) *Internationalization or interdependence of national economies*—consists of internationalization of markets (movements, mobility, stocks), of intergovernmental and market-oriented institutions, and of externalities, with serious consequences for the efficiency of nation-state decision-making in stabilization, allocation, and distribution policies.[25] This becomes increasingly problematic for the national decision-maker given the demand for more centralized planning and control, resource scarcities, and the salience of internal distributional issues.

One cannot, of course, scientifically demonstrate the existence, or priority, of this particular set of heavy tendencies, although it can be asserted and defended more or less persuasively. At this stage of research, it is simply postulated in order to formulate an analytical model and to generate researchable hypotheses.

What we have here is a set of postulated tendencies or "privileged problems" that all advanced capitalist states will presumably be confronted with in one form or another. I see these as among the major sources of strain and tension and conflict that will alter the load/capability dynamics of advanced capitalist societies and that will crystallize or catalyze other ongoing changes, which have hitherto been too contradictory or formless to assess (e.g., value change, the service society).[26] But we cannot foresee the exact magnitude of these tendencies or problems, nor *how* they will interact with other dynamic trends, nor how they will be perceived, understood, responded to by men and women in different societies. These can and should be principal foci of political research.

How is the policy agenda or "load" of decision-makers changing and have their response resources or capabilities declined?

The developmental approach I have proposed asks how polities produce "solutions"—make decisions and choices through time—how via the intended and unintended efforts of leaders and others they adapt themselves to situational givens and seek by means of policy and institutional changes and strategies to stabilize those elements within their control.[27] Thus the trends postulated above will have political significance insofar as they substantially alter the number, intensity, or nature of policy problems the dominant elite or decision-maker must confront, and insofar as they reduce, alter, or increase their response capabilities. We would expect this to vary markedly from one country to another.

There is strong evidence that each of the "heavy tendencies" or "privileged problems"—and all of them in combination—cut across and put new strain on all sectors of modern public policy making. This is as true for government goal setting and the choice of policy instruments in the area of economic stabilization and management as for social policy, for policies designed to improve and rationalize governmental organization, planning, and evaluation, and for efforts to manage and stabilize relations with other countries and with international institutions and transnational processes. Similarly, there is ample reason for concern that public choice processes may be less and less capable of assuming the added burden. In the face of these new sources of strain they seem bogged down by the established interests, the political and economic power and limited vision of dominant elites, by conceptual barriers on the part of policy-makers (Vickers speaks of Western societies as being strangled "in the mythology we have evolved from market economics"),[28] by the breakdown of internal and external regulators, by the decline in the legitimacy of regimes, parties, and political authorities generally, and the erosion of "mutual appreciations of the situation" among elites, policy-makers, and publics.

Although space does not permit me to explore these effects, some of the principal ones are summarized in Table 1.

How will different societies respond to major changes in their decisional loads and capabilities?

Table 1.

Impact of Postulated Trends on Decision Loads and
Capabilities of Advanced Capitalist Societies

Postulated Trends	Loads	Capabilities
Primacy of politics	Strain on political organization, representational structures, information handling, policy evaluation, planning and forecasting capacities. Social complexity.	More active state intervention highlights existing structure of dominance and hierarchy. Increased salience of conflict, declining consensus on goals. Legitimacy loss.
Scarcity	Difficulties of economic management and stabilization, especially relation between employment and inflation. Conflicts and trade-offs among economic growth, employment, resource conservation, and environmental amenities. Claims for equity and fairness.	Increased conflict over allocation of scarce resources and the governmental budget (fiscal crisis of the state). Coalitions more difficult to form and manage. Legitimacy loss.
Equality	Increased militancy of demands for equality, of condition, equity, and fairness in distribution. Strain on existing social policies, welfare, health, transportation, housing.	Increased knowledge of existing inequalities and relative salience of such inequality. Strain on public budget, dominant coalition. Legitimacy loss.
Internationalization	New problems of economic management, especially regional problems	Declining efficiency of policy instruments to deal with

Table 1. (Continued)

Postulated Trends	Loads	Capabilities
	and structural unemployment and inflation. Control of multinational firms, shared policy space, international externalities.	inflation and balance of payments, to organize allocational and distributional policy. Declining national consensus on foreign policy goals.

Lindbloom[29] has recently observed that "a society's experience with forms of economic behavior and economic organization teaches it to change those forms, as also for parties, interest groups, and other political institutions." But, he goes on, we know very little about this "learning process." He suggests it ought to be of highest priority to investigate "sequences of social behavior and institutional organization" and "emerging patterns of behavior." In terms of the research focus being proposed here this would entail a series of longitudinal, in-depth analyses of what we might call nonroutine problem solving. We are interested in how new problems are perceived and handled in different industrialized nations, and in how policy and institutional change or innovation may be seen to occur over time in the ongoing trial and error process that characterizes political decision. "Learning" will involve not only rational problem-solving in the form of technical "solutions," but also the conflict-resolution and intergroup communications processes that prevail in each system—the patterns of compromise, bargaining, and domination, the norms of allocation and distribution that are invoked, the general societal goals in terms of which policies may be legitimated. I would anticipate that distinctive national political and institutional contexts for policy making will have a profound impact on the nature and outcome of such "learning" processes. We very much need to know more about how the political process characteristic of any nation will help define the issues that are considered problematic for purposes of public action, the scope of alternatives available as responses to new issues, and the constraints that focus the attention of policy makers.[30]

Over-time sequences of problem-solving can be analyzed at several different levels of abstraction.

(1) We may focus on policy strategies, changes, and innovations *per se,* across our universe of countries, trying to extract from such a comparison some kind of inventory of political responses to similar problems, assessing the circumstances under which given solutions are appropriate or not, and controlling for ideological, cultural, and structural differences. We would be centrally concerned with how political actors respond to a given set of circumstances, how they interpret demands and manipulate available resources. Comparative policy analysis conceived in this fashion would then be

> the inductive counterpart of the formal, deductive models of political economy and public choice, of game theory and coalition theory, which attempt to define the conditions of political rationality under the postulated abstract conditions.[31]

In terms of our postulated trends we can think of responses, strategies, innovations at the level of *policies* having to do with particular activities within the society, and of institutions structuring the decision-process and helping to determine which issues are accorded priority, which groups are represented and in what arenas, etc.

It is widely held in the literature cited that these trends imply either a cumulative instability of policy performance (e.g., LaPorte, Vickers) or a *de facto* structural adaptation in an authoritarian, technocratic, antiliberal direction (e.g., Gross, Heilbronner, many Marxists), or both. That is, there is wide skepticism, much of which I share, that advanced capitalist states can successfully adapt to these new circumstances while maintaining "bourgeois liberal" forms and policies. While this may be true it cannot be simply postulated and must become the focus of comparative empirical research. Table 2 will suggest some of the possible modes of response that might be investigated.

(2) Or the focus of analysis and comparison might be upon *domestic-international policy linkages,* upon the interaction in each

Table 2.
Possible Responses of Policy Makers
to Postulated Trends

Postulated Trends	Policy Strategies and Innovation	Institutional Strategies and Innovations
Primacy of politics	Use of science and social science research and development to refine decision systems, planning styles and structures, forecasting and evaluative capabilities. New laissez-faire and regulatory law (reintroduce the market).	Regulatory commissions rather than discretionary planning. Participatory planning. Representational systems of a quasi-corporatist type (as in incomes policies).
Scarcity	Rationalization of public sector expenditures. Evocation and development of norms of equity and fairness (a new social contract). Changes in conceptualization of GNP to account for externalities and depletion of nonrenewable stocks. No-growth or low-growth strategies.	Rationing and allocational systems. Representational systems.
Equality	New social contract. Redistributive policies, taxation reforms. "Positive" incomes policies. From equality of opportunity to equality of condition. Emphasize collective consumption over individual consumption, solidaristic over meritocratic norms.	Rationing and allocational systems. Representational systems.
Internationalization	Floating exchange rates. Introduction of produc-	New transnational institutions to manage

Table 2. (Continued)

Postulated Trends	Policy Strategies and Innovation	Institutional Strategies and Innovations
	tion and other subsidies (neomercantilism). New rules of international good conduct, coordination of interest rate, inflation and exchange rate policies.	the high seas, air, outer space, etc., to control international externalities, to regulate multinational firms, and to coordinate stabilization policies.

country between the demands/aspirations of domestic policy and the demands/aspirations of foreign economic and security policies. Our postulated trends imply a simultaneous rise in demands and aspirations for national planning and control, for the rational management of scarce resources and amenities, for greater attention to distributive justice, but also a simultaneous decline in the efficiency of the nation-state as a decision-making unit in stabilization, allocation, and distribution policies. This is due both to the fact that many instruments are ineffective when used by one nation alone (interest rate, exchange rate, indirect taxes, profit taxation, progressive income taxes, etc.), and also to the fact that many new domestic policy problems are caused by international or transnational processes (fall in profit margins, rate of structural change in economics, structural unemployment, regional policies, trend toward mergers and industrial concentrations, power of multinational firms, international externalities).

There is some reason to think that governments will perceive themselves as increasingly constrained by these internationalization effects as they attempt to innovate with policies and institutions designed to assure employment opportunities and relative incomes of underprivileged or disadvantaged groups or regions; with redistributive policies; with environmental policies (taxes and production restrictions lower external competitiveness); with introduction of public participation or control in production and investment decisions; with efforts to manage inflation, meet demands for expansion of public services, and so forth.

Already there are signs of the emergence of a "new mercantilism" [32]—a process surely accelerated by the 1973–74 petroleum crisis. (This latter event—and its long-term consequences for strategic and alliance policies, the pursuit by nations of self-sufficiency in energy or guaranteed supplies, etc.—is widely perceived in Europe as the most important and portentous since the Marshall Plan.) On the other hand, governments will also try to evolve new transnational policies, and institutions to cope with international externalities, and will also try to maintain such existing structures as the European Community.[33] It is not at all clear how the conflicts and trade-offs will be perceived and what the outcome will be, but the next decade will perhaps see a turning-point in the postwar internationalization process with consequences about which we can now only conjecture.

(3) My argument has been that the four postulated trends are of such compelling significance that they will not only structure the terms of the political debate over the next decades, becoming the central focus of public choice, of conflict, of the formation of new cleavages or the consolidation of old ones, but that the way in which they are managed by particular polities will be a principal determinant of the quality of political institutions, of political and social life more generally, of the style and pattern of economic policy, of environmental and other amenities, indeed of social justice and political stability. If the next decades will indeed be decisive in these regards, it behooves us well to chronicle and evaluate the processes as they unfurl in each country and to assimilate them to the corpus of theory on democratic performance and stability. Such analyses can be undertaken at the level of the nation-state and different patterns of response—of innovation or of failure to innovate—explained and compared. In this regard we will be especially interested in possible patterns of structural change in these polities, for example, in systems of interest representation (is there a trend toward neocorporatism?),[34] in politically relevant cleavage lines, in the concentration of power, planning, and control.

(4) But we may also conceptualize the problem at the level of *societal learning*, seeking to develop a general understanding of what constitutes an "adaptive" or an "active" society, of what are the determinants of an ability to invent and carry out new policies, to combine items of information into new patterns and to make

uncommitted resources available to the system. What factors induce "learning" in modern political systems? Does it require societal disruptions of a particular nature or intensity? Particular elite or mass values, ideologies, beliefs, or attitudes? Particular attitudes toward authority, information and communication networks, media systems, or institutional arrangements? Particular patterns of elite consensus/dissensus, or of existing mass cleavages and social-psychological distance? Or is it related to the nature of participation, e.g., the role of *ad hoc* groups, or to the existence of an overall value consensus in society? Or does it ultimately depend on the availability of "prophetic leadership," or upon the achievement motivation, self-confidence, or "loss of nerve" of dominant elites? What factors block learning? How and why do pathologies arise? What are the roles of such factors as uncertainty, organizational complexity, demand overload?

Donald Schon has argued that the most critical and the least understood stage of the process of "public learning" is "that barely visible process through which issues come to awareness and ideas about them become powerful." [35] This is when conflicts crystallize, issues are identified, solutions made available, sides defined and chosen. "These antecedent processes are as crucial to the formation of policy as the processes of discovery in science are central to the formation of plausible hypotheses." [36] They are essential to change in public policy and thus to public learning. Indeed, Schon suggests that a close analysis of these processes will give one basic insights into the vitality of a society's capacity for public learning.

> A learning system must transform its ideas in good currency at a rate commensurate with its own changing situation. More broadly the adequacy of a learning system is in part shown by how far its ideas in good currency are adequate to the situation actually confronting it. [37]

Schon's emphasis on what we might call "early learning" seems to me particularly suggestive in view of the emphasis I have given to a set of postulated trends and how they are likely to intersect advanced capitalist societies. He posits a sequence that might well become a framework for research on how new ideas about needs, priorities, and policies come into currency and become powerful for public policy: systems at any point in time are "dynamically

conservative" and are characterized by some set of ideas in good
currency; disruptive events or a crisis produce a demand for new
ideas; ideas already present in "free or marginal areas of society
begin to surface," they are mediated by "vanguard roles" which
move ideas to public awareness; diffusion depends on interpersonal
networks and the media of communication; ideas become powerful
as centers of policy debate and political conflict when organizations grow around them; ideas gain widespread acceptance through
the efforts of those "who push or ride them through the fields of
force created by the interplay of interests and commitments." [38]
The above recalls Karl Deutsch's suggestion that

> very serious challenges to the functioning of a society or state . . .
> may have only those solutions that are fairly unlikely to be discovered
> by means of the standardized and accepted habits, preferences, and
> cultural patterns existing in the society.[39]

They are often more likely to be found by deviant members of the
community. But these groups are not likely to be able to form
stable, cohesive, and influential social groups, and therefore their
role in learning is to persuade others. If I am correct in postulating
that the present period is one of serious challenges to the
functioning of advanced capitalist systems, then Western Europe—
in combination with and in comparison with North America and
Japan—provides an indispensable laboratory for developing truly
reliable and systematic, imaginative theory about social change
and policy responses thereto.

NOTES

1. For further detail see Stephen Blank, "Afterword: The Future of
European Studies" in Martin O. Heisler, ed., *Politics in Europe* (New York:
David McKay, 1973), pp. 388–400. See also publications of the Council for
European Studies, especially the *European Studies Newsletter*.

2. Martin O. Heisler, "Comparative and European Politics" in
Heisler, ed., ibid., pp. 18–22.

3. The most careful and comprehensive critique was done by a group
at the Science Policy Research Unit at the University of Sussex and has

been published as Christopher Freeman, ed., *Models of Doom* (New York: Universe Books, 1973). See also Peter Passell and Leonard Ross, *The Retreat from Riches: Affluence and Its Enemies* (New York: Viking Press, 1973), and John Maddox, *The Doomsday Syndrome* (London: Macmillan, 1972).

4. See Geoffrey Vickers, *Freedom in a Rocking Boat* (Harmondsworth, Middlesex, England: Penguin Books, 1972); Donald Schon, *Beyond the Stable State* (London: Temple Smith, 1971); Todd LaPorte, ed., *Organized Social Complexity: Challenge to Politics and Policy* (Princeton, Princeton University Press, 1974); Fred E. Emery and Eric Trist, *Towards a Social Ecology* (London and New York: Plenum Press, 1972); Eric Jantsch, *Technological Planning and Social Futures* (London: Associated Business Programmes, Ltd., 1972); Robert L. Heilbronner, *An Inquiry into the Human Prospect* (New York: W. W. Norton, 1974).

5. Samuel P. Huntington, "A Change to Change," *Comparative Politics*, April 1971, p. 293.

6. Daniel Bell, *The Coming of Post Industrial Society* (New York: Basic Books, 1973).

7. Bertram M. Gross, "Planning in an Era of Social Revolution," *Public Administration Review*, May/June 1971, pp. 259-297.

8. "The Human Prospect," *New York Review of Books*, January 24, 1974.

9. For details see Leon N. Lindberg and Stuart A. Scheingold, *Europe's Would-Be Polity* (Englewood Cliffs, N.J.: Prentice-Hall, 1970).

10. Donald T. Campbell, "Reforms as Experiments," *American Psychologist*, vol. 24, no. 4 (1969), and Donald T. Campbell and Julian C. Stanley, *Experimental and Quasi-Experimental Designs for Research* (Chicago: Rand-McNally, 1963).

11. Hugh Heclo, "Policy Analysis," *British Review of Political Science*, vol. 24, part 1 (Jan. 1972), pp. 83-108.

12. The distinction between prediction and forecasting is from Otis Dudley Duncan, "Social Forecasting—The State of the Art," *The Public Interest*, no. 17 (Fall 1969), pp. 107-108. On conjectures see Bertrand de Jouvenel, *The Art of Conjecture* (New York: Basic Books, 1967). On futurology more generally see Albert Somit, ed., *Political Science and the Study of the Future* (Hinsdale, Ill.: The Dryden Press, 1974), Charles de Hoghton, William Page, and Guy Streatfield, . . . *and now the future* (London: Political and Economic Planning, Aug. 1971), and Wendell Bell and James A. Man, eds., *The Sociology of the Future* (New York: Russell Sage Foundation, 1971).

13. Vickers, cited, pp. 56-57.

14. Ibid., p. 182.

15. Samuel P. Huntington, "Postindustrial Politics—How Benign Will It Be," *Comparative Politics*, Jan. 1974, pp. 4-5.

16. Ibid., p. 168.

17. For a summary of the literature bearing on this argument see Martin O. Heisler, "The European Polity Model" in Heisler, cited, pp. 27–89. See also Leonard Binder et al., *Crises and Sequences in Political Development* (Princeton: Princeton University Press, 1971), Barrington Moore, Jr., *Social Origins of Dictatorship and Democracy* (Boston: Beacon Press, 1966), Seymour M. Lipset and Stein Rokkan, *Party Systems and Voter Alignments: Cross-National Perspectives* (New York: Free Press, 1967), Stein Rokkan, "The Structuring of Mass Politics in the Smaller European Democracies," *Comparative Studies in Society and History*, 10, 2 (Jan. 1968), pp. 173–210, Arend Lijphart, *The Politics of Accommodation: Pluralism and Democracy in the Netherlands* (Berkeley and Los Angeles: University of California Press, 1968), Ralf Dahrendorf, *Society and Democracy in Germany* (Garden City, N.Y.: Doubleday, 1967).

18. Peter Wiles, "A Comment on Bell," *Survey*, vol. 17, no. 1 (Winter 1971), p. 42.

19. Ibid., p. 5.

20. Space does not permit a full exposition of this argument, nor of the citations from the literature and research from which it is derived. This formulation of trends or "wavy tendencies" is a preliminary one, representing a stage in my own thinking. For more elaborated conceptualizations and derivations of this analytic scheme and a report on preliminary research applying it to policy formation and policy debate in Britain, France, Sweden, and the U.S., see my forthcoming book, *System Change and Policy Response in Advanced Capitalist Nations* (Cambridge: Winthrop Publishers, EDP, 1975). See also Leon N. Lindberg, Robert Alford, John Goldethorpe, and Claus Offe, eds., *Patterns of Change in Advanced Industrial Societies: Research Priorities for the 1970's and 1980's* (forthcoming).

21. On the concept of crisis see Sidney Verba, "Sequences and Development" in Binder et al., *Crises and Sequences in Political Development* (Princeton: Princeton University Press, 1971), esp. pp. 298–307.

22. Geoffrey Vickers, *Value Systems and Social Process* (Harmondsworth, Middlesex, England: Penguin Books), p. 70.

23. Kenneth Boulding, "The Shadow of the Stationary State," in *The No-Growth Society*, a special issue of *Daedalus*, Fall 1973, pp. 89–102. See also Herman E. Daly, ed., *Toward a Steady-State Economy* (San Francisco, W. H. Freeman, 1973).

24. See Vickers, *Freedom in a Rocking Boat*, pp. 156–157, S. M. Miller and Pamela Roby, *The Future of Inequality* (New York: Basic Books, 1970), Christopher Jencks, *Inequality* (New York: Basic Books, 1972), A. B. Atkinson, *Unequal Shares* (London, Allen Lane: The Penguin Press, 1972).

25. For a good treatment see Assar Lindbeck, "The National State in an Internationalized World Economy," Institute for International Economic Studies, University of Stockholm. See also Harold and Margaret

Sprout, *Toward a Politics of the Planet Earth* (New York: Van Nostrand Reinhold, 1971), Robert O. Keohane and Joseph S. Nye, Jr., "Transnational Relations and World Politics," *International Organization*, vol. XXV, no. 3 (Summer 1971), C. Fred Bergsten, *The Future of the International Economic Order: An Agenda for Research* (Lexington, Mass.: Lexington Books, 1973).

26. It is for example difficult to know how to interpret Ronald Inglehart's findings about value change in Western Europe in the abstract, that is, in the absence of some actual or postulated set of issues or conflicts around which political opinions and attitudes might be expected to cluster. See his "The Silent Revolution in Europe: Intergenerational Change in Post-Industrial Societies," *American Political Science Review*, LXV, Dec. 1971, pp. 991–1017. The same is true of Samuel Huntington's efforts to identify possible "post-industrial" political trends. See his "Post Industrial Politics—How Benign Will It Be," cited, passim.

27. William C. Mitchell, "The Shape of Political Theory to Come: From Political Sociology to Political Economy," in S. M. Lipset, ed., *Politics and the Social Sciences*, p. 124.

28. Vickers, *Freedom in a Rocking Boat*, p. 163.

29. "Integration of Economics and the Other Social Sciences through Policy Analysis" in James C. Charlesworth, *Integration of the Social Sciences through Policy Analysis* (Philadelphia: American Academy of Political and Social Science, 1972), p. 12.

30. For a discussion of new issues and policy responses in different societies see Leon N. Lindberg, ed., *Politics and the Future of Industrial Society* (New York: McKay, forthcoming), especially essays by Charles W. Anderson, Taketsugu Tsurutani, and M. Donald Hancock.

31. Charles W. Anderson, "System and Strategy in Comparative Policy Analysis: A Plea for Contextual and Experiential Knowledge" (unpublished manuscript), p. 19.

32. See Lindbeck, cited.

33. For surveys of the problems and relevant literature see C. Fred Bergsten, *The Future of the International Economic Order,* cited, passim.

34. See Philippe Schmitter, "Still the Century of Corporatism?" (forthcoming).

35. *Beyond the Stable State*, p. 123.

36. Ibid., p. 123.

37. Ibid., p. 123.

38. Ibid., pp. 128–136.

39. Karl W. Deutsch, *The Nerves of Government* (Glencoe, Ill.: The Free Press, 1963) p. 173.

Index